THE BIBLE

IN

SCOTTISH LIFE AND LITERATURE

THE BIBLE

IN

SCOTTISH LIFE AND LITERATURE

Edited by

DAVID F WRIGHT

with the assistance of
IAN CAMPBELL and JOHN GIBSON

THE SAINT ANDREW PRESS
EDINBURGH

First published in 1988 by
THE SAINT ANDREW PRESS
121 George Street, Edinburgh EH2 4YN

Copyright © 1988 The Saint Andrew Press

ISBN 0 7152 0695 X

British Library Cataloguing in Publication Data

The Bible in Scottish life and literature.
1. Scottish culture. Influence, history of Bible 2. English literature. Scottish writers. Influence of Bible to 1987 I. Wright, David F. (David Frederick) II. Campbell, Ian, 1942- III. Gibson, John S. 941.1

This book is set in 10/11 pt Times

Typeset by Bookworm Typesetting Ltd, Edinburgh.
Printed by Bell & Bain, Glasgow.

Contents

List of Contributors

Professor George W Anderson, Professor Emeritus of Hebrew and
Old Testament Studies, University of Edinburgh

Dr Ian Campbell, Reader in English Literature,
University of Edinburgh

Dr Sarah M Carpenter, Lecturer in English Literature,
University of Edinburgh

Professor Alec C Cheyne, Professor Emeritus of Ecclesiastical
History, University of Edinburgh

Michael Chibbett, Organist and Choirmaster, Greyfriars, Tolbooth
and Highland Kirk, Edinburgh

Professor John C L Gibson, Professor of Hebrew and Old
Testament Studies, University of Edinburgh

Dr Máire Herbert, Lecturer in Early and Mediaeval Irish,
University College, Cork

The Revd Fergus Macdonald, General Secretary of the National
Bible Society of Scotland

Dr Donald E Meek, Senior Lecturer in Celtic,
University of Edinburgh

The Revd David D Ogston, Minister,
St John the Baptist's Church, Perth

Professor G Ross Roy, Professor of English, University of South
Carolina, Columbia, SC

David F Wright, Senior Lecturer in Ecclesiastical History,
University of Edinburgh

Introduction

The old heartlands of Christianity in the West are apt to be unaware
that the Bible is *the* book *par excellence* for a growing multitude of
people throughout the world. Standard measures of its appeal and
fascination—the zeal to read and study it for oneself in one's own
language, the clamour to buy it, the passion to publish its teachings—
register an all-time high on a universal scale. The Bible Societies
cannot cope with the demand, whether in the burgeoning churches of
Africa or among the post-Marxist peoples of Eastern Europe,
searching again for a long-overlaid religious heritage.

Yet there is a chilling truth in the label 'the world's least read
bestseller'—one of the snappiest of quotable tags that the Bible has a
gift for attracting. Not least read in Scotland, one might have thought,
but hard evidence suggests otherwise. The *Lifestyle Survey* conducted
recently for the Church of Scotland's Board of Social Responsibility
revealed that almost 70 per cent of the Church's members who were
canvassed seldom or never read the Bible; only a tiny proportion (7.5
per cent) read it daily.[1]

It was against this sombre backcloth (hardly unveiled for the first
time by the *Survey*, which merely served to tabulate what keen church-
watchers in Scotland have long discerned) that 1988 was designated the
Year of the Bible by virtually all the Scottish churches with the
National Bible Society in the vanguard. The aim was to raise the profile
of the Bible among the people of Scotland and to promote its use
within and beyond the membership of the churches.

Celebration of Scotland's Bible

This volume owes its inception to the Year of the Bible, not as part of its official programme (which has been second to none in imagination and enterprise), but as an endeavour, on the part of a group of individuals whose professional commitment keeps them in different ways close to the Bible, to pay tribute to its role in Scottish life. In its own fashion the book sets out to offer a celebration, evoked by this special year, of the Bible's place in Scottish religion and culture over hundreds of years. It may thus undergird the various projects of the Year of the Bible with much-needed historical depth and breadth. The Year takes place not as an isolated occasion but as an urgent and timely focus in a story older, almost, than Scotland itself.

That story—of the Scottish people's engagement with the Bible—is admittedly so extensive and so multi-faceted that no single collection of essays can do it justice. This one opens only selected windows. Reviewers may be expected to find its sins of omission numerous and various. It says next to nothing, for example, of the Bible and the visual arts, both plastic and graphic—from the biblical scenes carved on the great Celtic stone crosses to Robin Philipson's dazzling stained-glass canvasses and the newly-revived craft of banner-making. A footnote might be reserved for the burning bush encountered by Moses (*cf* Exod. 3:2)—symbol, for no very obvious reason, of the Church of Scotland (and much earlier of Mary's perpetual virginity).[2]

Nor does the symposium record, except for the nineteenth century, the history of biblical scholarship in Scotland. This, for example, could not omit Archbishop Robert Leighton's seventeenth-century commentary on 1 Peter: 'so truly spiritual . . . so fresh and suggestive, so interestingly illustrated, so generous in its spirit, so free from pettiness and nearsightedness'.[3] It would also have to encompass, for all the learned disdain it sometimes enjoys, the late William Barclay's monumentally popular *Daily Study Bible*, as well as that evergreen resource of the Bible preacher and writer, *The Expository Times*, founded (in 1889) by James Hastings, minister of the Free and United Free Churches and prolific midwife of multi-volume biblical dictionaries.

The Preacher's Bible

Some will never forgive us for neglecting to find a place for the Bible in the Scottish pulpit. It was here that the 'sword of the Spirit' (*cf* Eph. 6:17) was wielded by Wishart and Knox and Robert Bruce in the sixteenth century, and by luminaries of the Highland host like John

MacDonald of Ferintosh and John Kennedy of Dingwall (names still liable to be uttered in tones of hushed awe);by the short-lived Robert Murray McCheyne of Dundee, and by the moderns who made their mark in the metropolis—Edward Irving in London, James Black, Alexander Whyte and James S Stewart in Edinburgh. (I can still hear the last-named's sermon on Nicodemus: 'Listen to the wind, Nicodemus, listen to the wind . . ..')[4] It is difficult to know where to stop in this veritable 'nation of preachers', in which for a period the indispensability of the expositor in effect made the Scriptures 'so obscure in things necessary to salvation that they might not be read to the people without an human gloss'.[5] With 'a corner of a verse by way of a text for I cannot tell how many sermons',[6] preaching ruled in the church, not the Bible.

Nor have we covered the devotional literature of Scotland, perhaps not one of the country's richest genres, but capable in such contrasting figures as Samuel Rutherford and John Baillie of producing works of perennial worth and inspiration. Rutherford's luxuriant imagery is sometimes cloyingly precious, but few Scottish writers have displayed a finer touch with biblical images—the cross, for example: 'Christ hath honoured you to bear His chains, which is the golden end of His cross'; 'no man hath a velvet cross'; 'the apples and sweet fruits, which grow on that crabbed tree of the cross, are as sweet as it is sour to bear it'.[7] And what of the Bible's use in popular religion? Regard for the material book could outreach sound piety, in divination, for example, or in 'making a lottery of the Holy Scriptures' by random oracular trial. The much-worn, much-travelled bosom companions ('Bible-black' of course) of the fugitive Covenanters earned the reverence almost of sacred relics.

If the poets and novelists of Scotland have done better by us, Stevenson gets scant mention, Edwin Muir and George Bruce even less, and Gaelic literature is only lightly touched upon. Nor did the editors' best efforts succeed, in the short timescale available, in recruiting a study of the King James Bible's deeply-etched imprint upon the common speech of the Scottish people. Broad indeed are the tracts of the Scottish landscape that this volume makes no stab at surveying; narrow, by comparison, are the paths we have chosen to tread.

But recognition of our limited perspectives serves other ends than the doubtless vain hope of disarming critics in advance. It is an invigorating reminder of the vastness of the terrain—of the heights and depths and breadths and lengths of Scotland's interaction with the Bible. Has any nation's culture (in the broadest sense of that term) been as thoroughly informed by the Bible as Scotland's? If this is the case, then the abysmal ignorance of the Bible into which we have lapsed will not be unrelated to the disorientation and malaise diagnosed by perceptive analysts of Scotland's national psyche in the dying twentieth century.

For Future Investigation

Acknowledgement of the untouched dimensions of our subject has the further value of signposting the way to future research. Some at least of the avenues we have chosen not to follow have yet to be adequately explored. No suitable brief study, for example, of the biblical colouring of the spoken language of Scotland was at hand for a straight reprint or adaptation. There is scope for a handful of fresh treatments of the Scottish pulpit. And even within the confines of the present collection of essays, pointers to fruitful areas of new enquiry will be found—for example, on the use in sixteenth-century Scotland of early (pre-Genevan Bible) English versions.

Yet the contributors have not set out to produce research papers. We have tried to bear a general readership in mind, even when, as is certainly true of some chapters, material is presented which has never previously been published in any form. William Lorimer's *New Testament in Scots*, for instance, has never before been assessed except at review length. The subject impinges too broadly on the Scottish scene, past and present, for it to be restricted to a specialised circle of readers. The writers span a range of disciplines and include, in addition to academics active and emeriti, a parish minister, a professional musical administrator and a Bible Society leader.

The need for such a contrived concentration as the Year of the Bible would have appeared strange to earlier generations of Scots. The novel English Bible in the sixteenth century made 'all the din and play in our Kirk' (or, in another version, 'all this ple and commer'), and even if this pitch of excitement could not last, the Geneva Bible and then the Authorised Version exerted for centuries a mastering hold on Scottish hearts and minds (even though the latter never received official authorisation from the Church of Scotland). The fading traces of that imprint can still be detected in unlikely places; I have frequently been surprised in some university committee at the biblical phrases or allusions contributed almost instinctively by colleagues not conspicuous for their churchmanship. William Smith's heroic spirit believed that 'we need never tremble *for* the word of God, though we may tremble *at* it'.

Yet it is a sad irony that knowledge of the Scriptures should be a fast wasting asset in an age when biblical translations have multiplied and publishers' versatility in marketing them has known no bounds. The Bible has never been so abundantly available—but must contempt be the price of familiarity? If Prime Minister Thatcher's credal address to the Kirk's General Assembly of 1988 succeeds in driving Scottish churchmen back to the text of Scripture, to ascertain if it really says what they, or she, think it does, it will not have been in vain.

Sense of Identification

One of the themes running through several of these essays is the sense of identification with the biblical story: Adomnán's assimilation of Columba to the miracle-working company of the prophets and apostles; Gaelic highlanders experiencing a new exodus; John Knox re-enacting the Israelite prophet's admonitory defiance of the powers-that-be; the Covenanters reading their struggles through the fortunes of the uniquely covenanted people of God. From Calvin onwards the Psalter has been read autobiographically in the Reformed tradition—but changes in Scottish Presbyterian hymnody threaten even the centrality of the Psalms in worship. Samuel Rutherford's letters from his Aberdeen exile were first published under the title *Joshua Redivivus* ('Joshua Reborn'); he saw himself as 'sent . . . as a spy into this wilderness of suffering, to see the land and try the ford'. He had an intense conviction that 'Christ got a charter of Scotland from His Father, and who will bereave Him of His heritage, or put our Redeemer out of His mealing [tenancy], until His tack [lease] be run out?' The year 1988 marks also an anniversary of the National Covenant of 1638. Perhaps Scotland's ancient and modern freedoms lie closer to its biblical heritage than we realise.

DAVID F WRIGHT

Notes

1 A Robertson (ed) (Edinburgh, 1987).
2 cf G D Henderson, *The Burning Bush. Studies in Scottish Church History* (Edinburgh, 1957), ch 1.
3 Henderson, 'The Bible in Seventeenth-Century Scotland' in his *Religious Life in Seventeenth-Century Scotland* (Cambridge, 1937), p.30.

4 Published in J S Stewart, *The Wind of the Spirit* (London, 1968).
5 George Garden (1703), cited by Henderson in *Religious Life*, p 11.
6 John Sage (1704), cited ibid.
7 T Smith (ed), *Letters of the Rev. Samuel Rutherford* (Edinburgh, no date).

I

Scotland's Bible

1

The Gaelic Bible

But, furthermore, we, the Gaels of Scotland and Ireland, have ever
endured a great disadvantage and deficiency beyond the rest of the world
in that we have never before had our Gaelic languages in print, as all
other peoples in the world have had their tongues and languages in print;
and we suffer from a lack greater than all other lacks, in that we do not
have the Holy Bible in Gaelic print, as it is printed in Latin and English,
and in every other tongue besides . . . [1]

Thus wrote John Carswell in the 'Epistle to the Reader' in his epoch-
making work, *Foirm na n-Urrnuidheadh* (*The Form of Prayers*),
published in 1567, seven years after the meeting of the Scottish
Reformation Parliament. Carswell's book, a translation of the *Book of
Common Order*, made literary history as the first work in Gaelic to be
printed in Ireland or Scotland. The *Book of Common Order* was
intended as a service book for the worship of the Reformed Church,
and its relatively quick translation into Classical Gaelic is a testimony
to the existence of active, Gaelic-speaking Reformed ministers in
certain parts of the Highlands. The most conspicuous of these was
Argyll, where Carswell laboured as a Superintendent of the Reformed
Church, and enjoyed the patronage of Archibald, Fifth Earl of Argyll.
The Earl's patronage had ensured the beginning of Gaelic printed
texts.[2]

As a Protestant reformer, Carswell was right to emphasise the
need for a Gaelic translation of the Bible. Translations of the
Scriptures lay at the heart of the Reformation, both in bringing it about
and in furthering its aims. A Gaelic Bible would have been more
influential than a service book aimed primarily at ministers and office-
bearers of the Church. Yet, while the need was recognised as early as
1567, the Gaelic speakers of Scotland had to wait a full two centuries

for the New Testament to be translated specifically for a Scottish readership. For the complete Bible they had to wait until 1801.

The delay in producing a distinctively Scottish Gaelic translation of the Scriptures stands in contrast to the expeditious manner in which the Bible was translated into Welsh. In 1567, the year in which Carswell produced his work, Wales received a translation of the New Testament and of the *Book of Common Prayer*, largely through the labours of William Salesbury. By 1588 Bishop William Morgan had completed the translation of the whole Bible into Welsh. Behind this remarkable activity lay an Act of Parliament of 1563 which authorised the translation of the complete Bible into Welsh.[3] In Ireland, a translation of the New Testament into Classical Gaelic, completed by William O'Donnell, became available in 1602, and a translation of the Old Testament in similar style by Bishop William Bedell was published in 1685. Beyond the Celtic areas, the English-speaking inhabitants of Britain were provided with a number of translations of the Bible, some dating from before the Reformation, and several appearing thereafter. The best-known English translation was the King James Bible (the Authorised Version), published in 1611.[4]

Why should the Gaelic-speaking areas of Scotland have fared so badly in the matter of a translation of the Bible? The application of a fundamental principle of the Reformation—to provide Bibles in the languages commonly spoken by ordinary people—was obstructed primarily by the prejudice of central government against the Gaelic language. Unlike Wales, the Scottish Highlands did not have the benefit of an Act of Parliament to ensure a translation. In addition, the attitude of the Established Church to Gaelic was ambivalent, and much depended on individual presbyteries and synods. The General Assembly of the Church could not ignore the government's view that the removal of Gaelic, and its immediate replacement by English, was a necessary part of 'civilising' the Highlands. It is, however, difficult to believe that this policy was held uniformly throughout the Church, and its implementation may have varied with time and place. In spite of the antipathy of James VI, many bishops and ministers in the Highlands in the early seventeenth century would have used Gaelic for religious instruction. Attitudes at various levels probably hardened in the disturbed years after 1660.[5]

The task of translating the Bible into Scottish Gaelic eventually fell to the Society in Scotland for the Propagation of Christian Knowledge (SSPCK). The Society was established in 1709, and it too aimed to 'civilise' the Highlands. This was to be achieved through the advancement of the national Presbyterian Church in the region and by the specific agency of the Society's teachers and catechists. The SSPCK was strongly anti-Catholic and anti-Jacobite, and it strove initially to replace Gaelic with English. The removal of Gaelic would make Gaelic books unnecessary; the Society therefore put its weight behind the English Bible, and its teachers tried to teach English reading.[6]

By 1750, the anti-Gaelic stance of the SSPCK was beginning to crumble, since it was meeting with minimal success in the teaching of English. The possibility that it might be easier to teach Highlanders to read and write their own language was being entertained. Literacy in Gaelic, it was realised, might provide a back-door route for the introduction of English. In addition, the Society had to pay attention to the labours of the Synod of Argyll, which had been engaged in a programme of Gaelic translation since the early seventeenth century. Although the Synod was an integral part of the Established Church, it was trying hard to produce, among other things, a Gaelic translation of the Old Testament, and by the 1670s it had come tantalisingly close to success.

The Translation Programme of the Synod of Argyll

The Synod of Argyll, erected in December 1638, had jurisdiction over no less than five presbyteries, namely those of Inveraray, Kintyre, Dunoon, Lorn and Skye (including Lewis).[7] Its influence therefore extended over all of the Hebrides and the Argyll mainland. Gaelic was strong throughout these areas, and there is clear evidence that in the seventeenth century the Synod could call on the services of a considerable number of ministers who were literate in the Gaelic language. In addition, there were still men on the Argyll mainland who could read and write Classical Gaelic, the dignified literary language which was used in the composition of important works. Some of these men were laymen; others were quite probably to be found among the ranks of the clergy (like John Carswell in the previous century). The Synod therefore possessed the necessary literary expertise to embark on a scheme of religious translation.

The Synod's main programme was aimed at producing some basic tools for teaching and memorising Reformed doctrine, and it followed a pattern which was already well established. Some eight years before the creation of the Synod, a Classical Gaelic translation of a major catechism, namely John Calvin's *Catechismus Ecclesiae Genevensis* (*Catechism of the Church of Geneva*), was published in Edinburgh. The translation was probably made in Argyll, but details of its production remain obscure. In 1653 the Synod distributed printed copies of its own translation of the Westminster Assembly's *Shorter Catechism*. No copy of the first edition survives. A second edition was printed in 1659. While preserving classical forms, the language of this edition is much closer to spoken Scottish Gaelic than that in Calvin's *Catechism*. The Synod's work provided the basis of the Gaelic *Shorter Catechism* which became so familiar to many Gaelic speakers in later years.[8]

Even more familiar to present-day Gaelic speakers are the Gaelic metrical Psalms, and these too were originally translated by the Synod of Argyll. *An Ceud Chaogad* (*The First Fifty*), the translation of the first fifty Psalms, was published along with the *Shorter Catechism* in 1659, but the whole Psalter was not available until 1694. Ten years earlier, the Revd Robert Kirk, the Episcopalian incumbent of Aberfoyle, had published his own version of the Gaelic metrical Psalter (which employed the Synod of Argyll's *First Fifty*, with Kirk's translations following thereafter). Nevertheless, the Synod of Argyll's complete translation, with subsequent revisions, became the popular rendering, and it forms the core of the existing Gaelic Psalter.[9]

In 1657 the Synod of Argyll passed a resolution calling for a Gaelic translation of the Old Testament, evidently as part of a plan to translate the whole Bible. The Synod then believed that relevant 'sundry parcels translated already by some in former times' could be located by diligent search, and in October of that year the Revd Archibald MacCalman of Muckairn claimed that he possessed a translation of the Books of Job, Proverbs, Ecclesiastes and the Song of Solomon. The evidence therefore suggests that even before 1657 attempts were being made in Argyll to translate the Old Testament. The project was put on a firmer footing in November 1660, when the Synod appointed an impressive team of translators consisting of several of its ministers. Their progress was seriously disrupted by the Restoration of 1660, which led to the ejection of almost all the translators. Yet, by 1673 a complete translation of the Old Testament evidently existed. This was mainly the work of the Revd Dugald Campbell of Knapdale, the only minister in the Presbytery of Inveraray who was prepared to accept episcopacy.[10]

The publication of Campbell's text, now lost, was probably hindered by a lack of finance and by the religious and political turmoils of the times. The desire to publish it doubtless waned further because of the appearance of another work, namely William Bedell's translation of the Old Testament, published in London in 1685 as part of the complete Bible in Classical Gaelic. The Synod's desire to translate the Old Testament, rather than the New Testament, as the first part of its project suggests strongly that it already had access to a Gaelic translation of the latter. Such a translation had, in fact, become available in Ireland in 1602.

The Classical Gaelic Bibles

The Old and New Testaments published in London in 1602 and 1685 respectively are customarily referred to as parts of the 'Irish' Bible. This is correct in respect of their place of origin, but, if applied to their language, it can create an unhelpful distinction between Scottish Gaelic and Irish Gaelic at the literary level. Throughout the Middle Ages, Ireland and Gaelic Scotland shared the common literary language of Classical Gaelic, and this made it possible for texts written in Ireland to be readily understood by the literate class in Scotland and vice versa. The use of the literary language overcame the difficulties of employing the spoken, everyday language of both countries, which had developed in different directions by the beginning of the Middle Ages. The spoken languages now known as Irish and Scottish Gaelic were, however, both different from Classical Gaelic, and, even if a Bible in Classical Gaelic came to Scotland, it might not be wholly understood by a person unversed in the classical language. Even so, it is possible to exaggerate the problems of comprehension; seventeenth-century Highlanders, even if they could not read Gaelic, had an infinitely greater familiarity with Classical Gaelic than their present-day counterparts. Through their hearing and memorisation of folk-tales and heroic ballads, they would be able to move readily to a level of language close to that of the classical tradition.[11]

The 'Irish' Scriptures were translated into a form of Classical Gaelic similar to that of the seventeenth-century Irish historian, Geoffrey Keating. Their appearance represented many years of effort by clergymen of the Church of Ireland. The New Testament, the work of four men at different stages, was finalised by William O'Donnell, and published in 1602. The Old Testament was translated mainly by William Bedell, Bishop of Kilmore and Ardagh, and, together with the Apocrypha (still unpublished), was complete at the time of his death in 1642. The Old Testament was brought to print through the benevolence of the Hon. Robert Boyle, seventh son of the Earl of Cork. Boyle, who is best known as a scientist and as formulator of 'Boyle's Law', was a supporter of many Christian enterprises, including Bible translation. Boyle also produced a reprint of

O'Donnell's New Testament in 1681.[12]

'Bedell's Bible', as the Old Testament was called, was introduced to the Scottish Highlands through the offices of James Kirkwood, an exiled Episcopalian clergyman living in Astwick, Bedfordshire, and a member of the English Society for Promoting Christian Knowledge (not to be confused with the SSPCK). Kirkwood, who was anxious to supply Gaelic Bibles for Highland use, arranged with Boyle a scheme whereby 207 copies of Bedell's Bible, accompanied by some copies of O'Donnell's New Testament, were dispatched to Scotland in 1688. The distribution of the books to Highland parishes was severely hampered by the Established Church's suspicion of episcopacy, especially after 1690 and the re-establishment of Presbyterianism. By 1710, eighty Old Testaments were still in Edinburgh.[13]

The Synod of Argyll, however, quickly distributed its share of the books. Copies of Bedell's Bible and O'Donnell's New Testament can still be seen in the library of Rothesay High Kirk, where they bear witness to a noteworthy Episcopalian initiative during the troubled years of the 'Second Episcopacy' in Scotland.[14] These years allowed the Classical Gaelic Bible to find a nervous toehold in the Highlands, but at the same time Presbyterian suspicion of episcopacy impeded its wider acceptance.

The Classical Gaelic versions of the Scriptures had disadvantages in the Scottish context. They were printed in a font based on Gaelic script, which was customary in Ireland, but not in Scotland where roman font was used in printing. The Gaelic font preserved regular scribal abbreviations which would have made reading more difficult, although such conventions were once widely practised by the literati of Gaelic Scotland. The books also consisted of two separate quarto volumes. A project to produce the two Testaments in roman font, with no abbreviations and in a single volume, was undertaken by Robert Kirk, the Episcopalian minister of Aberfoyle. 'Kirk's Bible', which made some alterations to suit Scottish Gaelic usage, was published in 1690, with a print-run of 3000 copies. One thousand New Testaments were also printed.[15]

The print-run of Kirk's Bible was probably based on the optimistic assumption that between ten and twenty copies would be distributed to each Gaelic-speaking parish. The distribution of the Bible was supervised by James Kirkwood, who drew up detailed lists of parishes which were to receive copies. However, the episcopal affiliations of Kirk's work, poor methods of distribution and the lukewarm response of the Established Church appear to have hampered its circulation in a manner reminiscent of its predecessors. Only in the Synod of Argyll was there any noticeable enthusiasm for it, although it did percolate to other parts, and established itself in the affections of some readers. This readership would have been restricted mainly to ministers, who read it to their congregations, and made extemporary modifications of its style and syntax to suit Scottish congregations. Some ministers attempted to fill the continuing gap by using the English Authorised Version as a basis for 'working translations' of verses and chapters relevant to their preaching.[16]

The publication of Kirk's Bible in 1690 was something of a landmark, and one can understand why James Kirkwood should have exclaimed when it appeared: 'At last the Bibles are printed, Blessed be God!'[17] Yet matters had not really made much progress. The remarkable initiative of the Synod of Argyll in trying to produce a Gaelic translation of the Old Testament perished in the 1680s, and the 'Irish' translations were a poor substitute for a genuinely Scottish Gaelic Bible. Kirk's Bible was essentially a compromise solution, the best that could be achieved at a time of fudged issues and lost opportunities. There was still no official backing for a much-needed translation of the Bible into Scottish Gaelic.

The Scottish Gaelic Bible: 1767–1801

Some 60 years after its publication, Kirk's Bible had an important part to play in the production of the first Scottish Gaelic New Testament. In 1754 the Synod of Argyll took the step of reprinting Kirk's version of the New Testament. The Synod's action was noted by the SSPCK, who were now aware of the failure of their English-only policy in Highland schools, and asked that the version should be modified to include an English translation alongside the Gaelic. This could not be done, and the SSPCK decided to commission their own translation of the Gaelic New Testament. They approached the Revd Alexander MacFarlane of Arrochar, the reviser of the 1753 edition of the Synod of Argyll's Gaelic Psalter, to undertake the task, but when MacFarlane made no progress, it was offered to the Revd James Stuart, Established Church minister of Killin. Stuart obtained the assistance of the Revd James Fraser of Alness, who revised the manuscript. Dugald Buchanan, the Gaelic religious poet from Rannoch, Perthshire, supervised the printing in Edinburgh. In June 1766, ten thousand copies of the first Scottish Gaelic New Testament rolled off the presses of Balfour, Auld and Smellie, printers to the University of Edinburgh.[18]

The publication of the Scottish Gaelic New Testament by the

SSPCK, with the financial assistance of the English SPCK, was an event of great significance for Scottish Gaelic literature. If the SSPCK ever thought of withdrawing support for the further translation of the Old Testament, the tide of influential public opinion now flowed firmly in favour of providing the Scriptures in Scottish Gaelic. There was no going back; even Dr Samuel Johnson had written to the directors of the SSPCK in 1766 to urge them to provide for Highlanders 'a translation of the holy books into their own language'. The aim of using the Gaelic Bible as a bridge to English was, however, endorsed by Johnson, and gladly accepted by the SSPCK.[19]

Work began on the translation of the Old Testament in 1783, but it proved to be a much longer and more difficult undertaking than the New Testament. The size of the Old Testament required that it be divided into four parts. The first two parts were translated under the supervision of the Revd John Stuart of Luss, son of James Stuart of Killin. The third part, which was not completed until 1801, was translated entirely by John Stuart, whose alleged tardiness gave rise to acerbic comments in the Minutes of the SSPCK.[20]

The translator of the fourth part of the Old Testament, the Books of the Prophets, was the Revd John Smith, the assistant minister of the parish of Kilbrandon and Kilchattan, and subsequently minister at Campbeltown. Smith was the translator of an influential Gaelic version of Joseph Alleine's work, *Alarm to the Unconverted*. In 1780 and 1787 he published two volumes of Ossianic verse. His 'translations' of Gaelic heroic ballads and other related material show a considerable flair for poetry and a willingness to participate in the contemporary game of pseudo-literary adaptation, developed to a fine art by James Macpherson, who gained fame (and notoriety) in the 1760s as the 'translator' of some of the alleged works of 'Ossian'. Smith also produced a revision of the Gaelic Psalter, published by the Synod of Argyll in 1787.[21]

Smith's volume of the Old Testament, published in 1786, provides a fascinating insight into the attitudes to biblical translation and textual criticism which governed approaches to the Gaelic Bible. The Scottish translators all worked from the original languages. Yet, while his fellow translators were happy to consult the Greek Septuagint version of the Old Testament and contemporary textual commentaries on matters of difficulty, Smith appears to have gone further than his colleagues in applying the fruits of scholarship relating to the Hebrew Massoretic text. Scholarly understanding of the Massoretic text improved greatly after 1611, leading to revision of Old Testament translations, notably in the King James Bible, which was extensively overhauled in individual works by such scholars as Dr Benjamin Blayney of Hertford College, Oxford. In the introduction to his volume, Smith disclosed that his version was different from the English one, and that he had consulted works by Blayney, Archbishop William Newcome, Father Charles François Houbigant, Bishop Robert Lowth and Dr Benjamin Kennicott. By 1802, when a second edition of the Gaelic Old Testament was required, the SSPCK had received complaints about Smith's translation, to the effect that it was 'too free, corresponding much more with Dr Lowth's translation than with the English one, which had a bad effect upon the minds of those who understand both languages'. Apart from ministers, few in the Highlands would have been in a position to worry about conflicting versions, but the 'bad effect' was nevertheless removed by allocating the offending volume to the Revd Alexander Stewart of Dingwall for an extensive revision. Stewart's work brought the fourth volume into line with the style of the other parts, and, more significantly, into closer conformity with the King James Bible in respect of difficult readings.

In retrospect, it is evident that, while Smith may sometimes have over-indulged his literary inclinations by inserting explanatory phrases which were not attested in the original Hebrew text, there were numerous instances in which he anticipated the readings in the Revised Version of the English Old Testament, published in 1885. This can be illustrated by his translation of Isaiah 38:12, which reads (in English translation):

> My dwelling-place has been taken away, and removed from me, like a shepherd's tent; my life has been cut short, as by the weaver; he will cut me from the loom; in the course [*or* departing] of the day, you will bring my cloth to completion.

The English Revised Version reads:

> Mine age is removed, and is carried away from me as a shepherd's tent: I have rolled up like a weaver my life; he will cut me off from the loom: From day even unto night wilt thou make an end of me.

Detailed analysis of the Hebrew text shows that Smith's rendering is, in fact, even closer to the original text than the English Revised Version.[22] It is also noteworthy that Smith very skilfully sustains the central image of the weaver and his loom—an image which would have been very meaningful in the Highland cultural context. In the subsequent revision by Alexander Stewart, the verse was recast to follow the King James Bible more closely (although not precisely), and the basic imagery was largely lost:

My age has departed from me, and it was removed like a shepherd's tent; my life was cut off as if by the weaver; he oppresses me with a wasting sickness; from day even until night you are making an end of me.

Original translation is also found in the work of Smith's colleagues. John Stuart's third volume contains examples of readings which differ from those of the King James Bible, and correspond to the English Revised Version, most noticeably in the Book of Job. Stuart, however, provided variant readings in footnotes, and, unlike Smith, he did not disclose his sources in his introduction. Stuart's distinctive renderings have, in fact, been retained to the present day in the main editions.[23]

The Style of the Scottish Gaelic Bible

The style of the Scottish Gaelic Bible, as it became by 1807, is indebted to its predecessors, both Gaelic and English. There can be little doubt that the translators had their eye on the Classical Gaelic translations of Bedell and O'Donnell. Nevertheless, their work was an original piece of translation, and, as such, was far more than a mere adjustment of the existing texts. The translators chose a vocabulary which, in general, was noticeably closer to Scottish Gaelic usage, and in the matter of grammar and syntax they adopted Scottish Gaelic vernacular practice in important areas. The verb-system, for example, retains comparatively few of the forms which characterise the classical language. The influence of Classical Gaelic lasted longer in the endings of nouns, especially in the plural, and in the forms of prepositions and prepositional phrases. In its phrasing and pointing, the Scottish Gaelic Bible probably owed most to the King James Bible, which was itself modelled on the liturgical styles of the Anglican Church.[24]

Within Gaelic literature, the Gaelic Bible is distinctive in its use of a type of vocabulary which sets it apart from day-to-day language. Gaelic 'Bible words' include *imich* ('go'), *labhair* ('speak'), *maille ri* ('together with') and *a-ghnàth* ('always'). The overall style is dignified but plain, and, at its best, it has a chiselled grandeur. This is particularly noticeable in the elegiac passages of the Old Testament, which owe their effectiveness in part to the well-developed tradition of elegiac poetry which already existed in secular Gaelic literature, and furnished appropriate vocabulary. Highlanders and Hebrews had much in common in their approaches to heroic verse and heroic narrative, and this gives the Gaelic Old Testament a piquancy which is, perhaps, not so obvious in the New. The Epistles of the New

Testament are possibly the part which the modern reader finds most difficult to assimilate, since there is a tendency (as in the Authorised Version) to translate technical terms literally, with a minimal amount of helpful paraphrasing.

In spite of its literary excellence, the Scottish Gaelic Bible was not accepted immediately in all parts of the Highlands. Although volumes were equipped initially with glossaries to aid comprehension among speakers of dialects different from the Argyllshire and Perthshire dialects of the translators, dialectal problems were encountered. It was alleged that the new work was not understood generally in Ross-shire, and the Revd Thomas Ross of Lochbroom attempted, unsuccessfully, to have his own translation accepted by the General Assembly in 1820. The Scottish Gaelic Bible also took time to find a place of esteem among congregations who were accustomed to the regular reading of Kirk's Bible or to their ministers' extemporary 'working translations'.[25] Today these difficulties are long forgotten, and the 1767–1801 translation is supreme, although it has been revised at regular intervals.

Revisions: 1796–1988

The process of revising the Scottish Gaelic Bible began soon after the publication of the first volumes. In 1796 the SSPCK published a revision of the New Testament, undertaken by John Stuart of Luss, and in 1807 a new edition of the Old Testament appeared, incorporating Alexander Stewart's translation of the Prophets. In 1820 John Stuart and Alexander Stewart completed a revision of the Old Testament as far as the First Book of Samuel. Sadly, both men died in the following year, and the expected thorough revision of the whole Bible, which depended on their expertise, was not carried out. Instead, the 1807 Old Testament and the 1796 New Testament were brought together in a single volume published in 1826. The 1826 edition incorporated spelling changes, made largely by the Revd John MacDonald of Comrie. A more extensive revision of the spelling and style of the Gaelic Bible was carried out by the Revd Thomas MacLauchlan of Edinburgh and the Revd Archibald Clerk of Kilmallie, and the resulting new edition was published in 1860. This edition included some modifications of vocabulary and syntax which were not well received initially, but which brought the text judiciously closer to Scottish Gaelic practice. MacLauchlan and Clerk also produced the Reference Bible of 1880.

An ambitious programme of revision, which applied to textual readings as well as to style and spelling, was initiated by the SSPCK in 1880. The work was entrusted to a commission, and the result was the 1902 Pulpit Bible. The revisers based their New Testament modifications on the Greek textual studies of B F Westcott and F J A Hort, which had also underlain the English Revised Version, and their Old Testament revision was based on the Massoretic text. The 1902 Bible was a fine example of modern textual revision, broadly in tune with the principles of the original translators. Nevertheless, its more radical departures from the previous mainstream Gaelic editions militated against general acceptance. The texts presently in use are based on the 1826 edition.

The monopoly of the SSPCK in the production and maintenance of the Gaelic Bible was broken in 1807, when the British and Foreign Bible Society published an edition. In the 1830s the Edinburgh Bible Society began publication, and responsibility later passed to the National Bible Society of Scotland, which sponsored the revision of MacLauchlan and Clerk.[26] In 1911 the Society published the Gaelic Pocket Bible, rooted in the 1826 edition, and edited by the Revd Dr Malcolm MacLennan. This has proved to be a popular rendering, and it forms the basis of the latest revision of the Gaelic Bible. This revision was initiated in the late 1940s by the National Bible Society, and operated through a panel of churchmen and scholars, led by the Revd Dr T M Murchison, who became the reviser (and later Moderator of the General Assembly of the Church of Scotland). The revision was primarily one of spelling, aiming at modernisation and consistency of orthography throughout the Bible.

When Dr Murchison died in 1984, two-thirds of the Old Testament had been revised. The work was continued in 1986 by the writer of this chapter, who was employed by the National Bible Society of Scotland for one year to set up a computer-based method of spelling revision. With the help of Edinburgh University Press and the type-setting company Speedspools, an efficient means of making spelling changes automatically in the typesetting process was developed. These changes are largely in accord with the guidelines for Gaelic spelling drawn up by the SCE Examination Board. Set in a very clear typeface, the revision is due to be completed in the autumn of 1988.

Translations into Present-day Gaelic

Although the translation of 1767–1801 was in a language which can be regarded as distinctively Scottish Gaelic in its principal features, it did not employ the everyday, spoken language of the Gaelic people.

Instead, it employed a style of language based on the Classical Gaelic literary tradition. A noticeable break with this tradition was apparent in 1875, when a translation of the New Testament, based on the Latin Vulgate, was published. This translation was the work of Father Ewen MacEachen, who died at Tombae, Glenlivet, in 1849, and it was published under the supervision of Father Colin Grant. MacEachen's work used a form of language which was based firmly on modern, spoken Gaelic.[27]

In making a translation of this kind, Father MacEachen was well ahead of his time, and his work was not widely used. It was only in the 1970s that the National Bible Society of Scotland initiated a programme of New Testament translation employing a form of contemporary Gaelic which would be readily understood by a wide cross-section of the Gaelic community. Behind this programme lay an awareness that young Gaelic speakers were not as familiar with 'Bible Gaelic' as earlier generations had been, and that they were liable to turn to English as the language of devotion and worship. A further stimulus towards a new Gaelic translation was provided by the example of the Bible Societies' 'Good News' Bible in modern English.

In 1977 a small team of translators began to work on Mark's Gospel, and *An Deagh Sgeul aig Marcus* (*Mark's Good News*) was published by the National Bible Society in 1980. In 1986 the Society published a further volume, *Facal as a' Phrìosan* (*A Word from Prison*) consisting of Paul's 'Prison Epistles': Ephesians, Philippians, Colossians and Philemon. The programme continues with a team which has recently been expanded to eight translators.

The translation of the Bible into Scottish Gaelic was undertaken more than two hundred years after the Reformation, and it took almost forty years to complete. Such chronology reflects the prejudices, both political and religious, which operated against the Gaelic language, and underlines the comparative scarcity of men who were willing and able to undertake the task of translation. After 1801, the difficulties were eased by the increasing responsibility of the Bible Societies for the production and maintenance of the text. In particular, the establishment of the National Bible Society of Scotland helped to sustain the revision and improvement of existing Gaelic versions. Since 1945, and especially in the 1970s and 1980s, the Bible Society has initiated important projects which will ensure that the Gaelic Bible will retain its place in the forefront of Gaelic literature and in the life of Highland churches.

DONALD MEEK

Notes

1 R L Thomson (ed), *Foirm na n-Urrnuidheadh* (Edinburgh, 1970), p 10.

2 D E Meek and J Kirk, 'John Carswell, Superintendent of Argyll: a Reassessment', *Records of the Scottish Church History Society* 19:1 (1975), pp 1–22.

3 M Stephens (ed), *The Oxford Companion to the Literature of Wales* (Oxford, 1986), pp 39–40.

4 F F Bruce, *History of the Bible in English* (revised edition) (London, 1970), pp 96–112.

5 See, in general, V E Durkacz, *Decline of the Celtic Languages* (Edinburgh, 1983), pp1–44, and J. Kirk, 'The Jacobean Church in the Highlands, 1567–1625' in L MacLean of Dochgarroch (ed), *The Seventeenth Century in the Highlands* (Inverness, 1986), pp 24–51.

6 C W Withers, 'Education and Anglicisation: The Policy of the SSPCK toward the Education of the Highlander, 1709–1825', *Scottish Studies* 26 (1982), pp 37–56.

7 H Watt (ed), *Fasti Ecclesiae Scoticanae* 4 (Edinburgh, 1923), p 1. The Presbytery of Skye became part of the Synod of Glenelg in 1724.

8 R L Thomson (ed), *Adtimchiol an Chreidimh: The Gaelic Version of John Calvin's Catechismus Ecclesiae Genevensis* (Edinburgh, 1962).

9 D MacKinnon, *The Gaelic Bible and Psalter* (Dingwall, 1930), pp 3–41.

10 Ibid., pp 42-4; John MacKay, *The Church in the Highlands* (London, 1914), pp 140–2.

11 K H Jackson, 'Common Gaelic', *Proceedings of the British Academy* 38 (1951), pp 71–97.

12 R E W Maddison, 'Robert Boyle and the Irish Bible', *Bulletin of the John Rylands Library* 31 (1958), pp 81–101.

13 Ibid., pp 97–101; Durkacz, *Decline of the Celtic Languages*, p 19.

14 I am very grateful to the Revd Andrew Swan, Rothesay, for drawing my attention to the Rothesay Collection and for allowing me to see his background notes. The Kirk Session of the High Kirk kindly forwarded photocopies of the texts for consultation.

15 D MacLean, 'The Life and Literary Labours of the Rev. Robert Kirk, of Aberfoyle', *Transactions of the Gaelic Society of Inverness* 31 (1922–24), pp 328–66.

16 When he visited Coll in 1773, Dr Samuel Johnson found that the minister had been in the habit of using his own 'extemporary version', by which he made the text 'more intelligible' than that of the 1767 New Testament; see R W Chapman (ed), *Johnson's Journey to the Western Isles of Scotland* (Oxford, 1970), p 110.

17 MacLean, 'Rev. Robert Kirk', p 347.

18 Durkacz, *Decline of the Celtic Languages*, pp 66–7. Dr Durkacz erroneously attributes the New Testament to John (rather than James) Stuart.

19   Ibid., p 76.
20   James and John Stuart made an outstanding contribution to the translation of the Scottish Gaelic Bible, and their commitment to the project, despite many difficulties, was crucial in ensuring its success.
21   D S Thomson (ed), *The Companion to Gaelic Scotland* (Oxford, 1983), pp 268–9; MacKinnon, *Gaelic Bible and Psalter*, p 15.
22   See, for background, A C Partridge, *English Biblical Translation* (London, 1973), pp 163, 166–9. References to the works of the eighteenth-century scholars who studied the Massoretic text and aspects of Hebrew poetry can be found in R K Harrison, *Introduction to the Old Testament* (Grand Rapids, 1969). Lowth published an influential work on Hebrew verse entitled *Lectures on the Sacred Poetry of the Hebrews*, first published in Latin in 1735 and from 1787 in English translation.
23   See, for example, Stuart's rendering of Job 19:26, which reads in translation, 'And after these have consumed my skin, yet in my flesh shall I see God', with no equivalents of 'though', 'worms' or 'body' (supplied in the Authorised Version, but not found in the Hebrew text). See further, J C L Gibson, *The Daily Study Bible: Job* (Edinburgh, 1985), pp 156–8.
24   For discussion of the style of the King James Bible, see Partridge, *English Biblical Translation*, pp 139–58.
25   MacKinnon, *Gaelic Bible and Psalter*, pp 66–71; see note 16 above.
26   Ibid., pp 76–84, 90-7.
27   Ibid., pp 85–90.

Further Reading

V E Durkacz, *Decline of the Celtic Languages* (Edinburgh, 1983).
J MacInnes, *The Evangelical Movement in the Highlands of Scotland: 1688–1800* (Aberdeen, 1951).
D MacKinnon, *The Gaelic Bible and Psalter* (Dingwall, 1930).
D MacLean, 'The Life and Literary Labours of the Rev. Robert Kirk, of Aberfoyle', *Transactions of the Gaelic Society of Inverness* 31 (1922–24), pp 328–66.
R E W Maddison, 'Robert Boyle and the Irish Bible', *Bulletin of the John Rylands Library* 31 (1958), pp 81–101.
C W Withers, *Gaelic in Scotland, 1698-1981: The Geographical History of a Language* (Edinburgh, 1984).

2

The Bible Societies in Scotland

The Bible Societies in Great Britain came into being as the result of a remarkable convergence of spiritual renewal in the Churches and a decisive development in printing technology.

The second half of the eighteenth century was marked by the Evangelical Revival, associated with the names of George Whitefield and John Wesley, which gave birth to the modern Protestant missionary movement late in the century with the founding of societies such as the Baptist Missionary Society (1792), the London Missionary Society (LMS—1795), similarly named Edinburgh and Glasgow Societies (both 1796), and the Church Missionary Society (1799).

In 1802 the invention of stereotype printing heralded a breakthrough for the printing industry, making possible for the first time the mass-production of books. Books had, of course, been printed in the West since Gutenberg (d. 1468), but prior to stereotyping each edition had to be re-set.

It was only to be expected that the growing evangelistic fervour in the British Churches should seek to grasp the new technological opportunities for mass-production of the Scriptures, and, in 1804, the British and Foreign Bible Society (BFBS) was formed in London. In 1802, at a meeting of the Religious Tract Society (founded 1799), the Revd Thomas Charles of Bala—inspired by the example of young Mary Jones who had walked 25 miles for a Bible—had presented the urgent need for Welsh Bibles. The Revd Joseph Hughes of Battersea asked: 'Surely a Society might be formed for the purpose; and if for Wales, why not for the Kingdom; why not for the whole world?' An appeal was issued, a constitution drafted, and finally on 7 March 1804, at a meeting held in the London Tavern, Bishopsgate Street (until recent years the site of the Royal Bank of Scotland), 300 people unanimously and enthusiastically founded the British and Foreign

Bible Society. The new body quickly set up a network of contributing 'Auxiliaries' all over Great Britain which enabled the fledgling Society to expand rapidly.

Beginnings

The earliest known Scottish Auxiliary of the BFBS, the Glasgow Bible Society (GBS), was formed in Glasgow in July 1805 under the chairmanship of David Dale, the enterprising Christian entrepreneur and philanthropist and the founder of the cotton mills at New Lanark. Some months earlier, Dale had made a fervent plea to the Presbytery of Glasgow on behalf of the BFBS with the result that it unanimously appointed an annual collection to be made in parish churches within its bounds. The offering was made on the last Sabbath of March 1805, when the eight parishes of the city contributed a total of £888.1.6d, which in present-day values is worth well over £200 000! However, Dale died the following year, and without his drive the Glasgow Bible Society began to lose momentum, and from 1808 it suspended operations.

The Presbytery of Edinburgh followed the example of Glasgow in January 1806. A collection for the BFBS raised £666.9.9d. These Presbyterial collections were indicative of the generous support the BFBS received from many parts of Scotland; indeed, in 1806 a total of £3399 was received by the BFBS from north of the Border, representing 46 per cent of its total income.

An Auxiliary of the BFBS was set up in Greenock and Port Glasgow in 1807, but it was in Edinburgh two years later that the first Bible Society bodies in Scotland were established on a basis firm enough to maintain a continuous record of service in the years ahead. On 4 August 1809, at a meeting chaired by John Balfour held in the New Rooms, Royal Exchange Coffee House (now the City Chambers), members 'formed themselves into a Society to be called "The Edinburgh Bible Society", having the same object in view with the British and Foreign Bible Society, and to act in concert with it or separately as circumstances shall require'.

This freedom of independent action incorporated in the constitution of the new Society was in later years to become deeply significant. One of the prime movers behind the formation of the Edinburgh Bible Society (EBS) was Christopher Anderson, founder and minister of Charlotte Baptist Chapel.

By a curious coincidence, another Bible Society had been

founded in Edinburgh only two days previously with almost precisely identical aims and, indeed, for a time with an identical name. This body, which a few months later changed its title to the 'Scottish Bible Society', was formed by ministers belonging to the Church of Scotland Presbytery of Edinburgh. It has been claimed that the two separate Bible Societies emerged in Edinburgh because some of the Church of Scotland ministers hesitated to associate with an organisation in which laymen and members of the dissenting churches played such a dominant role. A more significant reason may have been the desire on the part of the members of the Scottish Bible Society for a greater degree of independence from London—certainly the wording of its constitution seems to have placed more emphasis on separate action than on co-operation with the BFBS. 'The object . . . shall be the circulation of the Holy Scriptures either by separate means or by direct co-operation with the British and Foreign Bible Society, as shall be found most practicable and expedient.' In any event, as the two Societies developed over the years, they each found complementary roles: the EBS (together with the other local Bible Societies associated with it) became increasingly involved in overseas Bible work, while the Scottish Bible Society met a real need at home by providing ministers with heavily subsidised Scriptures for the poor.

The Glasgow Bible Society was re-established in 1812 at a meeting in the Black Bull Inn under the presidency of John Tennant, who had chaired the last meeting of 1808. It is noteworthy that the GBS was set up on a different basis from the EBS in so far as it was 'a simple Auxiliary of the BFBS'. Its *Fourth Annual Report* (1816) rather surprisingly highlights its subordinate role to the London body—a sentiment which contrasts markedly with that of its sister societies in the East of Scotland. Within 11 months the GBS had raised £1025.19.0d, of which £971.7.8d was sent to the BFBS for its overseas work.

Auxiliaries and Associations

Support for these new Bible Societies grew rapidly. A major of the Ross-shire Militia, stationed at Leith, forwarded to the EBS a donation of £29, a total representing one day's pay from the non-commissioned officers and privates of the regiment. At Aberdeen the 'Female Servants' Society for Promoting the Diffusion of the Scriptures' was instituted, and by February 1811 it had 110 members each contributing one penny per week to Bible Society work.

The GBS received its support from a series of affiliated Associations, some of which had a geographical base and others a congregational connection: 'The Barony of Gorbals Bible Association' and 'The Dovehill Relief Congregation Youth's Auxiliary Bible Society' are two examples. Like the Female Servants' Society in Aberdeen they were organised on the assumption that members would each contribute one penny per week. There was also a proposal to form a Ladies Association in Glasgow but this proved to be too revolutionary a suggestion for the time:

> Far be it from your Committee to recommend any scheme for your adoption, incompatible for that retiring delicacy, which is the loveliest beauty of the female character—any scheme that would divest the Christian fair of that ornament 'which is in the sight of God of great price, the ornament of a meek and quiet spirit'—that would 'quench the blushes' of feminine sensibility, or fix in the openness of masculine effrontery, the downcast eyelids of modesty.[1]

Both the EBS and the GBS steadily developed a network of supporting Auxiliaries and Associations throughout the country which by 1820 amounted to over one hundred, ranging from Stranraer to Kirkwall. Some contributions were also received from overseas, the first coming in 1813 from the Scots congregation at West River, Pictou, Canada, which sent £22.17.0d.

Until 1815, Britain was engaged in the Napoleonic Wars on the continent and both the EBS and the GBS saw the distribution of Scriptures among the prisoners of war as part of their mandate. Indeed, the very first act of the EBS was to distribute Scriptures in Danish, French and Dutch among prisoners in the prison camp at Greenlaw. Every prisoner was given a New Testament in his own language. A letter of thanks from a Danish prisoner stated:

> I shall never forget this piece of brotherly friendship, and when our day of peace shall return, I shall be happy to make it known in Denmark, as a proof of that fine spirit of humanity which shines bright in the midst of war.[2]

The Glasgow Bible Society presented a French Bible to the French General Simon, who was held a prisoner of war in Dumbarton Castle. They also made available Bibles and New Testaments to British soldiers at half-price and placed Bibles in soldiers' quarters at the Glasgow barracks and Dumbarton Castle.

There was also extensive distribution of the Scriptures among the poor in Edinburgh and Glasgow. Bibles were supplied to the Destitute Sick Societies of Edinburgh and Leith as well as to the Royal Infirmary and the Lying-In hospital. In Glasgow, prisoners and the inmates of asylums received Bibles, and between 1815 and 1822 the GBS met requests from the Catholic School Society—which was set up to teach the uneducated among Roman Catholics—for a total of 1049 Bibles and 1400 Testaments.

Gaelic Scriptures and Schools

A very important part of the early Bible Society work in Scotland was supplying Gaelic Scriptures to the Highlands (see also chapter 1 above). At that time there were some 335 000 people living in the Highlands, 300 000 of whom understood Gaelic only. The Society in Scotland for the Propagation of Christian Knowledge (SSPCK) in 1767 had published the first Gaelic New Testament—translated by the Revd James Stuart of Killin—in spite of the fears of some of its members that it might inflame Jacobitism. Many Highland parishes were without schools and churches, and the popular religion was 'a strange medley of half forgotten Catholicism and the fragments of a more ancient Nature worship'. It is not surprising, therefore, that the distribution of Gaelic Scriptures became an early priority of the Bible Societies together with strong support for the promotion of Gaelic schools. The SSPCK, which published the first Gaelic Bible in 1801, had established 159 schools throughout the Highlands by 1777. But the emphasis in these schools was on anglicising the Highlanders (which was, of course, government policy since the beginning of the seventeenth century), so it is not surprising that after 1804 responsibility for the Gaelic Scriptures passed to the Bible Societies. Shortly after its inception in 1809, the Edinburgh Bible Society took over from the BFBS the task of distributing the Gaelic Scriptures and set up depots for this purpose in Edinburgh and Inverness.

Many of Scotland's Gaelic speakers were non-readers. There were few parochial schools and the SSPCK schools never really took root, mainly because of their anglicising objective. A significant step forward was taken in 1810 when the Edinburgh Society for the Support of Gaelic Schools was set up, and, once again, Christopher Anderson was one of the leading promoters. These Gaelic schools took on in a way the SSPCK schools never did. They catered for all ages and the principal text book was the Gaelic Bible. All of them were 'circulating schools' (*ie* they moved round the parish going to the people rather than expecting the people to travel to them).

From Kiltearn in Ross-shire a farmer wrote that the announcement of a gift of Gaelic Bibles prompted many in the parish to learn the language properly. They decided to devote two hours per week after 6 pm to improve their knowledge of the language in preparation for the arrival of the Bibles. At first, children aged from 9 to 14 attended, but numbers steadily increased and soon other schools were started until seven were operating in a parish seven miles long. The more expert Gaelic readers went round the schools once or twice a month when it was moonlight and helped the others. Soon there were more than 300 people of all ages engaged in reading the Scriptures in their mother tongue.

In addition to supplying circulating schools with Bibles, the Edinburgh Bible Society responded to individual requests. The Revd W Findlater of Durness wrote that of the 1200 people in his parish, all except five families were Gaelic speakers, yet in the whole parish there were only nine Bibles. In Glengarry a correspondent reported that he had personally witnessed 20 people sitting around the fireside listening to the man of the house reading aloud Isaiah 40—the only leaves of the Scriptures he possessed.

The following extracts from early reports of the Edinburgh Bible Society provide ample testimony to the effectiveness of these circulating schools:

> In two populous townships, 12 miles from the Parish Church, where, except in one house, not a single Bible was to be found, by the following year there was not a house in which a portion of the Word of God was not read and His worship performed twice a day.[3]
>
> Their local situation [in Tolsta, Lewis] prevented their receiving any benefit from church or school. Having no roads, and there being several waters, sometimes impassable, between them and the Parish Church, it is but very seldom that they can attend. Some old people told me they had not heard a sermon for 20 years. . . . Now they all collect on the Sabbath in the Schoolhouse where the teacher reads to them a portion of Scripture, and in almost every family they have now someone to read to them at home.[4]

Expansion Overseas

The Scots who left their native shores in the early nineteenth century for Canada, Australia and New Zealand were by no means forgotten by the Bible Societies. Bibles in English and Gaelic were regularly offered to passengers on emigrant ships leaving Greenock and Leith. For many years, convicts leaving Leith for Botany Bay were also given copies of the Word of God. There was a hitch in 1837 when it was discovered that the Bibles presented in Edinburgh were being confiscated on the ships reaching London. The Directors of the EBS protested to the Prime Minister of the day, Lord John Russell, about 'this amazing piece of senseless English bumbledom'[5]—apparently successfully, because the practice of supplying Bibles to convicts was later resumed.

From its inception, the Edinburgh Bible Society regarded the world as its parish. Its Directors desired to 'excite compassion for the deplorable conditions of millions who have no Bible'. So, in addition to making regular remittance to the BFBS, which by 1824 had totalled £20 100, the EBS became increasingly involved in direct support of Bible work abroad. In its first year £200 was sent to the Hibernian Bible Society and a grant of £100 was made through the BFBS towards the printing of the Bible in Icelandic. It also made a donation of £200 to William Carey's translation and publication ministry at the Serampore Press in India. The following year a gift of £100 to the Evangelical Society in Stockholm (later the Swedish Bible Society) enabled 3400 Swedish Testaments to be given to those 'who were destitute of even a shilling to pay for a copy for themselves'. In 1813 the Society provided German Roman Catholics with £50 to print the Psalms of David in German. In 1815, in association with the London Society for Promoting Christianity among the Jews, the Society provided copies of the Gospels in Hebrew for Jewish communities on the continent.

During these early years the EBS and the GBS were in continual contact with the BFBS in London. They not only sent regular and substantial contributions towards the work of the parent Society, but also offered suggestions as to how that work might be undertaken. For example, in 1821 the EBS proposed that the BFBS should publish a Bible in Spanish—a suggestion which was acted on.

Other proposals were not taken up. An enterprising Scottish missionary, James Thomson, had made his way in 1818 to South America. After establishing many schools and Bible work in Argentina, Uruguay and Chile, he passed on to Peru (where his name was recently commemorated in the newly-founded 'Diego Thomson' Teacher Training Institute in Lima). In 1824, Thomson wrote from Lima to the EBS asking for a grant of £200 to pay for the printing of the New Testament in Quechua, the language of the fabled Inca empire. He had arranged for a native of Cuzco to make the translation. The Edinburgh Director passed on the request to the BFBS, who were unable to respond to it. It was not until 56 years later, in 1880, that the BFBS published John's Gospel in Quechua, and the 'Quechuistas'—

the largest indigenous community in the Americas—had to wait until 1947 for the New Testament. The full Bible in Quechua: Cuzco was not published until 1988. While fully recognising that in 1824 the BFBS decision was taken reluctantly, and in the light of other claims on its limited resources, one cannot help but wonder how different the history of the Quechua Bible might have been had the EBS taken the initiative themselves.

In a curious way a Scottish connection has been maintained with the development of the Quechua Scriptures over the years. The translation of the New Testament was undertaken by Len Herniman, and the 1971 revision was co-ordinated by Leslie Hoggarth, both of whom later became Scottish Secretaries of the Evangelical Union of South America. In fact, Leslie Hoggarth taught Quechua at the School of South American studies at St Andrews University. And the translation of the Old Testament, and a further revision of the New, were co-ordinated by William Mitchell of Ballingry, Fife, who is currently a Translation Adviser with the United Bible Societies.

A Period of Controversy

Between 1823 and 1826 the Bible Societies in Scotland became caught up in two complicated controversies: first over the monopoly of Bible provision. In 1824 His Majesty's Printers for Scotland—Sir David Hunter Blair and John Bruce—obtained an interdict to make it impossible for Bibles printed in England to be sold in Scotland. This was in retaliation against the King's Printers in England who, in 1821, had taken advantage of a previous legal ruling prohibiting Bibles printed in Scotland being sold in England.

The Directors of the Edinburgh Bible Society immediately realised that the Scottish interdict would severely limit their work since they depended heavily on English supplies. With the strong support of the other Bible Societies in Scotland, they appointed Dr John Lee, minister of the Canongate Church and later Principal Clerk of the General Assembly, to draw up a *Memorial for the Bible Societies in Scotland* (Edinburgh, 1824, followed by *Additional Memorial on Printing and Importing Bibles*, Edinburgh, 1826). This *Memorial* tersely and eloquently summarised the opposition to the interdict. But in spite of Lee's cogent arguments, both the Court of Session and the House of Lords upheld the monopolists' case, with the result that from 1828 to 1839—when the monopoly was abolished—the Scottish Societies were compelled to purchase Bibles from a single source which offered inferior quality in insufficient quantities and at exorbitant rates. Inevitably distribution figures fell during these 10 or 11 years.

The second great controversy concerned the printing of Bibles containing the Apocrypha—the 12 additional books which are found in the Greek translation of the Old Testament known as the Septuagint, but not included in the Hebrew canon. The Roman Catholic Church regards these books—which it calls the Deuterocanon (for it the 'Apocrypha' is another collection)—as part of the canon of Scripture. The Orthodox Churches also accept these books, although the degree of authority offered them varies from one Orthodox Church to another. Lutherans and Anglicans permit them to be printed in a section between the Testaments, but do not regard them as part of Holy Scripture.

The Edinburgh Bible Society claimed that publishing Bibles with the Apocrypha was in breach of the rule which limited the BFBS funds to the circulation of the Holy Scriptures exclusively without note or comment. However, it seems to have been prepared initially to adopt a pragmatic line with regard to those Bible Societies on the continent which were circulating Bibles, containing the Apocrypha placed between the Testaments, on the assurance from the BFBS that all grants provided would be used exclusively for the printing of 'the Books of the Old and New Testaments as generally received in this country'.[6]

However, a subsequent decision in 1824 by the BFBS to give a grant of £500 towards a Roman Catholic German Bible with the Apocryphal books interspersed, resulted in the EBS writing to the BFBS to express the hope that they 'would not again agree to support any edition of the Scripture along with which the Apocrypha was to be circulated'.[7]

By this time the controversy was a matter of extensive public debate in Scotland and England. A vast array of pamphlets from both 'anti-Apocryphalists' and 'philo-Apocryphalists' were widely read throughout Scotland and England and beyond. The leading anti-Apocryphalists in Scotland were Robert and James Haldane, founders of a movement which led to the establishment of Congregational and Baptist churches in Scotland, and Andrew Thomson, minister of St George's Church, Charlotte Square, Edinburgh, editor of *The Christian Instructor* and a leading abolitionist in the slavery debate. The BFBS committee were divided as, indeed—although to a much lesser extent—were the Scottish Societies. However, by 1826, the Directors of the EBS felt that they were left with no alternative but 'with much anxiety and deep regret' to withdraw formally from the association with BFBS. Later in the year the GBS followed suit. The great majority of the Scottish Bible Societies and Auxiliaries supported the Edinburgh Bible Society, although alternative pro-BFBS auxiliary Bible Societies appeared briefly in Edinburgh, Glasgow, Aberdeen, Elgin, Inverness, Stirling and Fife.

Although by the time the break came, the BFBS had in fact bowed to the pressure of public opinion in England and Wales and decided 'not to print or circulate the Apocryphal books', the change was too late to restore Scottish confidence in the parent Society. With the passage of time and the death of the leading contenders, trust and co-operation were eventually restored, although to this day Scotland has retained its full independence in the world fellowship of Bible Societies.

Consolidation

The Scottish Bible Societies, having dissolved their links with the BFBS, faced a formidable task. Previously they had very largely left overseas circulation of the Scriptures to the parent Society in London, but now they were on their own. And the times were not propitious for setting up a new international network. It was a period of social upheaval at home with working-class unrest and Chartist riots. On the continent revolutions and wars were commonplace, marking an era of profound political change. Outbreaks of cholera aggravated the already fraught situation. During these early years of independence, support of Bible work in Ireland continued. In addition to grants to the Hibernian Bible Society and the Trinitarian Bible Society (a break-away from the BFBS in 1831), the EBS directly circulated 30 251 Bibles and Testaments. On the strong recommendation of the Synod of Ulster, an agent for Ireland was appointed, and soon several EBS Auxiliaries were set up there.

In spite of formidable difficulties, work in Europe was begun in Switzerland. In 1830 the newly-formed Evangelical Society of Geneva sought affiliation with the EBS which readily supplied it with Scriptures. By 1839, this Society had 21 colporteurs and had sold 44 748 Bibles and Testaments.

In 1834 the French and Foreign Bible Society came into being with a constitution similar to that of the EBS, which provided it with 1013 French Bibles and 447 Testaments. Associations of the new Bible Society were formed in Paris, Lyons and Bordeaux, each member promising to sell one New Testament each week.

In 1829 the EBS Directors were fortunate enough to secure the services of the Revd J C Oncken as their agent in Germany. He was to remain in the employment of the EBS (and later of the National Bible Society for Scotland—NBSS) for over 50 years, during which he rendered outstanding and faithful service in the face of great opposition and hardship. He opened a depot in Hamburg from which he supplied in his first ten years 52 302 Bibles and Testaments in various languages to Prussia, Mecklenburg, Hannover, Westphalia, Rhineland, Holstein, Holland, Bohemia, Hungary and Poland. Oncken himself travelled widely, sometimes in a one-horse carriage used as a travelling sales van.

The Edinburgh Bible Society also began work in Italy and Spain and the Glasgow Bible Society printed an edition of the Spanish New Testament. Carey's press at Serampore continued to receive regular support from Edinburgh, and Scottish missionaries recently arrived in India were supplied with Bibles. Close links were maintained with Scottish settlers in Canada. By 1839 there were seven Auxiliaries of the EBS in and around Pictou. Cape Breton, Prince Edward Island, New Brunswick and Glengarry County (Ontario) all received significant numbers of Scriptures, some of them in Gaelic. Scriptures were also sent to the West Indies, British Guiana, Colombia, Brazil, Venezuela and Uruguay. The GBS provided grants for the Kaffraria Missions in South Africa. Over 5000 Scriptures were supplied by the EBS to Scottish settlers in Australia, and even Pitcairn Island received 50 Bibles. Direct links with Canada, Australia and New Zealand carried on well into the twentieth century due to a demand for Bibles with the metrical Psalms among people of Scottish descent.

The monopoly of the King's Printers was finally broken in 1839 thanks in large part to a popular protest movement spearheaded by the Revd Adam Thomson, Secession minister in Coldstream. With the monopoly gone, Scriptures were again introduced from England resulting in a 40 per cent reduction in price. Adam Thomson went on to form the Free Bible Society in Coldstream with the object of printing Scriptures as cheaply as possible. At first the Coldstream Press was extraordinarily successful. In 1845 as many as 178 200 Bibles were produced and sold at unprecedentedly low prices. But the English printers retaliated by locking the Coldstream Bibles out of England, Ireland and the Colonies (the English monopoly was still in force), and by underselling the Bibles they supplied to Scotland. Such economic pressure was too strong and the Free Press went bankrupt. In Coldstream today there is a housing estate named after Adam Thomson.

Union

After the break with the BFBS in 1826, the Glasgow Bible Society recognised the need for 'a common Association, or a variety of Associations co-operating with one another, which shall . . . continue to disseminate the pure Word of God at home and abroad'. But it was not until 1845 that representatives of the EBS and GBS agreed to propose a union under the name of 'The Bible Society of Scotland'. The Directors of both Societies warmly approved the idea in principle, but not surprisingly the GBS found unacceptable the proposal in the plan of union put forward by the EBS in 1847 that 'there shall be a Central Committee or Board of Directors and Head Office in Edinburgh, with a Standing Committee in Glasgow, which would have the right of attending the meetings in Edinburgh'.[8] The matter was left in abeyance for ten years until the Revd Dr A N Somerville, Honorary Secretary of the GBS, sent a memorandum to all Bible Societies in Scotland proposing a union. Once again, the EBS insistence that the headquarters of the new society be in Edinburgh prevented the union from materialising. However, the religious revival that swept the country in 1859 and brought new vigour to the churches had created a widespread desire among Christian people for a united missionary endeavour which was impatient with petty rivalries. Accordingly the Glasgow Bible Society proposed a new route to union: if it had proved difficult to unite Societies as they stood, why not form a new national society and then invite the existing Societies to join the new one? So on 9 May 1860, at a meeting held in the Merchants Hall, Glasgow, the National Bible Society of Scotland was floated with leading ministers from all denominations on the board and the Duke of Argyll as Honorary President. The invitation to existing Bible Societies to join was readily accepted by the Edinburgh and Glasgow Societies and by many other smaller Societies throughout the country. The new Society was formed on 22 May 1861. Only two Societies declined to join: the Scottish Bible Society and the West of Scotland Bible Society (founded in 1849).

In view of the rivalry between the east and the west which had foiled earlier attempts to unite, the new constitution and rules provided for two committees, Eastern and Western, each having its own field of work. Regular meetings of the whole board of directors would deal with matters affecting the work of both committees. The Eastern Committee took over the work previously carried out by the Edinburgh Bible Society, and the Western assumed responsibility for the activities previously undertaken by the Glasgow Bible Society.

Later history would demonstrate that this union was to enable Scotland to play a key role in the global development of Bible Society work alongside the British and Foreign, American and Netherlands Bible Societies.

The work of the new united Society expanded rapidly. Distribution continued apace in Scotland. Seventy Bible women were employed in Edinburgh and Glasgow who, in eight years, sold over 20 000 Bibles and Testaments. Arrangements were made for the very poor to pay for Bibles in instalments, and for those who could not afford these terms a lending system was devised. The New Testament was published in one-penny parts, and large numbers of Bibles and New Testaments were distributed free of charge in missions, schools and hospitals. The Society helped in the support of over 200 colporteurs of the Tract and Book Society (later the Scottish Colportage Society), who operated in many parts of rural Scotland including the Western Isles, Orkney and Shetland. In these more outlying parts, money was not always available to buy a Bible: Bibles sold in St Kilda were paid for in woollen stockings which were later purchased by a Director of the Society and sent to Highland colonists in Labrador!

International Horizons

The work already established in continental Europe was consolidated and extended into Portugal, Belgium, Scandinavia, Finland, the Baltic States, Russia, Austria, Czechoslovakia, Yugoslavia, Rumania, Greece and Turkey.

The NBSS began to develop many more contacts in Africa. In 1862 the Efik New Testament was printed for the people of Calabar in West Africa (with whom Mary Slessor was later associated), followed in 1868 by the complete Bible. This was to be the first of many new translations of the Scriptures into foreign languages published by the recently united Society. Other West African languages published by the Society included Umon, Lobi, Songoi, Mumuye, Meninka and Kanuri. In Central Africa the Society's first publication was John's Gospel in Nyanja (1884) translated by Dr Robert Laws of Aberdeen. The New Testament followed in 1886, but the Bible did not appear until 1922. Other Central African languages published included Tonga, Mwamba, Tumbuka, Konde, Luba-Sanga, Namwanga, Bemba, Biza-Lala and Lomwe. The Kikuyu New Testament was produced for East Africa and jointly published with the BFBS in 1926.

Mark's Gospel in Tamachek, a North African language, was published in 1934.

After the adjustment of responsibilities for the Far East in 1948 between the BFBS, the ABS (American), the NBS (Netherlands) and the NBSS, the NBSS became jointly responsible for work in what is now Malaysia, Singapore and Brunei. Support was also given to the NBS work in Indonesia.

It was in China, however, that the NBSS developed the most extensive overseas operation. The link with China began in 1863 with the arrival in Chefoo of the Revd Alexander Williamson of the United Presbyterian Church of Scotland. Williamson undertook a series of strenuous journeys into the interior, visiting Tientsin, Peking, Manchuria and Mongolia. He was joined by Robert Lilley in 1868 and by William Murray (previously a colporteur in the Scottish Highlands) in 1872. Others were to follow. Accounts of their pioneering journeys, made often in atrocious conditions and sometimes subject to grave danger, make thrilling reading and did much to stir up a growing interest in China among Bible Society supporters in Scotland.

As early as 1867 Williamson printed Gospels in Peking Mandarin (later known as Kuoyu), and in 1879 he published the first Chinese Testament to have chapter headings, references and maps. In 1883, the NBSS published the first Scriptures in Easy Wenli (a simplified form of written Chinese), and work on the more literary High Wenli was jointly undertaken by the BFBS and ABS, culminating in the Union Version of 1919. To facilitate its work in China the Society set up a printing press in Hankow which was to produce many millions of Scriptures over the coming decades.

NBSS work in the Far East extended from China into Korea and Japan. In 1865 the Revd R Jermain Thomas, a Welsh LMS missionary in China seconded to the NBSS, visited Korea disguised as a Chinese traveller. At that time Korea was the 'hermit kingdom' and excluded all foreigners and foreign books. Nevertheless, Thomas succeeded in distributing Chinese Scriptures along the west coast of the Korean peninsula. However, this pioneer ministry was soon cut tragically short. Returning to Korea the following year, Thomas' ship foundered in the Taedong River, and passengers and crew were massacred by Korean soldiers. It is said that Thomas' last act was to offer a Bible to his murderer; today he is remembered as the first Protestant martyr of the Korean Church. In 1873 the Revd John Ross, a native of Nigg, Ross-shire, and a United Presbyterian missionary to Manchuria, made contact with Korean exiles and learned their language. With the help of a young Korean trader, So San Yun, Ross translated the Gospels of

Luke and John. These were the first Korean Scriptures published by the NBSS, in 1882. Their smuggling into Korea and the subsequent growth of the Protestant Church in that land are an exciting story.

In 1876 a NBSS agent was established in Yokohama, Japan, by Robert Lilley, who had previously worked in China. Today the Japan Bible Society looks back to the founding of the Yokohama agency as the beginning of Bible Society history in their country.

During the first half of the twentieth century, four major Bible Societies were working on a global basis: the British and Foreign, American and Netherlands Bible Societies and the National Bible Society of Scotland. By the second half of the century the situation had changed dramatically. In 1946 the United Bible Societies (UBS) was founded. It has now grown to 75 full or associate member Bible Societies. Joining the four large missionary Bible Societies in 1946 were the European Bible Societies which traditionally had served only their own national constituency: Czechoslovakia, Denmark, Finland, France, Germany, Norway, Sweden and Switzerland. Many of these, particularly Germany and Norway, very quickly became major contributors to the new fund—to be known as the World Service Budget—through which the UBS-member Societies co-operate to meet the needs of the world for copies of Scripture, together rather than separately. Since 1946 the growth of new Bible Societies has largely been concentrated in the developing countries.

The National Bible Society of Scotland continues to play a full role in the United Bible Societies which in 1987/1988 operated a World Service Budget of US $33 million and achieved a global distribution of over 24 million Bibles and New Testaments, to say nothing of a much larger number of smaller selections of biblical text.

The Bible for Today

While continuing to recognise the tremendous strengths of the Authorised Version of the Bible, the NBSS has actively supported the translation of the Scriptures into contemporary English. It has been represented on the Joint Committee of the New English Bible and the Revised English Bible (due to be published in 1989), and is a co-publisher of the Good News Bible (GNB), which has turned out to be one of the publishing 'miracles' of the 1970s and 80s, achieving global sales of over 25 million (75 million New Testaments). Translated into 'common language' English on the basis of functional (rather than formal) equivalence, the GNB has provided the Churches with an invaluable educational and evangelistic tool in the secularised, post-literary West as well as among new literates in the developing world. The Year of the Bible campaign in Scotland in 1988 is a response to the apparent decline in Bible reading among the people of Scotland and aims to increase popular awareness of it as a relevant book for today. It enjoys the backing of Scotland's main Churches with support from sympathetic organisations and companies. Media advertising and a series of national events, backed up by many locally organised happenings, are giving Scottish Christians a unique opportunity to witness the power of the Word of God in their lives. Most of the denominations have organised their own complementary Year of the Bible programmes. An important publishing event of the Year will be the appearance of the Gaelic Bible in the new orthographic revision.

1988 was chosen for the Year of the Bible for two reasons. First of all, for the first time Scottish research data recently became available on Bible use and popular attitudes to it (from the NBSS's Church Attendance Census and the Church of Scotland's *Life Style Survey*, both undertaken in 1984). This research reveals both the need for, and the potential of, a special promotion of the Bible, as well as providing a base on which it will be possible to measure the effectiveness of the campaign. Second, various factors in our national life are combining to make people increasingly aware of the need for moral guidelines: the threat of an AIDS epidemic, growing pressures on family life, business scandals and the concern for justice and peace issues. Under the slogan 'Go by the Book', the campaign is encouraging people to take a fresh look at the Book which helped to shape Scotland's national identity and to discover its power to guide them into the twenty-first century.

FERGUS MACDONALD

Notes

1 Quoted from the *Sixth Annual Report* (1818) of the Glasgow Bible Society in the unpublished typescript by G A F Knight and W C Somerville, *The History of the National Bible Society of Scotland*, part 1: *1809–1900*, pp 27f. This is cited below as *History*.
2 *History*, p 19.
3 *History*, p 37.
4 *History*, p 38.
5 *History*, p 61.

3

James Moffatt: Bible Translator

The Translator

In 1915 an appointment to the Chair of Church History in the United
Free Church College in Glasgow was pending. Referring to one of the
candidates, Principal James Denney wrote in a letter to William
Robertson Nicoll, 'in some quarters the Historical New Testament is
counted to its author for anything but righteousness still'.[1] The
candidate was James Moffatt, who at that time was Professor of Greek
and New Testament Exegesis at Mansfield College, Oxford. He was
born at Glasgow in 1870 and educated there, passing from the
Academy to the University, where he graduated with honours in
classics, before proceeding to the study of theology at the Glasgow
College of the Free Church. During his theological course he was
profoundly influenced by the Professor of New Testament Language
and Literature, Alexander Balmain Bruce, of whom it was said that 'he
belonged to the slender group of the original and quickening minds in
the Scotland of his generation'.[2]

In 1896 Moffatt was ordained and inducted as minister of the Free
Church at Dundonald in Ayrshire. It was during his time there that he
produced the work to which Denney alluded: *The Historical New
Testament, Being the Literature of the New Testament Arranged in the
Order of Its Literary Growth and According to the Dates of the
Documents. A New Translation Edited with Prolegomena, Historical
Tables, Critical Notes, and an Appendix*. It was published in 1901 and a
second edition was called for in the same year. By some it may not have
been counted to its author for righteousness, but in 1902 the University
of St Andrews recognised the quality of the scholarship displayed in
the book by conferring on Moffatt the honorary degree of Doctor of

Divinity. He was the youngest person ever to have received such an honour from any Scottish university.

In 1907 Moffatt left Dundonald to become minister of the United Free Church at Broughty Ferry. His massive *Introduction to the Literature of the New Testament* appeared in 1911, the year in which he moved to Mansfield College. In spite of Denney's misgivings, he was appointed in 1915 to succeed Principal T M Lindsay in the Chair of Church History in the Glasgow College. There he remained until 1927, when he was appointed to the Washburn Chair of Church History in the Union Theological Seminary, New York, from which he retired in 1939.

It was said of Moffatt, doubtless with truth, that he 'could have taken any chair in the Faculty at a moment's notice'.[3] Nevertheless, he was primarily a New Testament scholar and during the years in which he was a Professor of Church History he published nothing on that subject which is remotely comparable to his work in the biblical field, *eg The Approach to the New Testament* (1921), *A Critical And Exegetical Commentary on the Epistle to the Hebrews* (1924), *Love in the New Testament* (1929), and *Grace in the New Testament* (1931).

The best known of all his publications are his translations of the Scriptures. *The Historical New Testament* contained, as we have seen, a translation and rearrangement of the entire contents of the New Testament. *The New Testament: A New Translation* appeared in 1913. It was indeed new and not merely a reprint of Moffatt's earlier rendering. Eleven years later it was followed by *The Old Testament: A New Translation*, in two volumes. *The Complete Moffatt Bible* in one volume was published in 1926 and a final revision of the whole in 1935. Though Moffatt undertook no further revision of his own translation, his expertise as a translator was enlisted in the making of the American Revised Standard Version. He was executive Secretary of the translation committee and continued in this work until his death in 1944.

The Translations: (A) The Historical New Testament

The Historical New Testament was intended for scholars and students rather than for the general public. Moffatt's primary concern was to show the chronological sequence of the New Testament documents, since, as he rightly held, their relationship to one another is obscured by the traditional order. In his translation, which begins with 1 Thessalonians and ends with 2 Peter, the bulk of the epistolary literature comes before the first three Gospels and Acts, and Revelation comes before the Fourth Gospel and the Johannine Epistles. The critical questions which arise in connection with the character and dating of the documents are discussed at suitable points. Moffatt held that to be properly understood the New Testament must be seen within the context of the history of the period (roughly 200 BC to AD 200). His book contains numerous tables and diagrams presenting what he regarded as the essential data on these and other matters. All this is for the serious student. What is of supreme interest for our present purpose, the translation, was made as an afterthought.

Moffatt had intended to use the Revised Version in *The Historical New Testament*; but obtaining permission to print it proved to be difficult. Accordingly, he decided to make an independent translation. He described it as 'a difficult and audacious attempt' and offered it to the reader 'with extreme diffidence'. He realised that most of those who read it would compare it unfavourably with the Authorised Version, 'an English classic which has unrivalled associations of literary rhythm and of religious experience'. The one claim that he made for his rendering was faithfulness; but by 'faithfulness' he meant rather more than is commonly understood by the term, more even than appears from his own formulation many years later of his aim in his translation of the whole Bible: 'to present the books of the Old and New Testament in effective, intelligible English'.

Translating New Testament Greek
The claim is often made (sometimes by those who ought to know better) that the New Testament is written 'in the everyday Greek of the time' or words to that effect, giving the impression that the New Testament is written in unvarying colloquial style. New Testament Greek is indeed different in many ways from classical Greek; but there are important dissimilarities between different books, and sometimes between different parts of the same book. Furthermore, in the many passages which are quotations from the Old Testament there are additional differences of style and vocabulary. A translator who aims at reproducing not merely the sense of the original but the impression which it made upon its original readers, must take account not only of vocabulary and idiom but also of style. A rendering of poetry or elevated prose in the style of coffee-table chat just will not do, no matter how accurately the sense is reproduced. Moffatt declared that his aim was:

> to contribute something to that mental impression of change and progress in the NT literature which it is the aim of the whole edition to accentuate

and

> to make it [the translation] accurate and idiomatic, besides presenting, to some extent, the *nuances* of the individual writers.

Moffatt based his translation on the second edition of the critical text of the Greek New Testament prepared by Professor Eberhard Nestle, but did not follow it slavishly. When he preferred a different reading, he indicated this by a note. He also used brackets to indicate passages which he thought were later additions or had been displaced from their original contexts. We shall have occasion to notice his use of these and other devices when we consider his later translations of both the New and the Old Testaments. It is, however, possible to disregard these textual niceties and the critical discussions on authorship, date and the like, and simply to read the translation in its historical sequence with the help of the clear outlines which Moffatt prefaced to each book. To do so is to gain a general impression of the developing life of some of the earliest Christian communities and of the varying ways in which the ministry of Jesus of Nazareth was understood.

Opposition to *The Historical New Testament* was aroused mainly, if not exclusively, by Moffatt's whole-hearted acceptance of the critical approach to the New Testament writings. The last quarter of the nineteenth century was a time of bitter controversy in the Free Church of Scotland concerning the orthodoxy or otherwise of the critical approach to Scripture. [4] In 1881 the brilliant Old Testament scholar and Semitist, William Robertson Smith, had been deposed from his Chair in the Free Church College at Aberdeen because of the views expressed in his published works. In 1890 an unsuccessful attack was launched against two New Testament professors, Marcus Dods of New College, Edinburgh, and A B Bruce, Moffatt's own teacher in Glasgow. The General Assembly of the United Free Church declined in 1902 to institute a process of heresy against George Adam Smith, the Professor of Old Testament Language and Literature in the Glasgow College, to whom Moffatt was later to pay a graceful tribute in the dedication of his translation of the Old Testament. Heresy trials might no longer be likely to succeed; but there was still a strong groundswell of anti-critical opinion in some quarters. Doubtless this deflected from Moffatt's translation the criticism which would have been levelled at it, had it appeared separately and not been embedded in a work of formidable scholarship. Such criticism would have arisen in the main from prejudice in favour of the Authorised Version. Moffatt's rendering is both faithful to the original and independent of earlier English translations. It is also free of the colloquialisms which have been held to mar his later versions.

Two formal features are of considerable importance. Italics are used for quotations from the Old Testament and also for reminiscences of Old Testament expressions, *eg* in the Beatitudes in Matthew 5:3–12. This effectively draws the reader's attention to one way in which the New Testament is permeated by influence from the Old. The other feature is the printing of poetry as poetry. This applies not only to quotations of poetry from the Old Testament throughout the New Testament, but also to much of Revelation and of the teaching of Jesus, even when the Old Testament is not being quoted. It makes clear to the reader that Jesus often delivered his teaching in poetic form. Both the form and the spirit of Hebrew prophecy are there blended in a new and creative expression of the Hebrew poetic genius.

The Translations: (B) The New Testament—A New Translation

This translation was intended for general use. The books are in the usual order, and apart from notes on the Greek text at various places where Moffatt wants to indicate why he has chosen one reading rather than another, and some rearrangements of verses or paragraphs, there are no critical discussions. At two points in the Preface, Moffatt explains what he was trying to do.

> I have attempted to translate the New Testament exactly as one would render any piece of contemporary Hellenistic prose; in this way, students of the original text may perhaps be benefited.

As when he made his earlier translation, he was concerned to see the New Testament documents not simply as a closed canon of religious books, but as literary compositions from a particular period in the history of the Graeco-Roman world. Of course this would not be evident to the general reader; but it is important that the translator approached his task with this in mind. Later in the Preface he writes:

> Any new translation starts under a special handicap. It appears to challenge in every line the rhythm and diction of an English classic. . . . But intelligibility is more than associations, and to atone in part for the loss of associations I have endeavoured to make the New Testament, especially St Paul's epistles, as intelligible to a modern English reader as any version that is not a paraphrase can make them.

Here Moffatt indicates what is probably the chief merit of this translation, that it clarifies the meaning of the text at many points (chiefly in the Pauline Epistles) where the older versions leave it obscure. He does so without introducing a spurious smoothness into his rendering of St Paul's often terse and vigorous prose. His rendering of Galatians is an outstanding example of this. To read it straight through is to gain a vivid impression of the effect of the Greek original. One brief clause may serve as an illustration of Moffatt's achievement. Galatians 5:2 begins with five Greek words of which the literal translation is, 'Behold I Paul say to you'. In *The Historical New Testament* Moffatt had translated this, 'Behold, I Paul tell you'. In his later rendering it becomes, 'Here, Listen to Paul', which reproduces the emphasis and explosive force of the original. Wherever one turns in the great Epistles there are passages of which the meaning is illuminated by the clarity and liveliness of Moffatt's rendering. 1 Corinthians 9:26f provides a brief example:

> Well, I run without swerving; I do not plant my blows upon the empty air —no, I maul and master my body, in case, after preaching to other people, I am disqualified myself.

The force of the analogy from running and boxing is here brought out with considerably greater clarity than in the Authorised Version. Such short examples, however, do not adequately indicate the measure of Moffatt's achievement, which can only be appreciated if one reads several chapters or even an entire Epistle.

Modern translations of the New Testament which are independent and not revisions of earlier versions usually succeed, if they have any merit at all, in clarifying Paul's arguments. They are less successful in rendering effectively passages of profound simplicity such as the beginning of St John's Gospel, or on the other hand the noble eloquence of such passages as Ephesians 1; Hebrews 1; and 1 Peter 1:3–9. To some extent Moffatt shares this weakness. His rendering of John 1:1–18 is flat and prosaic by contrast with the Authorised Version; but this defect is less obvious in Hebrews 1 and 1 Peter 1:3–9. For one who has long been familiar with the Authorised Version, it is difficult to make an objective appraisal of such passages. Dr R Newton Flew used to recall that as a young minister he read Ephesians 1:3–23 in the Moffatt version at a devotional meeting. He did not mention Moffatt or give the reference to Ephesians. When the meeting was over an elderly minister asked him, 'What great work of devotion was it that you read from this evening?' Had the name 'Moffatt' been mentioned before the passage was read, the reaction would have been hostile; but anonymity made a favourable judgement possible. The fact that the question was asked showed that though the elderly minister had heard and read the passage in the Authorised Version many times, he had failed to grasp its contents well enough to be able to recognise it in a different translation. Ephesians 1 is a good example of Moffatt almost at his best in rendering a passage of sustained eloquence. His best is seen in his translation of 1 Corinthians 13, which is a perfect blend of accuracy and appropriate style.

Particular Words

The narrative prose of the Gospels and Acts is translated for the most part into lively modern English. Some of the terms used are worthy of comment. The *magi* in Matthew 2 are called 'magicians', as they had been in *The Historical New Testament*. The word has this meaning in Acts 13:6, 8; but 'astrologer' is more appropriate in Matthew 2. One of Moffatt's alleged Scotticisms is the use of the term 'factor' in Luke 16:1–8. In *The Historical New Testament* the 'factor' is called a 'steward'. It is perhaps worth noting that when Moffatt was living in Ayrshire he used the term 'steward', but preferred 'factor' when he was in Oxford.

How to translate biblical terms for money, weights, and measurement is always a problem for the translator. Should he simply transliterate the biblical terms and offer an estimate or an explanation in a note, or should he translate into modern terms? The problem about the latter method is that money values may change markedly and that new systems of measurement may be introduced. Moffatt uses in translation what were modern equivalents in his time. The one, five, and ten talents of Matthew 25:14–30 become £250, £500, and £1200 respectively; but by modern standards the sums involved were much larger. In the original, the sums involved are expressed in terms of 'talents', which is the word used in the Authorised Version. In the parallel parable in Luke 19:11–27, each servant received a *mna*, which the Authorised Version renders as a 'pound'. Moffatt's translation, 'a five pound note', sounds anachronistic for first-century Palestine, and even in 1913 was probably an underestimate.

In his Preface, Moffatt points out that some important Greek words in the New Testament have no exact equivalent in English, *eg logos* (word), *mysterion* (mystery), and *dikaiosynē* (righteousness). In some passages, notably the first chapter of St John's Gospel and the beginning of 1 John, he does not translate *logos* but simply transliterates it, claiming that in these passages *logos* is less misleading than 'word'.

Moffatt based his translation not on Nestle's text, as in *The Historical New Testament*, but on the critical edition of the Greek New Testament which had recently been published by Hermann von Soden. This was unfortunate from the textual specialist's point of view, for von Soden's text was open to adverse criticism. However, Moffatt did not follow von Soden slavishly. When he preferred a different reading, he adopted it and drew attention to the change in a footnote. There are many such footnotes scattered throughout the translation, mainly referring to relatively minor points.

Two conjectural changes which Moffatt made are of special interest. 1 Timothy 5:23 ('Give up being a total abstainer; take a little wine for the sake of your stomach and your frequent attacks of illness') is omitted from the text and relegated to a footnote, on the ground that it is 'either a marginal gloss or misplaced'. In *The Historical New Testament* the verse is retained in the text. Again, in 1 Peter 3:19, which in Moffatt's earlier translation is rendered 'in which also he went and preached to the spirits in prison', he now adopts the suggestion that the name 'Enoch' has dropped out (a few letters having been written once instead of twice) and that the verse refers not to Christ, but to Enoch, as visiting the imprisoned spirits: 'It was in the Spirit that Enoch also went and preached to the imprisoned spirits'. This is assumed to be a reference to the First Book of Enoch; but there is little to be said in favour of the change.

Rearrangement and Other Features

There has been much discussion among commentators concerning the correct order of John 13–16. Moffatt adopts a major rearrangement, transferring chapters 15 and 16 to the middle of 13:31, inserting 13:31b–38 after 16:33, then continuing with chapter 14. This undoubtedly produces a more convincing sequence of thought than the arrangement in the Greek manuscripts. It may perhaps be regarded as a permissible exception to the rule that a translator should not do what is properly regarded as the work of the commentator.

As in *The Historical New Testament*, quotations from and reminiscences of the Old Testament are italicised, and passages which Moffatt regarded as poetical in structure are so printed. In the Revelation of St John considerably less is represented as poetical than in the earlier translation.

The modern idiom in Moffatt's translation, which presented so marked a contrast with the Authorised Version, gave rise to much prejudiced criticism. Love for the familiar words and phrases prevented many readers from recognising that what was familiar did not convey a particularly clear sense, whereas Moffatt's rendering did. The opening clause of Philippians 3:20 provides a convincing example of this. The Authorised Version's rendering, 'For our conversation is in heaven', is at best obscure, at worst misleading. Moffatt's 'But we are a colony of heaven' conveys the sense in a particularly pointed way, since Philippi was a Roman colony. Qualities such as these caused the Moffatt New Testament to be widely used and brought the biblical text to life for very many readers.

One important by-product of the translation was the series of Moffatt New Testament Commentaries, of which Moffatt himself was the general editor and to which he contributed the volumes on 1 Corinthians and the General Epistles. Though the commentaries are based on Moffatt's translation, the commentators were at liberty to indicate their preference for other renderings. 'Our common aim,' Moffatt wrote, 'has been to enable every man to sit where these first Christians sat, to feel the impetus and inspiration of the Christian faith as it dawned upon the communities in the first century, and thereby to realize more vividly how new and lasting is the message which prompted these New Testament writings to take shape as they did'. In translation and commentary alike, Moffatt's aim was constant.

The Translations: (C) The Old Testament—A New Translation

The dedication of the first edition of Moffatt's translation of the Old Testament reads, 'To the Very Rev Sir George Adam Smith from whom I learned Hebrew and more than Hebrew'. George Adam Smith was Professor of Old Testament Language and Literature at the Free, later United Free, Church College in Glasgow from 1892 until 1909, when he became Principal of the University of Aberdeen. His commentaries in the Expositor's Bible on Isaiah, and on the Minor Prophets, contain eloquent and often moving translations; and the second volume of his great work on Jerusalem includes effective renderings of many passages from various parts of the Old Testament, most notably from Lamentations. In translating Hebrew poetry he could rise to the heights. Moffatt, it must be admitted, seldom if ever did so. Time and time again, Moffatt clarified passages which were obscure in the older versions and gave a new sharpness to others, the impact of which had been dulled by familiarity.

As the best qualities of his New Testament translation are seen in the Pauline Epistles, so in the Old Testament they are most evident in the prophetic books. Amos exhibits with particular effect his ability to transmit the urgency and passion of the prophetic message, both in stern denunciation and in solemn dirge. He is less successful in his translation of the Psalms, where the poetic structure is often unaccompanied by the poetic spirit, no matter how clearly the sense is conveyed. His terse, matter-of-fact style is well suited to much of the Wisdom literature, and by contrast, in the more eloquent passages he conveys much of their poetic quality. In the Authorised Version the description in Ecclesiastes 12 of the steadily increasing disabilities of old age, leading up to the solemn finality of death, is presented in language of great beauty, but at times the sense may elude the reader. In Moffatt's rendering, some of the beauty has been retained and the sense is more clearly presented. Those who are familiar with the Book of Job in the Authorised Version or, better still, the Revised Version of 1884, will feel that in Moffatt the glory has departed, but in many passages the gain in clarity and comprehensibility is considerable. It is a curious example of inconsistent pedantry that, although the book is still called 'Job', the man's name appears as 'Eyob', an attempt to reproduce the form of the word in Hebrew.

In both the narrative prose and the legal sections, Moffatt gives us clear and straightforward modern renderings, though sometimes the disappearance of familiar terms may be startling, as when Noah's 'ark' appears as a 'barge' and the 'tabernacle of the congregation' (AV) or 'tent of meeting' (RV) becomes the 'Trysting tent'.

The Name of God

A recurring problem for translators of the Old Testament is how to represent the name of the God of Israel. It is commonly held that the original form was 'Yahweh'. This may fairly be used in scholarly contexts but it is not appropriate in a translation of the Old Testament intended for general use. Moffatt decided to use instead (except in compound titles such as 'the Lord of hosts') 'the Eternal', which sounds impressive but may be judged unsuitable since the concept of eternity has no place in Old Testament thought. It seems best to retain 'the LORD' (which accords with long-standing Jewish usage) in a translation such as Moffatt's and to leave 'Yahweh' and explanations of its form and meaning to more technical works.

In the first five books of the Old Testament, Moffatt used italics, roman type, and square brackets to indicate the different sources from which passages were supposed to have been derived. Quite apart from the fact that those who held the standard hypothesis about sources often disagreed about the allocation of material to the different sources, and the possibility that the theory might be drastically modified or even overthrown, it was the commentator's responsibility, and not the translator's, to deal with sources.

It is because of this desire to indicate the sources that Moffatt's Old Testament begins with Genesis 2:4a, followed by 1:1. Elsewhere in the translation, and particularly in the prophetic books, passages are transferred to other contexts. This, again, is to usurp the commentator's task and is confusing for the reader, who may wish to consult a passage and find that it is absent from its accustomed place with no indication of where it is now to be found.

In spite of the blemishes which have been noted, Moffatt's translation of the Old Testament is a remarkable achievement. The merits of his rendering far outweigh its defects.

The Complete Bible

In 1935 a revised edition of the complete Moffatt Bible was published. Nearly 40 pages of introduction were added, describing the background and literary character of both Testaments and the principal versions. In the translation itself the paragraphing and punctuation had been reconsidered and altered, and in many places the English style recast and the translation modified; but the general character of the work is the same. It is still the Moffatt Bible.

It is particularly fitting that a chapter in the present volume should be devoted to James Moffatt, since he himself wrote a book entitled *The Bible in Scots Literature* (1924), a survey from the War of Independence to Sir Walter Scott, which is only one indication of his amazing versatility. It is, however, for his work as a translator of the Scriptures that he is best known. According to the history of Trinity College, Glasgow, Moffatt 'was not a particularly good teacher of students—he knew too much'.[5] However that may be, he reached through his translation a vaster audience than those who sat under him in the various centres in which he taught, fulfilling what he himself said ought to be the object of any version of the Scriptures, 'to stir and sustain present faith in a living God who speaks'.[6]

GEORGE ANDERSON

Notes

1   *Letters of Principal James Denney to William Robertson Nicoll, 1893–1917* (London, 1920), p 247.
2   S Mechie, *Trinity College Glasgow 1856–1956* (London, 1956), p 35.
3   Op.cit., p 33, quoting Principal W M Macgregor.
4   See Chapter 13 in this volume on these controversies.
5   Op.cit., p 36.
6   *The Moffatt Translation of the Bible Containing the Old and New Testaments* (London, 1935) p xlv.

Further Reading

The best commentaries on the character and aims of the Moffatt translations are to be found in Moffatt's own Prefaces to *The Historical New Testament*, *The New Testament: A New Translation*, *The Old Testament: A New Translation*, and *The Moffatt Translation of the Bible*.
Reference may also be made to:
F F Bruce, *The English Bible: A History of Translations from the earliest English Version to the New English Bible* (London, revised edition, 1970), ch 13.
A C Partridge, *English Biblical Translation* (London, 1973), ch 10.

4

William Lorimer's *New Testament in Scots:*
An Appreciation

Writing of the colourful imagery and the warmth of feeling to be found in the spoken words of Jesus, John Kelman of Edinburgh observes that 'When He addresses the dead damsel in the homely Aramaic tongue [Mark 5:41], we have the same tone in which a northern peasant of our own land might say "Lassie!" '[1] William Lorimer goes one better in his monumental translation of the New Testament into Scots: he has Jesus say, 'Rise ye up, lassock, I bid ye'. Now, at last, in the dying decades of the twentieth century, we Scots can hear in our own tongue the wonderful works of God; the northern peasant from Galilee has travelled farther still into our understanding and our affection.

The year of 1946 will always be a watershed in the chronicle of how the Bible enlarges its appeal to us. It was in 1946 that a parish minister from the Presbytery of Stirling and Dunblane prodded the General Assembly of the Church of Scotland to embark upon a new translation of the Bible 'in the language of the present day'. Thirteen years later the New English Bible New Testament (NEB) was ready for perusal. And it was in 1946 that a Classics Lecturer in St Andrews University began reading versions of the New Testament in a prodigious number of languages, from Afrikaans to Syriac, as a preparation for the task of translating it into Scots.

The Translator

Thirty years earlier William Lorimer had become fascinated with the struggle for survival and expression of the languages of linguistic minorities. By the late 1930s he had focussed this concern on the desirability, not to say the absolute necessity, of having the revival and

53

the strengthening of Scots consolidated by two things—the production of a reliable dictionary of the Scottish tongue, and the rendering of the New Testament into that same tongue, in all its diversity. Towards the end of 1957 he began in earnest to address himself to the latter; in 1983 a landmark in Scottish life and culture was arrived at with the publication of his Scots New Testament.[2] For some years, therefore, translations of Holy Scripture were proceeding in tandem, on two fronts: the one prompted by the national Church's General Assembly and involving panels of translators and literary advisers, the other issuing from one man's determination to test the sinews of his native language in a sustained prose-work which would encompass narrative, poetry, dialogue, discourse, argument, exhortation and reflection—a whole compendium of styles—all rolled into one. If ever Scots was to be proved a flexible and fulsome vehicle for contrasting modes of expression, there could be no better testing-ground than the New Testament.

William Lorimer brought many gifts to this exacting enterprise. His mastery of Greek was matched by a remarkable proficiency in the Scottish language. As a young boy he had begun to listen to, and to preserve, a vast store of Scots words, idioms, usages and definitions current in the everyday speech of people living not a stone's throw from his father's manse. He had kept a notebook; from being a chronicler of the vernacular he grew to be a true collector of the rich and rare varieties of words whose native element was conversation, description and information. Small wonder, then, that in his rendering of many passages in the New Testament—especially in the Gospels, naturally—we find the flavour of a lively, vibrant aural experience.

The translator of the Scriptures is far more than a messenger, simply handing on what he receives; the translator touches what he handles, and he leaves his imprint on it. He gives us the colouration of his own insights, the cast of thought peculiar to his own experience and his personal convictions. The translator, at every turn, reveals himself; he cannot dodge this tendency, nor should he wish to. He is both reporter and editor, sometimes unwittingly. To some extent, simply because he has to trust his instincts as well as his knowledge—because he must consult his inner life as well as his dictionaries—the translator is also a theologian. With wry humour, then, the Lorimer New Testament has as its frontispiece, in Greek capitals, *HĒ LALIA SOU DĒLON SE POIEI*, 'Your speech makes you come out into the open' (Matt. 26:73). We see the nature of the man himself when we read Lorimer's versions of some incidents and exchanges; but we remain conscious that he is forever striving to clarify his subject-matter, not simply trying to glorify the means. The Scots remains a servant of the labour thrust upon it.

Rediscovering the Familiar

There is a sense of culture-shock in picking up this volume; we encounter the familiar stories, but in a novel garb. This energises for us passages which have become wabbit and feckless with long usage. The Scots we find here is thorough, it is undiluted, and it is demanding. No one dialect is here, but rather all the versatility, the suppleness, of the old tongue. The classical and the colloquial blend together effortlessly. Reading this 'new' text we experience both recognition and discovery, and the awakening of that most precious faculty—curiosity.

Sometimes the Lorimer version of a passage startles us into cross-checking what he says with one of the English texts; sometimes we are driven back to the Greek quarry to investigate what mother-lode of meaning may be hidden there. For me the joy of reading the new version is something like the pleasure of watching Pier Paulo Pasolini's film 'The Gospel According to St Matthew', in which the players speak Italian but the English sub-titles are in the *verbatim* words of Matthew. One hears the rapid flow of Italian, one watches the images on the screen, and one reads the text of the Gospel. It is a multi-media experience—and so too with Lorimer. We read the Scots as it unrolls before us, we conjure up the images that spring to mind and the associations triggered off by words embedded in our own experience, and in the background we hear the text as we have grown accustomed to it, in English. The excitement lies in the comparison; we balance what we have formerly received against the novelty of what we see for the first time.

Inevitably, there is great gain here. New insights creep up on us, and a new warmth suffuses the activity of study in such a way that it ceases to be dry or disconnected. We embrace with feeling truths that formerly we merely lent assent to. If it is not too fanciful a way of putting it, the Word in English becomes flesh of our flesh in Scots. Lorimer breaks the chains of habit that have sometimes shackled our attention, and he shatters idols that sophistication and predictability have fashioned in us since our childhood.

More radically, Lorimer has stormed a citadel which has preserved for far too long a monopoly in spoken English: the parish worship of the Scottish churches. Whenever his New Testament is read and preached from, people are learning to forget the notion that Scots is not the medium for expressing heights and depths, profundity and insight. How well he knew, long years ago, that a nation which barricades its institutions against its own language is a nation ill at ease, a nation sundered and divided against itself. Did they sense it, those donors whose names are printed at the conclusion of Lorimer's volume, that they were and are co-conspirators in fomenting a revolution?

Vividness of the Original

What kind of revolution? For one thing, the public reading of this book in the context of worship will reflect the verve and vividness of the original utterances. We shall discover again, although we should never have abandoned him, a Jesus whose intensity, whose jocularity, whose animation, is impossible to conceal. Take, for example, the passage in Matthew where the Lord delivers his most scathing commentary on the conduct of the Pharisees: 'Woe to you, scribes and Pharisees, hypocrites!' (Matt. 23:13ff). Some would have us think that this is not invective, but merely a catalogue of some regrettable shortcomings. Lorimer will have none of it; in his view, these are words that are meant to wound: 'Black s' be your faa, Doctors o the Law an Pharisees, hypocrites at ye ar!' By way of contrast, the rebuke delivered to the wind and the waves, 'Peace! Be still!' (Mark 4:39), becomes in Scots the gentle but authoritative tone of voice a parent uses when reassuring a fretful child: 'Wheesht ye, be quait'. We glimpse afresh in these four words how Jesus' Lordship of the elements is a way of demonstrating that He is the One in whom and for whom all things were made.

In Mark 10:21 the rich young man is promised treasures in heaven if he will renounce his worldly wealth; the Scots employs a metaphor that would appeal to any capitalist (or any Aberdonian!): 'It will be an outly for ye i the bank o Heiven'. If there is humour there, albeit a sardonic flash of it, there is broad comedy in the parable of the judge who feared neither God nor man, but was terrified of a woman. A widow pesters him to give judgement in her favour; eventually he relents—in order to save his own hide!—and concedes, '. . . this widow's becomin a fair fash: I better gie the wuman juistice, or afore aa's dune, she'll come an gie me twa blue een' (Luke 18:5). By using the literal meaning of the Greek verb, *hypōpiazō*, 'to strike under the eye', Lorimer depicts a man fearful at the prospect of some real bodily harm. We can imagine (although we rarely do, much to our loss) how

Jesus' hearers greeted this sally, and picturing *their* laughter, we realise how strange, how pointless it would be for us to read this from a pulpit or a lectern with wooden features and solemnity.

In these four instances—the denunciation, the quietening of the waves, 'the bank o Heiven' and the judge's quandary, not only do we see in Jesus the contrasting aspects of his nature but we discern, in the Scots of Lorimer, the contrasting characteristics for which our Scottish language and our poetry are known and loved: the robust virility of 'Black s' be your faa!'; the gentleness of 'wheesht'; the touch of sarcasm in 'the bank o Heiven'; and the pictorial strength of 'twa blue een'. In all these cases, Lorimer stays close to his text; he is not embroidering.

In some quizzical passages, however, Lorimer demonstrates the sturdy mental independence of a man who knows he is obliged to many other voices, many diffuse interpretations, but beholden to none. He revels in his freedom to speak in accents of his own. The retort of Jesus, when his mother comes to him at the marriage-feast in Cana, reads like a rebuff: 'O woman, what have you to do with me?' (John 2:4). The Greek is cryptic: *Ti emoi kai soi*, literally, 'What is to me and to you?' Lorimer is daring here; he reads this question as being rhetorical, not interrogatory: 'Ye can lae that to me'—as if Jesus is musing out loud: 'What's mine is yours, eh? All right. I'll look after this'.

Sometimes the translator's freedom leads to our losing something, as in John 1:1 where *en archē* is amplified from 'in the beginning' to 'in the beginnin o aa things'. We lose the simplicity of the original words. Again, in John 9:9, when a quarrel starts about the real identity of someone who was healed of blindness, some saying that he cannot be the man they used to know, some asserting that he is indeed, the man himself insists 'I am the man'. Lorimer adduces the phrase, 'I'm the man—aa at there is o him'. In Scots this has a self-deprecatory ring to it, which is not at all the impression suggested in the Greek, *Ego eimi*.

Poetry in Prose

Where Lorimer excels is in his fondness for the phrase that has more poetry in it than the prose it deals with. A few examples will suffice: 'the abyss' (Luke 8:31) becomes 'the Boddomless Sheuch'; 'my Son, my Chosen' (Luke 9:35) becomes 'my Son, my Waled Ane'; 'Foxes have holes, and birds of the air have nests' (Luke 9:58) grips us by changing into 'Tod Lowrie hes his lair, and the miresnipe her bield';

C

the dog and the sow in 2 Peter 2:22 become 'Bawtie' and 'Grumphie'; 'Hades' (Rev. 6:8) is personified as 'The Lord o the Gane-Awa Laund'; 'the great tribulation' (Rev. 7:14) sharpens into 'the Days o Dree'; likewise, in 1 Corinthians 1:18 'those who are perishing' takes on a darker hue with 'them at is gaein the Black Gate'; who could not shudder at the dread import of 'the Deidlie Ugsome Thing' in Matthew 24:15—a more potent spectre than the ill-defined 'desolating sacrilege'?; and finally, in John 8:33 the economy of rendering 'we . . . have never been in bondage to any one' as 'we . . . hae ne'er been slaves tae the face o cley' is a masterstroke.

It seems excessively finicky to cavil at some isolated phrases which, to my mind, do not carry the real sense of the Greek into the Scots that Lorimer chooses for them. In John 1:14 'the Word . . . dwelt among us' is rendered as 'the Wurd . . . made his wonnin amang us'. The use of 'wonnin'—the chief house on a farmstead—suggests solidity and permanence, whereas the Greek verb *eskēnōsen*, with its root derivation from *skēnē*, 'tent', conveys more a sense of the Word sojourning with us for a temporary interval, even one lasting 33 years. The Word is eternal: the incarnation is in time and for a set time. In the Lorimer rendering we lose that contrast and the paradox is blurred. Again, in John 1:18 we find a lapse of concentration. Lorimer elects to translate the phrase 'the only Son . . . in the bosom of the Father' more literally: 'the ae an ane Son, at . . . liggs on the breist o the Faither'. The vexed question is the short Greek phrase *eis ton kolpon*. In New Testament times, this expression described a position on the immediate right of the host at a banquet, when guests reclined on their left elbows on couches angled away from the table. To be *eis ton kolpon* was to be closest to the head of the table; the Scots used here, it seems to me, has opted for the physical aspect of the metaphor instead of the symbolic meaning.

Lest any reader feel that to descend to the particular is to do scant justice to the achievement of the whole work, let me agree at once and leave this train of thought. And yet it does not need to be said that it is words and sentences that we engrave upon our memories and write upon our hearts. It is, too, words and phrases that we take as texts for the preaching of the Word; not surprisingly, then, it is to words and phrases that the reader of the Scots New Testament will turn expectantly. And we find here all the great sayings and the memorable word-pictures that we already love: Paul's universal Christ, who reconciles all races—'he has dung down the mairch-dyke o ill-will at keepit as sindrie' (Eph. 2:14); John's summons to authentic living—'Bairnies, latna our luve be frae the teeth . . . [but] . . . frae the hairt' (1 John 3:18); the visionary, stately metaphors of the Revelation of John—'I am the Shuit an Affspring o Dauvit, the glentin Stairn o the Dawin' (Rev. 22:16); the upheavals in the Magnificat—'he has sperpelt the heilie an heich . . . an heized up . . . the laich' (Luke 1:51, 52); the bravery of the faithful—'they dittit the mous o lions, slockent the bensil o fire . . . kythed feckfu in weir . . . ' (Heb. 11:33, 34); the images of Christ drawn by him from field and hillside—'I am the yett o the bucht' (John 10:7); the Christian's lifestyle—'Be cantie wi the cantie, an dowie wi the dowie . . . ' (Rom. 12:15); the apostles preaching their way into trouble—'Thir men . . . is turnin the haill toun tapsalteerie' (Acts 16:20); the risen Jesus coming to rejoin his friends—'the disciples wis fell gled tae see the Lord' (John 20:20).

Lorimer's Achievement

We can but echo that last remark, we Scots, when we assess the impact of this new translation. We have seen the Lord apparelled in the hodden grey of our own speech, and it is marvellous in our eyes. We have seen him, now on the rising tide of anger at the Pharisees, now provoking laughter, now teaching with laconic wit—'Ye canna sair God an Gowd' (Matt. 6:24), now taking on himself our human griefs and sorrows—'Jesus fell agreitin' (John 11:35). To possess a language which is distinctive and expressive, as we do, does not in itself confer upon us an added sense of individuality or identity: we need that language made available and accessible in the broad highway of ideas, in the open thoroughfares of common interest and shared concerns. Scots, while it is yet the occasional mainstay of some theatre repertoires, still the stuff of certain brands of comedy and the instrument in many poets' hands, still the living bloodstream of vernacular expression, must also be enabled to broaden its appeal to us by being allowed to demonstrate how capably it carries even such a weight as the New Testament.

In his life of Martin Luther, Roland H Bainton heaps praise on Luther's translation of the Bible into German.[3] He had started with the New Testament, and in great haste completed his assignment in three months. Bainton remarks: 'For the Germans, Luther's rendering was incomparable. He leaped beyond the tradition of a thousand years'. What made the translation by Luther so significant? In Bainton's words it was 'the majesty of diction, the sweep of vocabulary, the native earthiness, and . . . religious profundity'. He quotes the Reformer himself, saying with dubious, although admirable fervour, 'I endeavoured to make Moses so German that no one would suspect him to be a Jew'. Luther claimed for himself the same freedom as Lorimer exhibits: for Luther was insistent that 'the idiom of one language must be translated into the equivalent idiom of the other'. To this end, he gave the angel Gabriel's greeting to Mary as simply 'Liebe Maria' ('Dear Mary'), and claimed for such a sparse rendition the virtue that it was evocative and telling. 'What word is more rich than that word "liebe"?' demanded Martin Luther. Lorimer, I feel, has shown a mite more exactitude in his version of the angel's greeting—' "Fair guid-day tae ye," qo the angel'. The idiom is safeguarded, but so is the tone of the original.

For thus preserving the bonds of truth, so that his Scots is faithful to the spirit of the Greek text without being intimidated by pedantry, we have reason to be grateful to William Lorimer. We salute the qualities he shares with Luther—majestic diction, the sweep of vocabulary, earthiness and profundity. But over and above all these, we salute Lorimer's intention: to rescue Scots from the peripheral position to which it is too often relegated. A language dies when it is made to dance occasionally at feasts not held in its honour—when it comes to be regarded as a curiosity, an eccentricity espoused by a select few, a trick of rhetoric interjected into speech and speeches for effect or amusement.

It is in no sense, therefore, pejorative to describe the Scots New Testament as a seminal work: for leading on from what Lorimer has done, dawning upon us slowly, but inexorably, comes the realisation that with the Scriptures safely mapped and charted in the landscape of our knowledge of who we are, there is no reason now why we should not go on to tackle lesser peaks or make fresh forays into territory which is as yet unnamed. If we stay true to the convictions and the hopes that prodded William Lorimer into action, what prevents us from engaging in a process like the alchemists of old—except that we shall practise alchemy in reverse, and turn fine gold into everyday coinage? We can await—but not too long—the provision of a Scots liturgy, a Scots Book of Common Order, and a Scots Hymnal, to say nothing of the Old Testament in Scots! Then, indeed, we shall be singing the Lord's song, but not in any foreign land nor in any foreign language.

DAVID OGSTON

Notes

1   James Hastings (ed), *A Dictionary of Christ and the Gospels* (Edinburgh, 1908), vol II, p 373.
2   Translated by William Lorimer, *The New Testament in Scots*, first published by Southside Publishers (Edinburgh, 1983); revised edition, Canongate Publishing (Edinburgh) and Penguin Books (Harmondsworth, 1985).
3   R H Bainton, *Here I Stand. A Life of Martin Luther*, first published 1950; Mentor Books edition (New York, 1955), pp 255f.
All quotations of the New Testament in English are from the Revised Standard Version.
Thanks are due to the Revd David Reid, Minister of Cleish and Fossaway, for helpful advice and wise guidance.

Further Reading

The New Testament in Scots, translated by W L Lorimer; revised edition, Canongate Publishing, Edinburgh (hardback, ISBN 0 9000 2524 7) and Penguin Books, Harmondsworth (paperback, ISBN 0 1400 7571 2).
The above publication was edited by Lorimer's son, R L C Lorimer, who has contributed an Introduction. A memoir of 'William Laughton Lorimer (1885–1967)' by K J Dover appeared in the *Proceedings of the British Academy* 53 (1967), pp 437–48. Lorimer's papers have been deposited in the National Library of Scotland, Edinburgh.

No extended assessment of Lorimer's work has yet appeared. Among the numerous, nearly all enthusiastic reviews, the following can be mentioned:
Donald Campbell, in *Lallans* 21 (Mairtinmas, 1983), pp 36–39 (in Lowland Scots).
Alan Main, in the *Scottish Literary Journal Supplement* 20 (Summer–Autumn, 1984), pp 36–39.
Peter Levi, in *The Spectator*, 26 November 1983.
P H Scott, in *Weekend Scotsman*, 22 October 1983 and in *Books in Scotland* 14 (Spring, 1984).
George Bruce, in *Times Literary Supplement*, 23 December 1983 (followed by response from R L C Lorimer).
John Fowler, in *Glasgow Herald*, 22 October 1983.

A tape cassette of readings, 'Portions Waled Frae the New Testament in Scots', was produced by Scotsoun, 13 Ashton Road, Glasgow.

II

The Bible
in Scottish Literature

5

The Bible in Mediaeval Verse and Drama

God wishes his Scriptures to be shut lest a passage of entry into the
treasury of the Lord be exposed to enemies.

RICHARD ROLLE

In a profound sense, all early English writing, poetic as well as
practical . . . is written within the biblical ambience.

GEOFFREY SHEPHERD

These two apparently contradictory statements,[1] the first by a fourteenth-century mediaeval mystical writer, the second by a twentieth-
century critic, seem to sum up the relationship between the Bible and
literature in mediaeval Scotland. They characterise the state of affairs
throughout mediaeval Europe, in an international culture in which
Scotland shared.

On the one hand, then, the Scriptures were 'shut'. The Bible that
was used throughout Europe in the Middle Ages, the Vulgate, was
written in Latin, a language that was understood only by the educated;
even among the clergy only the more highly educated were fully fluent.
Books, until the spread of printing in the sixteenth century, were in any
case prohibitively expensive. For the majority of people, including
most readers of and writers of literature, there was no direct access to
the Bible.

But if few people read the Bible for themselves, almost everyone
would have a vivid familiarity with parts of it through a wide variety of
indirect sources. The most important of these was through the services
of the Church: the mass, the daily offices for the clergy, and the
services for baptism, marriage, death and the church festivals.
Probably most influential for ordinary lay people were the biblical
texts and phrases that were incorporated into the liturgy itself: the
versicles and responses, the daily Psalms and prayers. These fragments
of the Bible were encountered regularly, and in an almost dramatic

setting—they were often musical, some in dialogue form, some spoken or sung by the congregation themselves. So although they were lifted out of their context in the Bible, they acquired a vividness and intensity of their own, and whether or not verbally understood, they clearly entered the memory and language of even the least educated.

The services also included readings from the Scriptures which, although themselves in Latin, were generally explained and interpreted to the congregation by the preacher. The full programme of daily readings laid down in the service books was designed to cover the whole of the Bible each year, at least in selection. As with the liturgy, however, these readings did not follow the chronology of the Bible. Lessons were clustered around the festivals of the church year, with Old Testament readings chosen to complement New Testament ones. Few, even of the clergy, would read and know the Bible in sequence.

The contents of the Bible were also made available in other ways, especially visually, through pictures. Almost every church was decorated with carvings, wall-paintings and stained-glass, all relating to Christian belief, and many directly presenting episodes from the Bible. One of the best remaining examples in Scotland is the fifteenth-century chapel of Roslin, near Edinburgh, where the complex riot of carving includes, among many symbolic and allegorical scenes, the Annunciation, the Presentation, the Crucifixion and the Resurrection. Pictures like these, in churches, books, houses, wall-hangings and elsewhere, would have made many biblical episodes visually, although not verbally, familiar to almost everyone. In particular, of course, the crucifix, the ubiquitous symbol of Christianity, was a picture both of a Bible story and of a central body of belief.

So although few people personally read the Bible in Scotland in the Middle Ages, we cannot say that they were ignorant of it. Ordinary people were likely to be familiar, more so than today, with a variety of stories, ideas and texts from the Bible. But they would know them in a different way from a reader. Not only were they encountered in a different sequence and context; they were also filtered through layers of interpretation provided by Christian tradition and the church fathers. The Bible and its meaning were seen to fall into various patterns. Probably the most significant of these was a pattern which saw the events of the Old Testament as all foreshadowing and reflecting the events of the New Testament: Abraham's sacrifice of his son Isaac prefigured the sacrifice of the innocent Son of God; the sin of Eve who, approached by a serpent, disobediently took fruit from a tree and brought death to man was reversed by another virgin, Mary. She, approached by an angel, obediently accepted the fruit of God who died on a tree, bringing man life. Such patterns and parallels revealed the mysteries of God's divine plan; they also affected the way in which biblical stories were understood.

Another significant difference from later periods was that for most people the boundaries of the Scriptures were less clearly fixed. The Vulgate text itself includes additional Old Testament books like Tobias, Judith and Ecclesiasticus that have been excluded from later Protestant versions of the Bible. And far less distinction was made between genuine and apocryphal New Testament texts. Some of the most important and familiar aspects of mediaeval Christian belief, ideas about Judgement Day, the Harrowing of Hell, the early life of Christ and the Virgin Mary, that were regularly pictured and expounded in church, were found in such apocryphal texts, not in the official New Testament. For mediaeval Scots the Bible was not, as it is today, a directly accessible text confined by its covers. It was a fluid pattern of oral and visual stories, phrases and ideas that infiltrated their language and their lives.

Plays and Pageants

This, then, was the background from which the writers, readers and audiences of Scottish mediaeval poetry and drama were working. To some extent, both drama and literature were themselves used as vehicles for communicating understanding of the Bible. This is especially true of the biblical drama of the Middle Ages which Scotland shared with the rest of Europe. These plays, celebrating the summer feast of Corpus Christi and other church festivals, were performed by the people rather than professional actors of clergy. They generally dramatised and interpreted a sequence of episodes from the Old and New Testaments, probably beginning as a series of wordless pageants which processed through a city to its cathedral.

The records that survive in Scotland are too fragmentary for us to be sure whether these ever developed into full spoken and acted drama, but most Scottish cities had elaborate and spectacular pageants of some sort.[2] No texts survive, but we can piece together at least some idea of the subjects presented. The first recorded allusion is to the 'ludo de ly haliblude' ('play of the Holy Blood') at Aberdeen in 1440, while in 1471 a 'ludum de bellyale' ('play of Belial') is also mentioned. Aberdeen's sixteenth-century catalogue of Corpus Christi pageants presents a series of saints' martyrdoms, but intersperses these with pageants of the 'Coronatioun of our Lady', the Resurrection and

Crucifixion. The fifteenth-century Candlemas play includes, appropriately, the characters of Joseph and the Virgin, the three Kings and Simeon; but also Moses, saints, bishops, angels and 'wildmen' of the woods (woodwoses). At Perth, Adam, Eve and the Devil appear alongside a mermaid, St Erasmus (Elmo) and a cord-drawer (to draw out the martyred saint's entrails). It is clear that this drama was not trying to offer a consecutive biblical performance, but to create a more heterogeneous celebration in which crucial biblical events mingle with other holy stories, secular festivity and spectacle. This lack of division between sacred and secular, biblical and non-biblical, is characteristic of the mediaeval inclusive view of the world.

The most common focusses for these plays were on the events surrounding the Nativity, and the Passion, the biblical account of Christ's suffering and death. The records give us tantalising glimpses of the visual style in which the Bible events were presented: a payment made in Lanark for 'futyn off the cros' ('footing of the cross') in 1505, or the Dundee record of 'a credil and thre barnis [babies] maid of clath' (1520), suggest that the episodes of the Crucifixion and slaughter of the Innocents were played with an emotional realism. But the 'gold fulye [foil] to Cristis pascione' (Lanark, 1507), gilding either Christ's costume or scenery, and 'cristis cott [coat] of lethyr with the hoss [hose] and glufis' for a crucifixion pageant in Dundee (1520), show that the naturalism went along with a spectacular ritual splendour.

Sometimes biblical subjects were included in the pageantry designed by cities to celebrate the royal entries of monarchs. One of the pageants in Edinburgh in 1503 represented 'the Salutacion of Gabriell to the Virgyne, in sayinge Ave gratia, and sens after, the Sollempnizacion of the varey [true] Maryage betwix the said Vierge and Joseph'. Since this celebration marked the entry of Margaret of York to be married to James IV, this biblical (and apocryphal) pageant was used as an appropriate comment on the new Queen's secular and political situation, a characteristic mediaeval cross-fertilisation between biblical and secular which, in later times, would probably be regarded as sacrilegious. When Queen Margaret visited Aberdeen in 1511 she was similarly welcomed with pageants of the Annunciation, the Magi, and the expulsion of Adam and Eve from paradise. This apparently random selection probably had deliberate significance, for the expulsion from paradise was often presented as beginning the process of human tribulation, which was eventually resolved and reversed by the Annunciation to Mary. Aberdeen's biblical pageants were followed by scenes of Robert the Bruce and the Stuart monarchs, a political compliment to the Queen which was perhaps obliquely paralleled by the Salutation and Magi episodes. Mediaeval biblical drama was designed to give people an emotionally vivid insight into the events and truths of their faith; but it was never divorced from the concerns of the secular world. Not only the church, but national and local government, and often the trade guilds of the cities, all co-operated in its production.

Poetic Re-telling

Non-dramatic poetry was also sometimes used to teach the stories of the Bible. A popular fourteenth-century Scottish work called *The Pistill of Susan* is, for example, a fairly straightforward recounting of the story of Susanna and the Elders.[3] This episode, omitted from the Authorised Version, is told in the Vulgate in Daniel 13, and was a popular subject for both poetry and drama in the late Middle Ages. The story of Susanna, spied on at her bath by lustful Elders, resisting seduction, and falsely accused by them of adultery till the child judge Daniel uncovers their deceit by cunning cross-examination, has obvious popular ingredients: sensuality and scandal, wronged innocence, and tense court-room drama. As well as revealing God's mysterious ways, his protection of the innocent and the vindication of truth, it could also easily be given a contemporary political significance.

In fact the Scottish poem follows the Vulgate text very closely most of the time, offering its readers an almost direct access to the Bible story itself. Where the poet has made changes he pushes his poem in the direction of mediaeval romance. The Susanna story is already potentially romantic: he adds a long description of the beautiful garden in which Susanna is assaulted, and a touching scene of farewell between her and her husband:

> Thei toke the Feteres of hire feete,
> And evere he cussed that swete: [kissed]
> 'In other world schul we mete.'
>   Seid he no mare.

(lines 257–260)

Many mediaeval saints' legends were highly romantic, satisfying their readers' (or listeners') love of romance with stories that were also morally and spiritually edifying. It looks as if the Scottish poet of *The Pistill of Susan* was using the Bible for the same purpose.

A much more common kind of poetic re-telling of Bible events is found in the many devotional poems on the Passion. William Dunbar and Walter Kennedy, poets at the court of James IV, each wrote a long poem recounting with moving emphasis the sufferings of Christ at the crucifixion. Several other similar works in poetry and prose also survive. These meditations are part of a popular devotional movement throughout Europe in the fourteenth and fifteenth centuries. People were encouraged to contemplate the sufferings of Christ, and of the Virgin, dwelling in detail on the pains they underwent. This would provoke in them feelings of pity, sorrow, gratitude and love, and these human emotions would lead them towards a truer spiritual understanding of their personal involvement in Christ's sacrifice. One of these Scottish works, *The Contemplacioun of Synnaris*, explains to its readers how the meditation should be approached:

> And in this manere haif mynd with reuthful hart,   [pitiful]
> As you present his pane had herd and sene;
> Off all his passioun smyttyng sair and smert
> Thi hert suld pers in pietie throw the splene.   [pierce, liver—
>   seat of emotion]
>   (lines 929–932)

The poets focus vividly on the sorrow and horror of Christ's suffering in order to provoke this response:

> With bluid and sweit was all deflorde   [disfigured]
> His face, the fude of angellis fre;   [noble]
> His feit with stanis was revin and scorde,   [cut]
> O mankynd, for the luif of the.
>   (Dunbar, 'The Passioun', lines 53–56)

Dunbar's version of 'The Passioun of Crist' then goes on to describe his own responses to the vision of Christ's suffering, using allegorical figures to help his readers to understand the purpose of the meditation:

> . . . soir Contrition, bathit in teiris,   [sad]
> My visage all in watter drownit;
> And Reuth in to my eir ay rounde,   [whispered]
> For schame, allace!
>   (lines 99–102)

Poetic meditations like this follow the gospel narratives very closely, but elaborate and embellish the details in order to make the scene as immediate as possible. The poems seem to be meant for ordinary lay people. However, they are not concerned simply to communicate Bible narrative, but rather to lead readers through an emotional experience that will help them to an understanding of God.

In fact mediaeval poetry based on the Bible is very often as much concerned with interpretation and understanding as with the text itself. A poem on 'The Annunciation' (perhaps by Robert Henryson) is a good example of the way that a Bible story was presented through traditions of interpretation. The centre of the poem is a straightforward account of Gabriel's visit to Mary; but it is presented within a pattern of ideas about love, and honour of the Virgin, that shape our responses to the gospel account. The poem begins as if it were simply a love poem:

Forcy as deith is likand lufe,	[forceful, pleasing]
Throuch quhom al bittier suet is;	[whom, sweet]
No thing is hard, as writ can pruf,	
Till him in lufe that letis.	[To, stays]
	(lines 1–4)

Without being directly tied to it, this creates a resonant context for the account of the Salutation that follows. Later in the poem, Mary herself is presented in the language of secular love, as she often is in mediaeval literature:

O lady lele and lusumest,	[true, most lovable]
Thy face moist fair and schene is.	[bright]
	(lines 61–62)

So the joy of human love plays around the Annunciation. But as the poem continues this is gradually transformed into the mystic divine love of God for man, which inspired the Incarnation itself:

The miraclis ar mekle and meit	[fitting]
Fra luffis ryver rynnis;	[love's, runs]
The low of luf haldand the hete	[flame]
Unbrynt full blithlie brinnis.	[unburned, burns]
	(lines 37–40)

So the biblical event comes to us through a web of ideas about human and divine love that explain its significance for Christianity.

The poem also knits the gospel moment to a series of Old Testament parallels. The Virgin is referred to as Moses' burning bush (burned, but not consumed), the wand of Aaron (that blossomed although dead), and Gideon's fleece (that gathered dew although the ground was still dry). These are all traditional mediaeval figures for Mary, who conceived a son although remaining a virgin. They reveal the divine mystery and ordered pattern of God's plan for the human race that underlies the history of the Scriptures. The overall view of the Annunciation that emerges from the poem would scarcely be accessible to a simple reading of the Bible text itself.

Indirect Biblical Influence

The literature considered so far has all taken stories directly from the Scriptures; but the Bible's indirect influence is probably even more important in mediaeval poetry. The thinking and the language of writers and readers of the Middle Ages were permeated with biblical concepts that often contribute significantly to poetry which appears to deal with quite different subjects. One of the major mediaeval Scots poets, Robert Henryson, a subtle and moving storyteller writing at the end of the fifteenth century, shows some of the covert ways in which the Bible shaped non-biblical poetry in his collection of animal fables based on the work of Aesop. Each fable presents a lively animal story, followed by a *moralitas* explaining the moral, and sometimes the hidden allegorical or spiritual, meaning of the story. None of these fables is biblical, but in various ways the influence of the Bible can be seen at work in them.

At its simplest, Henryson will sometimes give his animal characters the authority of biblical quotations to support their arguments. As in all fables, his creatures are anthropomorphic, allowed as he says to 'spak and understude,/And to gude purpois dispute and argow' (lines 44–45). In 'The Wolf and the Lamb' the brutal wolf accuses the innocent lamb of increasingly unreal 'crimes': of polluting his water (by drinking downstream from him), of being the son of a sheep who once argued with the wolf, and finally of trying to defend his innocence. When the wolf accuses him of his father's sins, the lamb responds:

Haiff ye not hard quhat Halie Scripture sayis,
Endytit with the mouth off God almycht?   [written]
Off his awin deidis ilk man sall beir the pais,   [burden]
As pyne for sin, reward for werkis rycht.   [pain]
(lines 2665–8)

He is drawing from Ezekiel 18, which discusses hereditary guilt, pronouncing: 'The son shall not bear the iniquity of the father . . . the righteousness of the righteous shall be upon him, and the wickedness of the wicked shall be upon him' (Ezek. 18:20). The wolf hits back:

> I let the wit, quhen that the father offendis,   [know]
> I will cheris nane off his successioun,
> And off his barnis I may weill tak amendis
> Unto the twentie degre descending doun.
>
> (lines 2672–5)

He is sacrilegiously appropriating to his private revenge the words of God himself in Exodus 20:5, claiming to visit 'the iniquity of the fathers upon the children unto the third and fourth generation'. Although the moral point is serious and the fable is grim, with the helpless lamb savagely murdered by the unjust wolf, Henryson seems to use the Bible here almost humorously, giving his simple animals a sophisticated knowledge of the technicalities of the Scriptures.

But often the biblical echoes are both more obscure and yet more significant to our understanding of the fable. 'The Cock and the Jasp' tells of a cock who discovers a precious jasper carelessly thrown on his dung heap, but rejects it in favour of food. The *moralitas* tells us that the cock stands allegorically for fools who scorn the precious gift of knowledge in favour of mere physical pleasure. This initially slightly surprising interpretation is given the weight of implicit biblical support. The allegorical explanation, revealing a new level of meaning in the tale, resembles Christ's own use of parables. Henryson also manages to recall a particular parable which reinforces his moral. The stone found by the cock is called a jasper. But in explaining his foolish rejection of it Henryson compares him to:

> . . . ane sow to qhome men for the nanis   [on purpose]
> In hir draf troich wald saw the precious stanis.   [draff-trough; scatter]
>
> (lines 146–147)

He is referring to Christ's injunction not to 'cast your pearls before swine' (Matt. 7:6). These pearls were often associated with the knowledge that leads to salvation, the kingdom of heaven represented by that other 'pearl of great price' sought by the merchant in Matthew 13:46. By this very indirect echo of a familiar biblical parable, Henryson shows his cock's rejection of the jasper/pearl not as an act of commonsense, but as foolish blindness to spiritual truth.

If the Bible sometimes helped Henryson to shape the meaning of his fables, it also contributed, indirectly but significantly, to the way his readers might interpret them. Because the mediaeval Scriptures were 'shut'—mysterious words of God that were not to be lightly under- stood—complex ways of interpreting them were established to help reveal their truth. It was suggested that biblical texts offered four levels of meaning: the literal sense; the moral or 'tropological' sense that referred to the conduct of life; an 'allegorical' sense related to Christ or the Church; and the 'anagogical' level which related the original text to heavenly realities. An example would be the phrase 'the temple of the Lord'. Literally it refers to Solomon's Temple in Jerusalem; the moral sense sees each Christian's body as a temple (1 Cor. 3:16); allegorically the temple is the body of Christ (John 2:21); and anagogically it represents the mansions of heaven.

This complex method of reading was designed for the Bible, rather than other literature; but it suggests how ready readers were to search out meanings beyond the literal sense. Much mediaeval litera- ture—Henryson's *Fables* are an example—offers at least two mean- ings, literal and allegorical. And sometimes Henryson does tell a story that can be interpreted, like the Bible, at several different levels. In 'The Paddock and the Mouse', a mouse, wishing to cross a river, is persuaded by an ugly but flattering toad to tie herself to him as he swims across. Once in the water he dives to try to drown her; but as they struggle a hungry kite seizes them both. The *moralitas* first interprets this story morally: do not trust 'ane silken toung, ane hart of crueltie' (line 2922). Then it begins to develop an allegory: the pad- dock is man's body, the mouse his soul, bound together in conflict; the water is the world in which they struggle. The hungry kite 'is deith, that cummis suddandlie' (line 2962). This haunting allegory is not biblical. But it was the system of interpretation developed for the Bible that encouraged this many-levelled kind of writing.

The other most famous mediaeval poet, William Dunbar (c.1460– 1515), shows yet other ways in which the Bible shaped and influenced mediaeval poetry. Dunbar often builds his poems round biblical phrases and ideas that come through the liturgy. So the resonances of the church services, as well as the Bible itself, contribute to the force of the poems. This is especially clear in his two poems on the Nativity and the Resurrection, which each use a liturgical/biblical phrase as a keynote and refrain. The Nativity poem centres on the phrase, still familiar, *Et nobis puer natus est* ('Unto us a child is born', Isa. 9:6), taken from the Introit for the Christmas Day mass. But the poem does not follow our Christmas traditions. The baby in the manger is not mentioned; instead there is an intoxicated delight and energy of celebration as the world is summoned to honour its new spring. Dunbar has drawn, not on the Bible story of the Nativity, but on liturgical hymns and responses, themselves based on biblical texts. So the poem opens with a phrase taken from the Advent services, *Rorate caeli desuper* ('Drop down, ye heavens, from above', Isa. 45:8). It then calls in turn on angels, sinners, clergy, birds, flowers—'Hevin, erd, se, man, bird and best'—to celebrate Christ's coming, following the pattern of the great hymns of praise in the *Te Deum* and the *Benedictus* (*cf* Psalm 148). The triumph and mystery of the birth derives not from the Gospels but from the prophecies and the Psalms; the images from the biblical revelation that, by entering the liturgy, had become powerfully familiar.

Dunbar's Resurrection poem seems equally far from our Easter traditions, in spite of its familiar-sounding refrain: the triumphant *Surrexit Dominas de sepulchro* ('The Lord has risen from the tomb') is taken from the mass for Easter Day. The poem celebrates, not so much the Resurrection itself, as Christ's glorious descent to hell to defeat the devil and release captive mankind from death, between Good Friday and Easter Day. This episode, known as the Harrowing of Hell, was based on a widely-known apocryphal work, the *Gospel of Nicodemus*.[4] The story it tells of Christ's descent to overthrow the devil and lead mankind up from hell to heaven is elaborated from scattered and fragmentary biblical texts. Pictures of Christ beating down the gates of hell, battling with Lucifer, and leading Adam, Eve, and the prophets out of hell up to his Father, were familiar in churches and drama, and the legend was for most people almost indistinguishable from biblical truth, permeated with biblical words and ideas.

In Dunbar's poem, Christ is the 'lyone' ('he lay down as a lion, and as a great lion: who shall stir him up?': Num. 24:9) who has thrown down 'the deidly dragon Lucifer' ('and he laid hold on the dragon, that old serpent, which is the Devil': Rev. 20:2). By his triumph, 'The gettis of hell ar brokin with a crak'. This moment was generally dramatised in the words of Psalm 24:7–10, which sounded as Christ approached hell's gates: 'Lift up your heads, O ye gates; and be ye lift up ye everlasting doors; and the King of glory shall come in'. The Easter celebration has become a glorious paean of victory, thundering in lively vernacular Scots the beliefs of the Latin liturgy. Although saturated with biblical allusions, this idea of Easter does not come from any direct reading of the Bible, but obliquely through apocrypha, liturgy and legend, which have added a characteristic mediaeval enrichment.

Controversy and Reformation

All of this mediaeval literature and drama was based on the shared certainties of the Roman Catholic Vulgate. But during the sixteenth century, as the Reformation approached, the Bible itself became involved in religious controversy. Bitter debate grew up over the possibility and propriety of translating the Scriptures into the vernacular: did translation give every Christian his rightful access to God's truth, or did it distort and trivialise the true meaning of God's Word? At least one Scots version of the Wycliffite English translation of the New Testament was copied at this time.[5] The literature of controversy, reform and propaganda also began to use the Bible to express contemporary political issues. Robert Wedderburn's mid-sixteenth-century *The Complaynt of Scotland* [6] openly describes the problems of the country through biblical parallels: 'The feyrd [fourth] cheptour conferris [compares] the passagis of the thrid cheptour of Ysaye witht the afflictione of Scotland'.

The drama also took up biblical allegory for contemporary purposes. John Knox claims that a Friar Kyllour was burned at the stake for presenting a reforming 'Historye of Christis Passioun' in Stirling in 1535 that likened the Pharisees opposing Christ to the Roman Catholic bishops.[7] In Dundee in the 1540s James Wedderburn's tragedy of the beheading of John the Baptist was performed, an anti-papist play apparently using biblical allegory to dramatise the plight of reformers oppressed by tyrannical authorities. So the Bible was initially a dramatic weapon for reform. But as the forces of the Reformation developed, the theatre came to be considered an inappropriate, and falsifying, medium for the sacred reality of the Bible. In 1574 the General Assembly of the Church forbade all plays on the 'Canonicall Scripture, alsweill new as old'.

The most famous surviving mediaeval Scottish play, David Lindsay's *Ane Satyre of the Thrie Estaits* directly dramatises parts of the Bible controversy. This political allegory presents the chaos into which Scotland has fallen through the corruption of the clergy, who are failing in their vocation. When the virtuous Good Counsel challenges Spirituality (the clergy), 'Schir, red ye never the New Testament?', he is answered:

Na sir, be him that our Lord Jesus sauld
I red never the New Testament nor Auld.

(lines 2933–4)

And when Verity, the truth of religion, enters, the clergy react in horror to the book she holds:

> Out walloway, this is the New Testament,
> In Englisch toung, and printit in England,
> Herisie, herisie, fire, fire, incontinent.

(lines 1155–7)

Lindsay's play does not reject the older forms of religion and the Bible. Virtuous characters quote freely from the Latin Vulgate, and one of the greatest charges levelled against the clergy is that they do not preach the Scriptures and teach God's law to the people who have no other access to it. But by the 1550s, when the play was performed at the public playfield in Edinburgh, it was clearly identified with the new movement in religion, which culminated in the Reformation of 1560.

In that new world the Bible became, at least in English, increasingly available. The mosaic of biblical ideas, images, stories and phrases, filtered through the rich interpretative traditions of the Middle Ages, was replaced by a plainer but fuller acquaintance with a different version of the text. As that happened, the Bible gradually took on a new role in the language, the consciousness, and the literature of Scotland.

SARAH CARPENTER

Notes

1   Richard Rolle, *Tractatus Super Apocalypsim*, in Nicole Marzac (ed), *Richard Rolle of Hampole: Vie et Oeuvres* (Paris, 1968), p 122 (f123 v B); Geoffrey Shepherd, 'English Version of the Scriptures before Wyclif', in G W Lampe (ed), *The Cambridge History of the Bible*, vol 2 (Cambridge, 1969), p 367.
2   All recorded references to Scottish mediaeval drama can be found in Anna J Mill, *Medieval Plays in Scotland* (Edinburgh and London, 1927).
3   Details of texts cited in this chapter are given below, after the Notes.
4   *The Gospel of Nicodemus* can be found in E Hennecke, *New Testament Apocrypha*, W Schneemelcher (ed), English translation, R McL Wilson (ed), vol 1 (London, 1963), pp 444ff.
5   Thomas Graves Law (ed), *The New Testament in Scots*, 3 vols (Scottish Text Society, Edinburgh, 1901–5). On this, see References to Chapter 11.
6   Robert Wedderburn, *The Complaynt of Scotland*, A M Stewart (ed), (Scottish Text Society, Edinburgh, 1979).

7   David Laing (ed), *The Works of John Knox*, vol 1 (Edinburgh, 1846), p 62.

Further Reading

Texts

F J Amours (ed), *The Pistill of Susan* in *Scottish Alliterative Poems* (Scottish Text Society, Edinburgh, 1897).

J A W Bennett (ed), *The Contemplacioun of Synnaris* in *Devotional Pieces in Verse and Prose* (Scottish Text Society, Edinburgh, 1955).

James Kinsley (ed), *The Poems of William Dunbar* (Oxford, 1979).

Denton Fox (ed), *The Poems of Robert Henryson* (Oxford, 1981).

Peter Happe (ed), David Lindsay's *Ane Satyre of the Thrie Estaits*, in *Four Morality Plays* (Harmondsworth, 1979).

Studies

David C Fowler, *The Bible in Early English Literature* (Seattle and London, 1976).

Fowler, The Bible in Middle English Literature (Seattle and London, 1984).

G W H Lampe (ed), *The Cambridge History of the Bible*, vol 2 (Cambridge, 1969).

Anna J Mill, *Medieval Plays in Scotland* (Edinburgh and London, 1927).

Rosemary Woolf, *English Religious Lyrics in the Middle Ages* (Oxford, 1968).

6

The Bible in Burns and Scott

It is well known that the Bible played a major role in the education of all Scots in the eighteenth century when two of Scotland's best-known authors were growing up. Robert Burns could quote (and sometimes misquote) the Bible with great facility, and Walter Scott, with his photographic memory could, when he so desired, do the same. Perhaps because he grew up in cosmopolitan Edinburgh, Scott drew less upon the Bible in his poetry than did Burns with his rural background. At the same time, it is interesting to note that Burns referred to or quoted the Bible much more frequently in his early years than in his later ones.

As a frame of reference, Scots could be assured that their audiences would immediately recognise quotations from or allusions to the Bible. This served well in the writing of satire; biblical references could also have a political dimension, giving the Scot an edge over his English contemporary in this respect. (We think, for instance, of the political as well as religious aspects of the literature of the 1733 Secession from the national Church led by Ebenezer Erskine.) Perhaps, too, because religion itself leaned more heavily on the Bible, pulpit oratory in the eighteenth century itself had a strong Old Testament character.

Burns' Familiarity with the Bible

Growing up in rural Ayrshire in the 1760s and 1770s, Robert Burns lived in the fading years of the controversy among the Secessionists between adherents of the Auld Licht and the New Licht. His father, a Kincardineshire man, appears to have belonged to the old school; although at times he displayed remarkable liberality, he was deeply offended when Robert disobeyed his command and attended dancing classes in Tarbolton at the age of 17. Because they were needed to help on the farm, Burns and his brothers did not get much schooling, although their father sent them whenever possible. Thus, like most country children of the time, much of their reading and a good deal of their learning came at odd moments and was largely self-directed. In his famous letter to Dr John Moore of August 1787, the poet mentions 15 books which made up his 'knowledge' when he was about 17 years old; two of these would have supplemented the Bible (which, of course, he did not feel he needed to mention)—Thomas Stackhouse's *New History of the Holy Bible* and John Taylor's *Scripture Doctrine of Original Sin*. It is unfortunate that no list of Burns' library exists, but it was quite a considerable collection for a man of his means. From references to religious books in his correspondence, we know that he had read Thomas Boston's *Human Nature in Its Fourfold Estate*, William Guthrie's *Trial of a Saving Interest*, Marie Huber's *Letters on the Religion Essential to Man* and other devotional works, all of which presupposed familiarity with the Bible, if not with the doctrinal disputes of the day.

Not only did Burns read the Bible while a youth under his father's eye; he read and enjoyed it as an adult. In 1787 he wrote to Margaret Chalmers: 'I have taken tooth and nail to the Bible, and am got through the five books of Moses, and half way in Joshua. It is really a glorious book'.[1]

Kirk Satires

Burns' familiarity with the Bible stood him in good stead in the writing of his kirk satires, 'underground' poems which he did not publish but which went the rounds in manuscript copies to the delight of his friends. One of the earliest of these was 'Holy Willie's Prayer', written in 1785 while the poet was living at Mossgiel. The occasion of the poem, in the words of the poet, was as follows:

> Gavin Hamilton was what the world calls, a good, moral man, but a stranger to 'Effectual Calling' or 'the Newbirth'; so was very properly summoned before the kirk session. . . . The affair went to the Presbytery, where the uncircumcised Philistines overcame the people of God . . . and Holy Willie, the Lord's servant [was] . . . put to shame. . . .[2]

Not only does Burns destroy Willie in the poem, he also demolishes the

Auld Licht concept of predestination. The opening lines encapsulate the narrow idea of salvation which Burns was satirising:

> Oh thou that in the heavens does dwell
> Wha, as it pleases best thysel,
> Sends ane to heaven and ten to hell,
>   A' for thy glory!
> And no for ony gude or ill
>   They've done before thee.

(Poems I, p 74)

Burns then continues with a general statement of God's ways:

> When from my mother's womb I fell,
> Thou might hae plunged me deep in hell,
> . . . .
> Yet I am here, a chosen sample,
> To shew thy grace is great and ample.

(Poems I, p 75)

Willie then goes on to destroy his own reputation:

> But yet—O Lord—confess I must—
> At times I'm fash'd wi' fleshly lust;
> And sometimes too, in warldly trust
>   Vile Self gets in;
> But thou remembers we are dust,
>   Defil'd wi' sin.   *(Poems* I, p 76)

Having also admitted to his own drunkenness and fornication, Willie brilliantly turns the table on God with 'thy hand maun e'en be borne / Until thou lift it' (*Poems* I, p 76). Little wonder that this poem has been called the greatest short satire in the English language. Although Burns never sanctioned its publication (a pirated edition was published in 1789), the several holograph copies attest to its immediate popularity; word of it must soon have come to the butts of Burns' ridicule, William Fisher and the Revd William Auld.

Burns was not through with Auld, though. In 1786 the Revd Dr William McGill, a New Licht who held the second charge of Ayr, published *A Practical Essay on the Death of Jesus Christ*, a book which was denounced as heterodox and caused the General Assembly of the Church of Scotland to order an inquiry. Burns realised that he could not help McGill by openly siding with him, but he wrote and circulated 'The Kirk's Alarm' as well as having some broadside copies of it printed in the hope of rendering 'some of the Doctor's foes ridiculous' (*Letters* I, p 422).

As with the earlier poems, Burns opens with a general salvo:

Orthodox, Orthodox, who believe in John Knox,
  Let me sound an alarm to your conscience;
A heretic blast has been blawn i' the West—
  That what is not Sense must be Nonsense, Orthodox,
  That what is not Sense must be Nonsense.

(*Poems* I, p 470)

One by one Burns singles out the people who were persecuting McGill and deftly skewers them before roasting them over the fire of his scorn. Among the poet's victims we find 'Daddy' Auld and Holy Willie, who, we are told, 'pilfer'd the alms o' the poor' (*Poems* I, p 474). Even Burns himself comes in for some abuse: 'Poet Burns, Poet Burns, wi' your priest-skelping turns, / Why desert ye your auld native shire?' (*Poems* I, p 474). There were other satires directed at members of the Church of Scotland who Burns thought were betraying their trust. But these poems were always directed at the person, not the institution.

Metrical Psalms

Like all Scots, Burns knew the metrical Psalms well, and quoted them quite frequently, although oddly enough he misquoted them more often than he did citations from the Bible itself. In an exuberant letter of 29 July 1787 to Robert Ainslie on the joys of fatherhood, Burns misquotes Metrical Psalm 127:3–5, going on to say that Jean Armour (not yet his wife, but already the mother of his twins) is 'certainly in for it again' (*Letters* I, p 131). We may gather how well the metrical Psalms were known in Burns' day by a passage in the letter to Margaret Chalmers in which the poet says of Jean, 'she scarcely ever in her life, except the Scriptures of the Old and New Testament, and the Psalms of David in metre, spent five minutes together on either prose or verse' (*Letters* I, p 318).

Doubtless it was his familiarity with the metrical Psalms which challenged him to write two paraphrases of Psalms himself—the first Psalm in its entirety, and the first six verses of the ninetieth. These poems were written between 1774 and 1784 and were published in the Edinburgh edition of 1787. I quote the first two verses of the first Psalm (in the Authorised Version), followed by the same verses in the Metrical Psalter and lastly in Burns' paraphrase:

Blessed is the man that walketh not in the counsel
of the ungodly, nor standeth in the way of sinners,
nor sitteth in the seat of the scornful.
But his delight is in the law of the Lord; and
in his law doth he meditate day and night.

That man hath perfect blessedness
   who walketh not astray
In counsel of ungodly man,
   nor stands in sinners' way,
Nor sitteth in the scorner's chair:
   But placeth his delight
Upon God's law, and meditates
   on his law day and night.

The man, in life where-ever plac'd,
   Hath happiness in store,
Who walks not in the wicked's way,
   Nor learns their guilty lore!

Nor from the seat of scornful Pride
   Casts forth his eyes abroad,
But with humility and awe
   Still walks before his God.

(Poems I, p 24)

Burns wrote one other paraphrase of the Bible in 1786, a twelve-line poem entitled 'Jeremiah 15th Ch. 10 V'. There are other poems and songs in which both construction and phrasing seem to have been inspired by the Bible, but Burns produced no more paraphrases of the Scriptures.

To his friend Mrs Dunlop, Burns confided his thoughts on religion on several occasions: in 1788, he wrote, 'A Mathematician without Religion, is a probable character; an irreligious Poet, is a Monster' (*Letters* I, p 230), and two years later, 'We can no more live without Religion, than we can live without air . . .' (*Letters* II, p 57). In 1792 he wrote to her about his son, and her godson, Francis Wallace:

> I am so convinced that an unshaken faith in the doctrines of Christianity is not only necessary by making us better men, but also by making us happier men, that I shall take every care that your little godson, & every little creature that shall call me, Father, shall be firmly persuaded that 'God was in Christ, reconciling the world unto himself, not imputing unto men their trespasses'.
>
> (2 Corinthians 5:19, slightly misquoted;
> *Letters* II, p 144)

At about the same time as he composed 'Holy Willie's Prayer', Burns also wrote 'The Cotter's Saturday Night'. The portrait Burns draws of the patriarchal father, generally accepted as being based on his own father, and the extended passage about the Bible-reading, Psalm-singing and prayer after supper are too well known to need quotation here. This warm-hearted picture of the Scotland of the poet's youth underscores how well Burns knew his Bible as well as the humble people who guided their lives by its teachings. ('From Scenes like these, old Scotia's grandeur springs, / That makes her lov'd at home, rever'd abroad'—*Poems* I, p 151.)

Poetry obviously does not lend itself well to biblical quotations, and so we find only oblique references to the Scriptures in most of Burns' verse. He does use such words as 'holy', 'Scripture', 'religion', as often as not for satirical purposes. Burns felt confident, though, that his barbs could not harm the Church: in his poem 'To the Rev. John M'Math, Inclosing a copy of *Holy Willie's Prayer*', he made the point:

> All hail, Religion! maid divine!
> Pardon a muse sae mean as mine,
> Who in her rough imperfect line
>   Thus daurs to name thee;
> To stigmatise false friends of thine
>   Can ne'er defame thee.

> Tho' blotch't an' foul wi' mony a stain,
> An' far unworthy of thy train,
> With trembling voice I tune my strain
>   To join with those,
> Who boldly dare thy cause maintain
>   In spite of foes.

(Poems I, pp 125–6)

The Bible in Letters

I have already suggested that we must turn to Burns' correspondence to assess the impact which the Bible had upon him. Unlike Walter Scott, who was able to have many of his fictional characters quote or paraphrase the Bible, Burns wrote no novels, so that we have only his correspondence as a guide. In his collected *Letters* we find many dozens of quotations from Scripture, most of them from the Old Testament. Among his favourite books were Job and Proverbs in the Old Testament, and Matthew and Romans in the New.

One passage from Job particularly struck Burns and he quoted it more than once. To the Revd John Skinner, friend and fellow-poet, he wrote, 'The world may think slightingly of the craft of song-making, if they please; but, as Job says, "O! that mine adversary had written a book!" let them try' (Job 31:35; *Letters* I, p 167). Burns displayed a remarkable memory for passages which took his fancy, although he sometimes misquoted. At other times he appears to have mistaken remembered snatches of pulpit oratory for biblical passages. In one such misattribution he wrote, 'A few years ago, I could have lain down in the dust, careless, as the book of Job elegantly says, "Careless of the voice of the morning . . ." ' (*Letters* II, p 164). This was either quoted from another source, or so garbled as to be unrecognisable.

Burns also used Job and other passages in the Bible in a somewhat less honourable form, to court Mrs Agnes M'Lehose. In February 1788 he wrote to her, 'The hour that you are not in my thoughts—"be that hour darkness! let the shadows of Death cover it! let it not be numbered in the hours of the day!"' (Job 3:4–6; *Letters* I, p 241). As is the case with most writers, Burns altered the tone of his letters to suit the correspondent and the occasion. Having perceived that Clarinda took refuge from his ardent courtship by reminding him that she was a married woman and very attached to the Bible, the bard larded his billets-doux with biblical allusion and quotation. Since one cannot take the Clarinda correspondence very seriously (let us remember that on 14–15 February 1788 Burns wrote four letters to her and on the 23rd he set up house with Jean Armour in Mauchline and married her shortly after), I shall take no further account of biblical references in the poet's letters to the rather ill-treated Clarinda.

The poet's relationship with Mrs Dunlop was quite a different affair; nearly 30 years his elder, she treated him as a somewhat wayward son, and Burns responded in kind. But when Mrs Dunlop wrote, without elaborating, that her son Anthony had had a 'great disappointment', the poet tactfully responded, 'The heart knoweth its own sorrows, and a Stranger intermeddleth not therewith' (Proverbs 14:10, slightly misquoted; *Letters* I, p 301). A long-awaited letter from Mrs Dunlop brought forth another quotation from Proverbs (25:25): 'As cold water to a thirsty soul, so is good news from a far Country' (*Letters* II, p 61).

On another occasion, without actually quoting the Bible, Burns tried to cheer up his friend:

Would I could write to you a letter of comfort. . . . Religion, my dear friend, is the true comfort! A strong persuasion in a future state of existence; a proposition so obviously probable, that, setting revelation aside, every nation and people . . . have, in some mode or other, firmly believed it. In vain would we reason and pretend to doubt.

(*Letters* I, p 439)

Despite the many quotations from the Bible and references to his own belief to be found in his correspondence, Burns has been regarded as an unbeliever by many. As late as 1869 the Revd Fergus Ferguson published *Should Christians Commemorate the Birthday of Robert Burns?* in which he argued against doing so on religious grounds. The answer is to be found in Burns' frequent quotation from and reference to the Bible, his defence of religion, and to no small extent his pillorying of the 'Chosen swatch, / Wi' screw'd-up, grace-proud faces' ('The Holy Fair', *Poems* I, p 132).

Scott and Religion

It would be hard to think of two more different backgrounds than those of Burns and Walter Scott. The one was a peasant—self-taught; lionised, but often with a certain condescension; brought up by a strictly Calvinist father; born into poverty, and never comfortably off. The other was an advocate, son of a Writer to the Signet; university-trained; urbane; likewise lionised, but by his social equals; at ease with the more relaxed teachings of his Church; comfortably brought up, and, as an adult, leading the life of a wealthy man. Nevertheless the Church of his fathers and its Bible was of abiding interest to Scott and we see this reflected in much of his writing.

Old Mortality (1816) is the earliest of Scott's Waverley Novels to be concerned with religion in a major way. As we would expect, most of its references to the Bible are to the Old Testament. Early in the novel (Ch 6) John Burley of Balfour quotes five verses from the Apocrypha (Ecclus. 40:1–5). This, and other quotations from Ecclesiasticus, serves to point to the fact that Scott and his readers were familiar with the writings of the Apocrypha, as were the characters he drew from the seventeenth century. On the other hand, Scott did not rely heavily on the New Testament in his fiction.

Old Mortality is set in 1679, when the Covenanters rose at Drumclog and were defeated at Bothwell Bridge. The story confronts the hero, Henry Morton, with a choice between liberty of conscience and the claims of government. As he frequently did, Scott makes some of his religious points through his comic characters or by the use of irony. In *Old Mortality* Mause Headrigg is one of these; she links the fun of the wappenshaw and shooting at the popinjay with idolatrous worship and convinces her son Cuddie not to participate. Explaining to Lady Bellenden why her son did not take part, Mause refers to 'Ane abune whase commands I maun obey before your leddyship's' (Ch 7) and then goes on to cite Nebuchadnezzar and Shadrach, Meshach and Abednego (Daniel 3).

But the intolerance of the times is not always painted in comic vein; Balfour, one of those who had murdered the Primate of Scotland, Archbishop James Sharp, is an example. When Morton overhears Balfour speaking of the event in his sleep, the fugitive is dreaming in biblical terms: 'Thou art taken, Judas. . . . A priest? Ay, a priest of Baal, to be bound and slain, even at the brook Kishon' (Ch 6). No wonder Morton calls him a 'stern enthusiast'. If there is a thesis in Scott's novel, it is that of the necessity of toleration. Both Covenanters and redcoats under Claverhouse are fanatics, and Scott does not make either side look attractive to the reader. But moderation was a dangerous thing in the Scotland of the time as Scott drew it; Morton's attempt to bring it to the Covenanters put him in mortal danger, as did his defence of the rights of Scotland before Claverhouse. Morton's personal victory in the novel is the stuff of fiction, as Scott knew. The father of the historical novel did not hesitate to show the bitter end of many of the zealots—Mucklewrath, for instance, who dies content, covered in blood.

Critics, such as Edgar Johnson, have pointed out that, while Scott certainly did not sympathise with the fanatic Covenanters, he did not burlesque them either.[3]

Favourite Parts of the Bible

In *Rob Roy* (1817) we see the troubles between Catholic and Presbyterian, and here, too, Scott deals even-handedly with both denominations, although the characters he paints do not. Thus Francis Osbaldistone's servant, Andrew Fairservice, was mightily prejudiced against Catholics, even though his master was eventually to marry one, Diana Vernon. In speaking of her cousin, Rashleigh Osbaldistone, Diana, who is appropriately hunting at the time, describes him as 'a mighty hunter . . . after the fashion of Nimrod' (Ch 7), in a reference to Genesis (10:8–9). Scott seems to have been rather fond of the Book of Genesis, for he quoted from it several times in his poetry and fiction. Other favourites were the Books of Samuel, in which Scott the story-teller found much to his liking and which he cited more than once. Bailie Nicol Jarvie, while he does not quote from these books, likes allusion to Scripture because it allows him to make reference to statute and gospel law, both dear to his heart, although he could overlook both on occasion. His advice to Francis Osbaldistone is that he should:

> take the counsel of those who are aulder and wiser than yoursell, and binna like the godless Rehoboam, who took the advice o' a wheen beardless callans, neglecting the auld counsellors who had sate at the feet o' his father Solomon . . ..
>
> (referring to 1 Kings 12:13–14; *Rob Roy*, Ch 26)

The Heart of Midlothian (1818) pits David Deans, father of Jeanie and Effie and an unbending Presbyterian of the Auld Licht school, against Reuben Butler, who was trained for the ministry, but is a schoolmaster as the story opens. The young man is possessed of little drive, and it seems unlikely that Deans will allow him to marry Jeanie.

When, near the end of the story, Deans has it in his power to name a minister on the Argyle estate, where he is to become factor, and despite the fact that Butler will soon wed Jeanie, he still feels it incumbent upon himself to catechise the candidate. Deans has reservations, based on his distaste for lay patronage, and it will be recalled that the time of the story of *Midlothian* is exactly the time of the Secession, led by Ebenezer Erskine and others. The old man runs through

> the doctrines and belief of the Christian Church [beginning] with the very Culdees, from whom he passed to John Knox,—from John Knox to the recusants in James the Sixth's time,—Bruce, Black, Blair, Livingstone,—from them to the brief, and at length triumphant period of the presbyterian church's splendour . . ..
>
> (*Midlothian*, Ch 43).

Here Scott, in the *persona* of Deans, shows himself to be familiar with Scottish Church history as well as the Bible.

We find another scriptural reference when Jeanie debates with herself about the propriety of entering a church in England:

> The prophet, she thought, permitted Naaman the Syrian to bow even in the house of Rimmon. Surely if I, in this streight, worship the God of my fathers in mine own language, although the manner thereof be strange to me, the Lord will pardon me in this thing.
>
> (*Midlothian*, Ch 31)

Scott was fond of this biblical story (from 2 Kings 5), referring to it also in *A Legend of Montrose.*

Jeanie's simple faith is in the Bible and also in the mercy, rather than the narrow justice, of the law. Effie, though, is prepared for a sterner interpretation of life. When Jeanie visits her in prison, she has her sister open the Bible at a spot which she has marked (Job 19:9–10): 'He hath stripped me of my glory, and taken the crown from my head. He hath destroyed me on every side, and I am gone: and mine hope hath he removed like a tree' (Ch 20). When it comes to drink, Jeanie sticks to the letter of the Bible, as we should expect of her. Declining a drink from the Duke of Argyle, who playfully quotes the saying 'wine maketh the heart glad', she counters with a reference to Jeremiah 35:6, 'my father is like Jonadab the son of Rechab, who charged his children that they should drink no wine' (Ch 40). This allows the duke to get in a sly dig at teetotalism, 'I thought your father would have had more sense . . . unless indeed he prefers brandy'.

Dark Side of Religion

There are, of course, many more quotations from and references to the Bible in Scott's works. Steeped as he was in the history and legend of his country, Scott was interested also in the darker side of religion. His *Letters on Demonology and Witchcraft* were published in 1830, rounding out his interest in the occult which we may trace from his *Minstrelsy of the Scottish Border* of 1802.

There are also several references to superstition connected with the Bible which Scott's characters display. Effie Deans, for example, after her father had inveighed against dancing, promises herself she will never again go to Maggie Macqueen's, where she had danced with George Staunton: 'But I'll no gang back there again. . . . I'll lay in a leaf of my Bible, and that's very near as if I had made an aith . . .'. Uncertain that his readers would know what Effie meant, Scott added a footnote:

> This custom, of making a mark by folding a leaf in the party's Bible, when a solemn resolution is formed, is still held to be, in some sense, an appeal to Heaven for his or her sincerity.
>
> (*Midlothian*, Ch 10)

Scott employed the supernatural not infrequently in his fiction, although usually the belief in such things is on the part of the character,

D

not part of the narrative itself. There are exceptions, of course, as when Ravenswood tries to rationalise what happens at the Mermaiden's Fountain, in *The Bride of Lammermoor*. And we all remember one of the greatest of Scottish ghost stories, 'Wandering Willie's Tale' from *Redgauntlet*.

Although in no hurry to admit his authorship, Scott permitted George Huntly Gordon to publish two sermons he (Scott) had written for him in 1824. These appeared in 1828 as *Religious Discourses by a Layman*, with the profit from sales going to Gordon.

Like Burns, Scott, too, frequently quoted the Bible in his correspondence, although he often just worked a short passage into the text of his letters without using quotation marks as Burns almost always did. Among Scott's most-often quoted books were Genesis, Kings, Job, the Psalms, and Proverbs; in the New Testament he drew heavily from the four Evangelists.

Certain quotations he used several times. Psalms 37:35 ('I have seen the wicked in great power, and spreading himself like a green bay tree') was a great favourite; he quoted it at least eight times, and it should be recalled that only about half the known Scott letters are published in the collected edition. This verse, of course, lends itself admirably to political reference, or even business dealings.

The Psalter

Another Psalm which Scott quoted frequently was Psalm 137—he liked particularly the second verse ('We hanged our harps upon the willows in the midst thereof') and the fifth ('If I forget thee, O Jerusalem, let my right hand forget her cunning'); the former verse Scott quoted five times, the latter three. Oddly enough, Burns also quoted the fifth verse in one of his letters.

Scott was also fond of the metrical Psalms. In addition to quoting from them, he was invited in 1818 by the Revd George Husband Baird, Principal of the University of Edinburgh, to collaborate in a new metrical version. Pleading in part 'my total unacquaintance with the original language of the scriptures', Scott went on to defend the version then in use:

> . . . I am not sure whether the old fashioned version of the psalms does not suit the purpose of public worship better than smoother versification and greater terseness of expression. . . . The expression of the old

metrical translation though homely is plain forcible & intelligible and very often possesses a rude sort of majesty which perhaps would be ill exchanged for more elegance.[4]

In the event nothing came of the project.

Metrical versions of the Psalms have been seen as something of a challenge to Scots poets. In 1773 James Maxwell, a poetaster known to Burns, but apparently not to Scott, had published *A New Version of the Whole Book of Psalms in Metre*, and there were others. These versions of the Psalms were oddities, and were, of course, not designed to compete with the officially recognised version which bore the stamp of approval in these words: 'Allowed by the authority of the General Assembly of the Kirk of Scotland, and appointed to be sung in congregations and families'. Principal Baird obviously hoped that Scott would produce a work which the public would purchase as a matter of interest, not for devotional use.

Burns, Scott and the Bible

In Burns and Scott, Scottish literature possessed two *universal* writers: critics have often remarked on the extent to which translation and international republication have brought out in both men the themes which transcend barriers of politics, language and distance. Each speaks from a background intimately known and cherished; each speaks to wide cross-sections of society. They employ very different literary languages, but what they demonstrably hold in common is a familiarity with, and a skilled use of, the King James text of Scripture.

Where Burns heard the Bible regularly preached, and caught marvellously the everyday incorporation of Bible phraseology into the commonplace in Scottish speech, Scott was obviously surrounded by a more varied social ambience and was receptive to language drawn from a very wide variety of experience and education. For Burns, the use of biblical phraseology on the farm, in the village, in the church and in the tavern would be part of an everyday phenomenon familiar since boyhood. For Scott, memories of boyhood church and the Bible would be more ambiguous, yet clearly his creative imagination recognised not only the intrinsic grandeur of the King James translation, but also the necessity of reflecting, in his use of it, something so natural to the Scottish society he depicted, that biblical speech was simply indispensable.

Each, then, uses biblical quotation and reference with the ease of the everyday, although the incorporation in art (as we have seen) is no necessary reflection of the author's own position or practice. Burns and Scott both *used* the Bible as a wonderful source book, and used it for private devotion and for religious inspiration in a much less obvious and public way. In each author's case, the insight into biblical meaning for individual characters, seen sympathetically or satirically, suggests long familiarity with the text and an easy, automatic reflection of that familiarity. Like Hogg, like Galt, like all their literate contemporaries in Scotland, they would have found the common use of the Bible quite natural; its place in their writing is equally natural and illuminating.

ROSS ROY

Notes

1   G. Ross Roy (ed), *The Letters of Robert Burns*, 2 vols, 2nd edition (Oxford, 1985), I, p 183. Subsequent references will appear in parentheses in the text.
2   James Kinsley (ed), *The Poems and Songs of Robert Burns*, 2 vols (Oxford, 1968), I, p 74. Subsequent references will appear in parentheses in the text.
3   Edgar Johnson, *Sir Walter Scott: The Great Unknown*, 2 vols (New York, 1970), I, p 599.
4   H J C Grierson (ed), *The Letters of Sir Walter Scott*, 12 vols (London, 1932–7), V, p 166.

Further Reading

General
James Moffatt, *The Bible in Scots Literature* (London, 1924).

Robert Burns
Thomas Crawford, *Burns: A Study of the Poems and Songs* (Edinburgh, 1960).
Hoxie Neale Fairchild, *Religious Trends in English Poetry*, 6 vols (New York and London, 1939–68), III, pp 19–65.
G. Ross Roy, 'The "Sighan, Cantan, Grace-Proud Faces": Robert Burns and the Kirk', *Scotia: American-Canadian Journal of Scottish Studies* 6 (1982), pp 26–40.

Walter Scott

Nicholas Dickson, *The Bible in Waverley, or Scott's Use of the Sacred Scriptures* (Edinburgh, 1884).

Richard French, 'The Religion of Sir Walter Scott', *Studies in Scottish Literature* II:1 (July 1964), pp 32–44.

Edgar Johnson, *Sir Walter Scott: The Great Unknown*, 2 vols (New York, 1970).

7

James Hogg and the Bible[*]

The Private Memoirs and Confessions of a Justified Sinner (1824) by James Hogg (1770–1835), the rural poet and novelist from Ettrick in the Scottish Borders, is now widely accepted as a masterpiece of Scottish fiction. In an earlier study of Hogg's use of the Bible in this work I reached the following tentative conclusions[1]: Hogg's use of the Bible could 'reflect an intensely religious childhood'; it could strengthen the author's bond to his audience in complex ways; the characters could use 'technical' words and phrases the better to explain themselves to the reader; the author could generate and control reader-response through the use of biblical and technical language.

> Just as the characters are made to reveal their beliefs by their language, and also their perversions and distortions, so Hogg is able to forecast his readers' distrust of them, and disgust at their extremity and hypocrisy, by drawing on the common fund of language based on the Bible and forms of worship at his time.[2]

This presupposes a reader-response based on detailed biblical knowledge (reasonable enough at the time), and a very interesting response based on Hogg's own childhood, which was unique in important ways. Even the parody of Hogg, which formed John Wilson's 'Ettrick Shepherd' in the *Noctes Ambrosianae*, could fume at the attempt by a dishonest bookseller to charge for 'a grawtis copy o' the Word o' God'[3]—small wonder, for in bitter poverty in his own childhood Hogg had had access to little else than the obvious family book. 'I neither read nor wrote nor had I access to any book save the Bible'. His pitiful

*Reprinted (with minor amendments) from the *Scottish Literary Journal* 10:1 (May 1983), pp 14–29. Thanks are expressed to the Council of the Association of Scottish Literary Studies and the Editor of the *Journal*.

schooling stopped short at 'the class who read in the Bible', having conquered 'the Shorter Catechism and the Proverbs of Solomon' along the way.[4] The Scriptures, Catechism, Psalms and Paraphrases were the staples of his early contact with literature. Critics have pointed to Hogg's command of 'English with Biblical overtones',[5] his ability to write of a devil who 'speaks out of Scripture', and of Robert Colwan who 'has a ready command of Puritan cant', and noted that Hogg 'had evidently read with attention the Paraphrases and Hymns at the end of his Bible'.[6] Hogg himself wrote of his early love of the Psalms, and his brother William reinforced the point heavily:

> Our mother's mind was well fortified by a good system of Christian religion . . . yet her mind was stored with tales of spectres, ghosts, fairies, brownies, voices &c . . . .These songs and tales which were sung and told in a plaintive, melancholy air, had an influence on James's mind altogether unperceived at the time, and perhaps indescribable now . . ..

> [James] was fond of reading and before he was able to read, could have said several of David's Psalms, which his mother had taught him partly to instil religious impressions into his mind, and no doubt partly to keep him peaceable and quiet when darkness and wet days kept him within doors. When he learned to read he read much on the Bible; this was a book which our mother was well acquainted with, and was in it better qualified to detect him when he went wrong, than if he had been reading any other book. And I can assure you, that in all the circle of my acquaintance, either among old or young people, I never was conversant with any one who had as much of the Bible by heart, especially of the Psalms, or could have told more readily where any passage was recorded than my brother James could have done. And, in my opinion, the beautiful descriptions of the nature and excellencies of the Divine Being, the sublime addresses to His grace and goodness that are interspersed through that invaluable work, more disposed his mind to utter his feelings in harmonious and poetic effusion than any native energy derived either from father or mother.[7]

His Mother: Teacher of the Bible

Several points call for emphasis. The first of these is the oft-noted status of Hogg's mother as repository of folktales and songs, source of much in Sir Walter Scott's published collections, and author of the famous rebuke to Scott that her tales were made to be sung and not printed—and that the tales once printed would never be sung more.[8] Hogg shared Scott's access to this source, but obviously drew from it much more copiously, whatever the results in published work. A short acquaintance with his published tales will soon confirm the point.

Yet alongside this point has to be put William Hogg's emphasis on Mrs Hogg as a Christian educator, one of a pair of parents concerned to give her children access to the Bible from an early age. Thus we have the curious picture of Hogg, illiterate, very poor, repeating parts of the Bible by heart from an early age, and drawing poetic inspiration from the Psalms of David in their English form. Whether this is the Psalmody of the Scottish Reformed Church or the Book of Psalms in the Old Testament is not really important—the truth was probably that Hogg drew inspiration from both. Certainly he knew the sung versions well enough to parody them splendidly in the *Confessions*.[9] In writing his own life, Hogg reinforced the point:

> I neither read nor wrote; nor had I access to any book save the Bible. I was greatly taken with *our version* of the Psalms of David, learned the most of them by heart, and have a great partiality for them unto this day.[10]

Here, completing the quotation we had earlier (and with my emphasis), is Hogg's own recollection, with no doubt some exaggeration—he is hardly likely to have memorised Psalm 119 in either version! It is just the sort of familiarity with Scottish Psalms which could give him inspiration for 'The Shepherd's Dog', chapter 20 of *The Shepherd's Calendar*, which concerns a precentor who knew only one tune, St Paul, for the Psalms of weekly worship.

One overall important point cannot be stressed enough. Hogg knew his Bible, early in life, the same way that he knew parts of his mother's enormous stock of folk literature—he learned it by hearing it, by repetition, by question-and-answer sessions with his mother. It was not the learned Bible of prolonged private study, a much-loved personal copy, the kind of study which presupposes literacy; it was the unconsciously absorbed familiarity with a central family text known to all from earliest youth.

English and Scots

This point is central to the present discussion. Briefly, I wish to differentiate between a common view of biblical influence on Scots authors, and the view which emerges from a brief study of Hogg's early life. The received position on the influence of the Bible on Scottish letters is that a gulf developed, and widened since 1611, between 'serious' English-language writing which is heavily influenced by the Bible, and 'relaxed'

Scottish writing which is vernacular, easy-going, and unconscious. That this thesis can do much to account for the poetic practice of Robert Burns and Robert Fergusson is self-evident. But applied to Hogg, the thesis is a dangerously simple one. And the reason is the one stated in the preceding paragraph; the Bible influence on young Hogg, as on presumably thousands of his contemporaries, is the influence of an orally-transmitted text probably absorbed in public recitation (and preaching) and its received form firmed up in family question-and-answer sessions, and public and family catechising in school, in church and in the home.

Thus the English, formal biblical language Hogg uses in his stories, and the informal natural Scots, come from the same area of his life. Our tendency to make the one formal, the other informal, is contradicted by the testimony of both the author and his brother. Thus the man who wrote in his farewell notes to *The Spy* that he 'went to service at seven years of age, and could neither read nor write with accuracy when twenty'[11] would have been at home at twenty in English and in Scots, even in that condition. Vulgarity would hardly enter into his thinking; the equation of Scots with vulgarity and English with gentility that was to dog the image of the Ettrick Shepherd in the *Noctes Ambrosianae* would hardly interest the Ettrick poet who would know both languages equally imperfectly, and accept them naturally. Had he known that Walter Scott was writing with regret of the disappearance of unembarrassed Scots, 'that is all gone and the remembrance will be drowned with the elders of this existing generation', he would probably have agreed.[12]

The picture we have of Hogg in private life is of a natural, well-balanced, Scots-speaking man who knew his literature, in Scots and English, and enjoyed both. Here is J M Wilson, describing Hogg as late as 1831, and it is interesting to see how religious topics take their minor place in the catalogue of his virtues:

> He is one of the greatest poets of his age, an indifferent novelist, a worse practical farmer, a tolerable astronomer, as good an angler as a poet, a bad archer, though wishing to be a good one, a poor manager of the things of this world, an amiable man, a warm friend, a tender husband, too good a master, a fond father, beloved by his neighbour, a humble christian, and a man who, if he has one, does not deserve an enemy.[13]

This is the man who learned his Bible from his mother, and incorporated it into his Scottish day-to-day experience quite unconsciously. What is of the greatest importance is that he incorporated it bilingually, mastering its English idiom while retaining his day-to-day neighbourly Scottishness. He rejoiced in his beloved metrical Psalms, partly because they bridged the gap between Englishness and Scottishness, as he made clear in 1830 in a letter to the *Edinburgh Literary Journal*:

> I never read any poetry in my life that affected my heart half so much as those sublime strains of Zion, sung in what I conceived to be the pure spirit of their ancient simplicity, and the antiquated rhymes and Scotticisms at which Mr. Tennant sneers so much, are to me quite endearing qualities.[14]

Naturalness

It is his natural love for poetry, including the Bible, his unembarrassed acceptance of it as poetry, even as honorary Scottish literature, which marks out Hogg's biblical usage as exceptional. J G Lockhart, who was always ready to make fun of Hogg, noted with surprise how good an impression the unaffected poet made in London society. 'The Shepherd, if he retires soon, will have left a good impression of himself here.' But Lockhart perhaps underestimated his man; Thomas Carlyle, who was to wage his own war against being misunderstood in his Scottishness while in London, had a shrewd perception of Hogg when the two men met in 1832. Hogg, he wrote:

> appears in the mingled character of Zany and raree-show. All bent on bantering him, especially Lockhart; Hogg walking thro' it as if unconscious. . . . Is the charm of this poor man chiefly to be found herein, That he *is* a real product of Nature, and able to speak *naturally*, which not one in the thousand is?[15]

The same Thomas Carlyle made an oblique reference, in his *Reminiscences*, to the secret of our discussion. Probing the secret of his father's blazing prose style, he wrote:

> none of us will ever forget that bold glowing style of his, flowing free from the untutored Soul; full of metaphors (though he knew not what a metaphor was), with all manner of potent words (which he appropriated and applied with a *surprising* accuracy, you often could not guess whence). . . . Nothing did I ever hear him undertake to render visible, which did not become almost ocularly so.[16]

Is this not the same tribute as the tribute paid to Hogg, though in more generous terms? Both men are memorable through their unconscious, natural command of language, and even satirical Wilson characterised Hogg in that way in the *Noctes Ambrosianae*, allowing the Ettrick Shepherd the odd fit of 'natural' eloquence to counterbalance the frequent bathos and anticlimax which was his lot, making him all too often the 'scapegoat', in his own words.[17] James Carlyle was never a scapegoat, for he was too much master of the arts of verbal self-defence and could argue, or denounce, his way out of trouble. Hogg, we must surely assume, could have done the same, given the enormous stylistic talent displayed in the *Confessions*, the more memorable set-pieces of the *Three Perils of Man*, the fastidious ear for language in 'Kilmeny'. But he chose not to. He chose rather to wear the mask of the Shepherd, in London and in Edinburgh, and in private life to maintain the balanced and natural approach which made him beloved of his friends, whatever his readers and his city friends might think of their scapegoat.

Hogg's educated contemporaries were certainly aware of the difficulties of their attitudes to their Scottish social inferiors. John Wilson's treatment of working-class Scottish characters falters often in the *Lights and Shadows of Scottish Life*—most notably in stories like 'The Shealing'[18]—though in his prose writing he noted the positive influence on the moral character of prolonged contact with nature. Thus ornithologists produce writings which 'are the gospel of nature . . . in it, too, there is felt to be inspiration—and when, in good time, purified from error, the leaves all make but one Bible'.[19] In his 'Reflections on Religion', Wilson also pointedly compared the urbanite with the countryman:

> Surely the astronomer may worship God in the stars and the manifest temple of heaven, as well as a Scotch elder in a worm-eaten pew, in an ugly kirk of an oblong frem [sic: form?], sixty by forty feet; yet the elder is a true man and pure.[20]

There is the same extraordinary faltering of tone here as is evident in *Adam Blair*, where Lockhart introduces the urbane reader to the worshippers of Cross-Meikle, or in *Old Mortality* and Scott's treatment of the Covenanters which so upset Hogg. It is the tone of an outsider, the man whose English—and Bible knowledge—are the product of wider experience and literate study, not the misapplied Scripture of Burley and the fanatics. Just the same attitude is subtly transferred to Wilson and Lockhart in the *Noctes* in their ridicule of the Shepherd.

The Oral Biblical Tradition

What we have reached, then, is a point of view where Hogg appears on one set of evidence—his own, and his family's—to be a man of natural acquirement of an astonishing range of language and learning, including Scots folklore and biblical English. On another set, that ascribed to the wider audience of his time (and we should not underestimate the size of the audience for the *Noctes*) and the educated critics, he is a countryman who may have picked up from nature some influences which give him inspiration and occasional felicity, but the operations of his writing genius threaten the operation of the laws of normal good taste. From such attitudes spring the condemnation of Hogg as a good poet but an indifferent novelist—or the hostile reception of the *Confessions* and their subsequent mutilation and near-suppression by Hogg and his editors. Only Thomas Carlyle, like Hogg the product of a peasant Scottish background of strong native gifts, educated to a degree (a degree far higher than Hogg, it should be pointed out) yet retaining strong emotional ties to his native Scottish experience, saw through the pretence sufficiently to put his finger on Hogg's natural endowment which put him ahead of so many of those who laughed at him. And the source of the endowment, the natural gift of speech, surely included the central literary text which Hogg himself paid tribute to—the Psalms, the hymns, the Scriptures. Where else, surely, did Thomas' father, James Carlyle, find the metaphors which enriched his language, even though he knew not what a metaphor was? It was no coincidence that when his son rebutted a false account of influences on his style, he asserted that

> the most important part by far was that of Nature, you would perhaps say, had you ever heard my Father speak, or very often heard my Mother & her inborn melodies of heart and of voice.[21]

This was written in 1866, by a man who had lived in London over 30 years, yet retained the cool self-appraisal which made him such a memorable autobiographer. And Carlyle's father and mother were barely literate, despite their painful penmanship. Their style, too, such as it was, came from communal oral tradition, from folksong and daily Scottish speech, and unmistakably, daily, weekly, in church and in home, from the Bible. And in that, if not in the quality and intensity of their speech, they would be typical. They would be like Hogg's fictional Duncan Campbell, who 'could not then read, but [had] learned several psalms from Mary by rote . . . ',[22] or the precentor in

'The Shepherd's Dog' who had to conduct the business of worship from a defective memory—and against the howls of his dog who tried to join in public worship.[23] In 'Sound Morality', the two shepherds who argue on moral subjects do so with a close attention to detail, and an easy facility in quoting biblical terms. Like Basil Lee, they might, if lucky, have received 'such an education as was generally bestowed on the sons of farmers in those days'. Basil 'could read the Shorter Catechism and even the Bible with great fluency, though with a broad and uncouth pronunciation. I could write a fair and legible hand . . .'.[24] Perhaps Basil was luckier than many, luckier than his creator at that age, but it is noticeable that no one protests at the cotter in Burns' poem reading from the Bible in conducting family worship, however many have commented uncomfortably on the shifts of language level in that poem as Burns accommodated Bible worship into a picture largely of domestic relaxation. The activity of Bible-reading and family worship (including public Psalm-singing, in English) is depicted as completely natural and universal in that most universal of poems, reinforcing the patronising comment of Hogg's nineteenth-century editor that:

> The Englishman, to whom much of the Shepherd's writings are in a strange language, can yet perceive their worldwide expression of nature, their beauty, and their truthfulness, and be as zealous in his admiration as the inhabitant of Ettrick or Teviotdale.[25]

Confessions of a Justified Sinner

So how does this position, partly understood both inside and outside Scotland, affect Hogg's finest writing, which I take to be unquestionably *The Confessions of a Justified Sinner*? Mrs Oliphant in 1897 wrote her history of the Blackwood family, naturally including Hogg in her survey. Hogg, she wrote, was

> no doubt steeped, like almost every other shepherd on the Scotch hills, in Biblical language, and also a little touched with that profane familiarity with sacred phraseology which is the reverse of the medal, and has given the opponents of the Bible in schools their strongest argument.[26]

This is very revealing indeed. It follows naturally from our earlier insistence on the completely natural way in which Hogg picked up his knowledge of the Bible, and Bible-English-phraseology from the everyday example of home and community. Like Burns, he could easily pervert that phraseology to satiric purposes, though he would not have dreamed for a moment of excluding the Bible from schools on account of the danger that children might thus be equipped to misuse Scripture. While Scott resorted to ridicule to characterise the Covenanting fanatics, Hogg, in 'The Covenanting Preacher's Tale', could show how sympathetically these devoted Christians incorporated biblical language into everyday speech without misuse or parody, though to outsiders the 'damned whining psalm-singing race' of *The Brownie of Bodsbeck*[27] could be ludicrous. Scott certainly made them so in chapter IV of *Old Mortality* in Bothwell's interrogation of the Covenanters, and indeed throughout these early chapters.

What Hogg reserved his parody for was *misuse* of this completely natural biblical speech which he had so picked up. In *The Brownie* his extremists use speech naturally, their convictions expressed thoroughly by their religious phraseology; and the burden of ridicule is transferred to the other party, whose language is far from the elegant normality ascribed to Claverhouse and his party in *Old Mortality*.

Device of Misapplied Language

In the *Confessions*, ridicule is spread much more widely, and the ridicule of misapplied language is one of the primary means by which Hogg achieves his major fictive excellence—the blurring out of the sharp edges of plot and character, of the ability of the audience to judge and estimate the plot and novel as a whole. If, as has been argued, the achievement of the novel in escaping too dated an effect and too narrowly religious an application has been through the transferring of decision-making to the audience, and the deliberate abrogation of that duty on Hogg's part, then the misuse of language levels is a clever weapon in the writer's armoury.

Take the following. Young Wringhim is, while still a schoolboy, catechising his mother:

> 'Ineffectual Calling is, *the outward call of the gospel* without any effect on the hearts of unregenerated and impenitent sinners. Have not all these the same calls, warnings, doctrines, and reproofs, that we have? and is not this Ineffectual Calling? . . . *Has not the Laird of Dalcastle and his reprobate heir* the same? And will any tell me, that *this is not* Ineffectual Calling?'
> 'What a wonderful boy he is!' said my mother.
> 'I'm feared he turn out to be a conceited gowk', said old Barnet, the minister's man.
>
> (Confessions, p 99)

Young Wringhim has every advantage of schooling and literacy but plainly he is well-advanced in the process of absorbing biblical language and phraseology, 'calls, warnings, doctrines and reproofs' and the rest of it. Learned from a household where 'it was the custom . . . to ask the questions of the Single Catechism round every Sabbath night' (p 98), this talent on the part of the precocious child is not hard to understand.

Yet the typecasting use of language is not simple. John Barnet, who speaks simple good sense, punctures Wringhim's absurd wire-drawn theology with a simple Scotticism. Yet to say that English and the Bible equate badness and Scots goodness, tempting as it might be, is plainly wrong. Barnet can speak biblical language when he wishes, after all: 'Aw doubt we're a' ower little thankfu', sir, baith for temporal an' speeritual mercies . . .'; 'Man's thoughts are vanity, sir: they come unasked, an gang away without a dismissal' (pp 104, 106).

Perversely, good brother George speaks English as does bad brother Robert, and George can prove knowledge of the Bible, as he does when they struggle on the top of Arthur's Seat: 'Is it not consistent with every precept of the Gospel? Come, brother, say that our reconciliation is complete'. (p 45). George and his friends uniformly speak English between themselves, befitting the younger generation of urban Scots throwing off the bucolic manners of the generation of the Laird of Dalcastle: yet George can drop into Scots in anger ('so, friend, I rede you to be on your guard', p 221) or mockery, when he first meets his brother, 'Mercy be about us, Sir! is this the crazy minister's son from Glasgow?' (p 23), though when he apologises decently for this irritated jibe (p 24) he reverts to English.

'Good' characters such as the laird express themselves comfortably in English and thin Scots; Isabella Calvert is at home in both. Yet the trial scene with Bessy the servant maid is pure farce (pp 65–8), and patently absurd to an audience who would have known the judges to be as likely to be fluent in Scots as was Bessy, whereas in Hogg's novel they speak the stiffest English. Yet the pretence worked for Scott in *The Heart of Midlothian*, and Hogg was happy to use it in the *Confessions*.

Language, Class and Goodness

Plainly, Hogg is out to pervert any easy equation between language level and social class or degree of inherent goodness. The equation might work in the *Noctes Ambrosianae*, and he might be happy to go along with it in the salons of Edinburgh and London, but in his fiction Hogg was in control, and his command of biblical English, going back to his earliest years, co-existed in his creative imagination with his command of Scots to make the dialogue a most flexible and deceptive instrument.

To take several propositions:

1   Should we be tempted to assume that 'good' characters are defined by superior social class defined by superior 'English' language levels, such language is ascribed to Bell Calvert the thief and prostitute, the entire Wringhim family of despicable and morally dubious perverts—and to Gil-Martin, the devil figure. The Ettrick Shepherd, long the butt of his English or Englished tormentors, has his revenge.

2   Should we be tempted to assume that the good characters have the Bible at their command, then we are brought up short by the realisation that the most biblical characters, in terms of speech, are the Wringhims—and Gil-Martin.

3   Should we be tempted to assume that Hogg is showing a merely transitional time where the older orders are still speaking Scots but the younger ones are turning to English and despising the old vulgar Scots, then this movement is exemplified by the despicable Wringhim clan, whereas the vigorous appearance of Hogg at the end of the novel (p 247) is in natural Scots, a confident expression of the author's mastery of his material and his refusal to solve the mystery for his readers. The same author who has an entire command of colloquial Scots throughout his novel, has a sufficient command of, and psychological insight into, biblical English and the characters who depend on it for their everyday thought-processes, to depict both language levels from the inside.

Language level is certainly used as one of the tools of psychological penetration. Mrs Wringhim uses biblical English superficially to indicate her superficial character, 'One Scripture text followed another, not in the least connected' (p 5), and after the fresh use of such language from the devil, Wringhim 'turned from hearing her in disgust' (p 128), so hackneyed had she become. Yet his mother has the key to the mystery. After Wringhim first meets the devil-figure, he is visibly altered and his parents fear he has met something evil (p 121):

'. . . I have been conversant this day with one stranger only, whom I took rather for an angel of light'.

'It is one of the devil's most profound wiles to appear like one,' said my mother.

'Woman, hold thy peace!' said my reverend father: 'thou pretendest, to teach what thou knowest not. Tell me this, boy: Did this stranger, with whom you met, adhere to the religious principles in which I have educated you?'

'Yes, to every one of them, in their fullest latitude,' said I.

'Then he was no agent of the wicked one . . . '

If Wringhim had listened to his mother, he would have understood one of the author's chief satiric methods. The devil achieves his domination in this novel by mimicking the inappropriate speech levels. The devil can be anywhere at any time: he knows Blanchard's arguments in advance for he was there to hear them incognito (p 135); and he knows Wringhim's father's arguments in advance, and can trot out the perverted forms of antinomianism ready to deceive Robert Wringhim at a first meeting. For that matter, he can deceive Robert's father, who obviously judges people by their parroting forth second-hand biblical doctrines which, the narrator assures us, consisted in 'the splitting of hairs, and making distinctions in religion where none existed' (p 16). Such theology suits the devil's purpose admirably, for he can slip on such a disguise effortlessly.

Mrs Wringhim's warning goes unheeded because the Wringhims' ears are dull to parody and perversions of meaning, since this is the stock-in-trade of their daily conversation and—worse still—their family worship. Like Holy Willie they live their everyday lives by this strained biblical language, and like Holy Willie they are satirised not by open attack, but by the ridiculousness of their inappropriate lives and languages. Holy Willie's bar-room nudge to his Creator—'Oh Lord—yestreen—thou kens—wi' Meg'—is no worse than the rubbish which the Wringhims speak in the name of Christianity, particularly the scene where Robert's father perverts the story of Jacob wrestling with the angel to force it into an assurance of Robert's acceptance into the ranks of the justified (p 115). The outsider—and by this I mean the 'normal' Christian, not the zealot Wringhims—easily sees through this misapplied biblical language. Only the insiders do not: the devil easily twists language to suit the Wringhim normal syntax.

'You seem strangely affected, dear sir, by looking on my book,' said he mildly.

'In the name of God, what book is that?' said I: 'Is it a Bible?'

'It is *my* Bible, sir,' said he . . .

(*Confessions*, p 124)

Or else there is the irony of the following, very obvious from outside the text: '. . . You may call me Gil-Martin. It is not my *Christian* name, but it *is* a name which may serve your turn' (p 129). Thus the devil slowly leads; Wringhim openly admits to being conquered by language: 'I could not help thinking, that I perceived a little derision of countenance on his face as he said this, nevertheless I sunk dumb before such a man, and aroused myself to the task . . .' (p 137). The hypnotic power of the devil can do most things, but it is this power, combined with the torture of fear and sleeplessness, which eventually force Robert to the blasphemous 'tremendous prayer': 'I was instantly at liberty and what I am now, the Almighty knows! *Amen*' (p 239). Wisely, Hogg does not try to find words for such an equivocal prayer—or indeed Mrs Oliphant's criticism might be justly applied to him, that his familiarity with biblical English led him to inappropriate levity. Hogg's touch is too fine: the prayer is unrecorded, but Wringhim's first words after his self-damnation are in the equivocal double-speak of the devil, pseudo-biblical English with a separate meaning visible to the reader outside the novel itself.

Yet Hogg's texture is dense, for within the novel there are 'good' people who speak English, thin Scots, and broad Scots. Most notably, there is the magnificent denunciation of Wringhim's father by the Laird, who uncharacteristically delivers a passionate speech in pure biblical English: 'Go thou in peace, and do these abominations no more; but humble thyself, lest a worse reproof come upon thee' (p 15). The Laird's normal language is thin boisterous Scots, but plainly he has this English *in reserve*, thinking it appropriate only for special occasions. Blanchard, another 'good' character, uses biblical English at all times, as befits the fictional minister, from Adam Blair to the ministers of the kailyard and beyond.

Varying the Language Level

The point seems to be that everyone in this novel has multiple language levels potentially available, as the author did. Hogg could, and did, use standard English, and his poetry shows the range of delicacy open to him in each medium. The author of 'Kilmeny' and the magnificent parodies of the English Lake poets had nothing to be ashamed of in his command of English. At the same time, he clearly enjoyed the company of his Scottish compeers in the Borders, and wore the part of the Ettrick Shepherd in London and Edinburgh with varying good humour. People who met him were surprised to find how good-humoured, well-mannered and well-bred he was. Yet circumstances of poverty and easy-going good nature had trapped him into the stereotype of the bumbling Shepherd mouthing his absurdities in a magazine which, though Scottish, was more and more reflecting the taste of a generation which expressed itself in English.

Hogg had English too: his finest satirical language-use, in the *Confessions*, is an explanation of his complete ability to fight back, to have his revenge on those who wrote him down as a fool because of his preference for Scots, or his *persona* as Shepherd. Those whose language was socially acceptable are often the worst characters, though sufficient counterpoises such as Barnet and the Laird, not to mention Blanchard, ensure no easy equivalence of language to character. The English narrative framework is helpless in the face of several internal Scottish jokes, and the understandable wish at the end of the novel to have some finished answers to a baffling plot is frustrated by the author, appearing in his 'Shepherd' disguise, and impudently refusing the request—in the broadest Scots.

The overall point is that this satiric poise—the balancing game in the *Confessions* between English and Scots, Bible and everyday, Christian and perversion—is available only to the author who had his Bible, his Christianity, and his insight into Scottish urban and rural society as naturally as did Hogg. Like Gil-Martin himself, he could puncture the Wringhims because he knew at first-hand how they thought and, more importantly still, how they spoke their biblical cant. He could also modulate into the straightforward, the farcical, the 'editorial', the impenetrable.

The conclusion to the *Confessions* is entirely in keeping with this view, for the 'editor' gives up the task of completing his tale, 'for I do not understand it' (p 253). This surely is exactly what Hogg wished. His satiric distance is what has given the infernal plot its power, and his satiric distance is that of a man who has been distanced by social convention and has learned defence mechanisms which express themselves best, not in a society where he was disadvantaged, but in a literature where his mastery is unchallenged. The combination of this deft social revenge with the thorough biblical knowledge of a peculiar kind makes the *Confessions* a unique production, completely in keeping with the satiric intention of the 'Ettrick Shepherd' caricature figure, yet controlled artistically by the real man behind that facade who, as Carlyle saw in 1832, had the gift denied to all but one man in a thousand—to write naturally.

IAN CAMPBELL

Notes

This paper was first presented at an Association of Scottish Literary Studies conference on James Hogg and his Circle, held on 1 May 1982 at the University of Stirling.

1   I Campbell, 'Author and Audience in Hoggs *Confessions of a Justified Sinner'*, *Scottish Literary News* 2:4 (June 1972), pp 66–76. The argument has been continued in 'Hogg's *Confessions of a Justified Sinner'*, *Liturgical Review* II 2 (1972), pp 28–33, 'Burns, Hogg and the Dangerous Art', *Liturgical Review* IV 1 (May 1974), pp 34–45, and 'Hogg's *Confessions* and the *Heart of Darkness'*, *Studies in Scottish Literature* XV (1980), pp 187–201.

2   *Scottish Literary News*, pp 75–6.

3   J Wilson, *Noctes Ambrosianae*, R S Mackenzie (ed) (revised edition, New York, 1863), II, p 427.

4   James Hogg, *Memoir of the Author's Life*, D S Mack (ed) (Edinburgh and London, 1972), pp 5–7.

5   L Simpson, *James Hogg, A Critical Study* (Edinburgh and London, 1962), p 125.

6   E C Batho, *The Ettrick Shepherd* (Cambridge, 1927), pp 12–13.

7   A L Strout, *The Life and Letters of James Hogg the Ettrick Shepherd* (Lubbock, Texas, 1946) I, pp 8–9.

8   Hogg, *Memoir*, p 62.

9   Hogg, *Confessions of a Justified Sinner*, J Carey (ed) (Oxford, 1969), p 10. Parenthetical references in the text following a quotation are to this edition.

10   Hogg, *Memoir*, p 7.

11   *The Spy*, 24 August 1811.

12   W E K Anderson (ed), *The Journal of Sir Walter Scott* (Oxford, 1972), p viii.

13   J M Wilson's letter is here quoted from Strout's typescript for the unpublished second volume of his biography of Hogg, National Library of Scotland MS 10495, p 53.

14   *Edinburgh Literary Journal*, vol 3: quoted from editor's note to Hogg, *Memoir*, p7.

15   A Lang, *The Life and Letters of John Gibson Lockhart* (London, 1897), II, p 111; *Two Note Books of Thomas Carlyle*, C E Norton (ed) (New York, 1898), pp 250–1.

16   Thomas Carlyle, *Reminiscences*, I Campbell (ed) (London, 1972), p 3.

17   Hogg, *Memoir*, p 80.

18   *Eg* 'Arthur Austin' J Wilson, *Light and Shadows of Scottish Life* (Edinburgh, 1822), pp 369–88. A further discussion can be pursued in I Campbell, *Kailyard, A New Assessment* (Edinburgh,1981), pp 34–40.

19   [J Wilson], *Recreations of Christopher North* (Edinburgh, 1842), III, p 13.

20   J Wilson, 'Reflections on Religion', quoted from Konrad Hopkins and Ronald van Roekel, *John Wilson/Christopher North* (Paisley, 1979), p 21.

21 J Clubbe (ed), *Two Reminiscences of Thomas Carlyle* (Durham, North Carolina, 1974), p 59.
22 These quotations are from the 'Tales and Sketches' volume of *The Works of the Ettrick Shepherd*, Thomas Thomson (ed) (Centenary edition, London, 1865), p 272.
23 Hogg, *Works*, p 423.
24 Hogg, *Works*, p 237.
25 Thomson in biographical notice prefacing 'Poems and Ballads' volume of Hogg, *Works*, p 1v.
26 Mrs [M W] Oliphant, *William Blackwood and his Sons* (Edinburgh and London, 1897), II, p 118.
27 D S Mack (ed), J Hogg, *The Brownie of Bodsbeck* (Edinburgh and London, 1976), p 17.

Further Reading

J Carey (ed), James Hogg, *Confessions of a Justified Sinner* (Oxford, 1969)—with extensive bibliography.
Douglas S Mack (ed), Hogg, *Selected Stories and Sketches* (Edinburgh, 1982).
Douglas S Mack (ed), Hogg, *Memoir of the Author's Life* (Edinburgh, 1972).
D Gifford, *James Hogg* (Edinburgh, 1976)—the best extensive discussion.
K Miller, *Doubles: Studies in Literary History* (Oxford, 1985).
Studies in Scottish Literature (annually)—regular forum for articles.

8

The Bible, the Kirk
and Scottish Literature

Scottish literature is full of references to the Bible and, beyond that (and not easily separable from it), to the Calvinist brand of religion that developed on the basis of a set of particular readings of the Bible in the Reformation of the sixteenth century. In the previous chapter, the encounter of a prominent writer with the biblical text itself was explored. In this study it is the encounter with biblically-saturated Calvinism that is more to the fore.

The writers under review have given us a literature which, in rejoicing to recreate Scotland's religious past, finds room for historical scenes of religious warfare (Covenanting), of peacetime (Reformation), and of everyday Christian life (worship in the home). There are portraits of a Presbyterian country both admiring and satirical, the mainspring of the satirical art of a Hogg or a Burns, the more ambiguous touchstone of an author such as MacDiarmid or Grassic Gibbon. As villain in the Clearances, as hero-parish minister in the fiction of the eighteenth and nineteenth centuries, the man in the pulpit and representative of the Scottish Kirk is inescapable in Scottish literature. Exported to foreign countries, Scottish ministers continue to dominate, as missionary, as Canadian patriarch in an expatriate community.

Granted that the role of the clergy and preacher is inescapable in a realistic portrait of Scottish life, it may seem surprising how little serious critical attention has been paid to the interaction between that presence and the literature which embodies it. It is a poor Scotland indeed which appears in a literature routinely populated by a predictable kailyard cast of popular characters, minister, dominie, doctor, local laird; it is a Scotland immortalised in the easy (if cleverly-written) pages of Ian Maclaren, lambasted in George Douglas Brown's *The House with the Green Shutters* (1901). Brown simply used those stock characters to populate a town so horrible as to make people ask themselves what sort of realistic portrait could this be of a country? In Brown's town of Barbie the reader would have found an unexpected answer. The clergy are there all right, the statutory two ordained men, one from the Free Kirk and one from the Establishment. Yet being there is not the point; on closer inspection it is their role in the community which is being looked at, for the Established Kirk minister is a gourmandising fool, and the Free Kirk minister a botanising weakling. Barbie is ridiculed by their inclusion.

Yet as startling is the exclusion from Barbie, otherwise so realistically portrayed, of the brick-and-lime of the kirks themselves. No matter how keenly *The House with the Green Shutters* portrays Ochiltree in Ayrshire (and, despite the author's later denials, it does so exactly), there is no trace in the novel of the building which dominates the real-life high street, the church or churches which bestraddled the architecture of the Scottish village. There may be ministers—but their buildings are so irrelevant as simply to be undescribed.

From Fanaticism to Moderation

A subtle and extensive process is being invoked here. The shift caught by Scott in *The Heart of Midlothian* was one from kirk-centred life (for Davie and Jeanie Deans) to a more moderate, humane society in a peacetime Argyle country where the kirk was a respected, natural part of an ordered week. Already Burns had been preparing the ground for a kirk where fanatical attention to order and discipline would be replaced by a more moderate, balanced lifestyle: writing to Mrs Dunlop, he expressed strong admiration for Cowper's *The Task*:

> The Religion of The Task, bating a few scraps of Calvinistic Divinity, is the Religion of God & Nature; the Religion that exalts, that ennobles man.

To Clarinda, perhaps even more spontaneously,

> . . . mine is the Religion of the bosom.—I hate the very idea of contro-versial divinity; as I firmly believe, that every honest, upright man, of whatever sect, will be accepted of the Deity.[1]

The author of 'Holy Willie's Prayer' is very recognisable in these lines, and he is staking out territory of imaginative literature which is quite ignored in any easy assumption that the influence of Presbyterianism was to repress imaginative effort.

Burns' confessions underline two important attitudes: one is that the individual imagination is free to interpret the 'religion of the bosom'—and the other is that an individual can feel strongly about abuse of Christianity as he can about conformity. The second of these produces the psychological insight into Holy Willie, and an even greater insight into Robert Wringhim, pilloried by James Hogg in the *Confessions of a Justified Sinner* (1824) for just this over-strained religion of 'scraps of Calvinistic Divinity'. Hogg's narrative voice at the outset of the *Confessions* openly characterises the Wringhim family's Christianity as Presbyterianism run riot: the lady particularly is shown as holding

> . . . not the tenets of the great reformers, but theirs mightily over-strained and deformed. Theirs was an unguent hard to be swallowed; but hers was that unguent embittered and overheated until nature could no longer bear it. She had imbibed her ideas from the doctrines of one flaming predestinarian divine alone . . .[2]

Thus put, the religion of one of the main protagonists is unhesitatingly set aside from what one might call 'mainstream' Christianity, Presbyterian or not—it is as deviant as the snarling of Holy Willie at his prayers, calling down destruction and death on his enemies from the God of love. The same mean-spirited negativity is what really shocks the reader who expects from the 'justified sinner' a measure of recognisable Christianity. Bred by both mother and father to expect his own sinlessness at the Day of Judgement, he adds a heretical and appalling belief in the damnation of all others (including his own relatives) while a smiling devil-figure, a Bible text ready for the occasion with a plausible argument, gently nudges him on the path to the very hell he has threatened to others.

Hogg's *Confeisions* are rightly seen as a masterpiece today for their psychological insight into what amounts to mental aberration; but more to our point, it was an insight gained from an insider's position in the religious society of his time. This is what Burns and Hogg shared, living as they did in devout communities where church-going was expected, and where (records suggest) each played a normal part in that process. To go to church and share a decent tolerant Christianity was quite normal; to attack excess and perversion, particularly under the name of Christianity, was equally normal.

Variety of Responses

We thus early arrive at a point where we can see that writing about Christianity, or the Kirk, could involve a range of responses. That many ministers of the Kirk wrote from a feeling of unshaken personal conviction, and published copiously and widely, is no reason to disbelieve the sincerity of feeling behind the work of a John Home or an Alexander Carlyle who found pastoral duty and Christian ministry to co-exist with a lively literary and social life. Scottish literature is the richer for this diversity of response. What links Burns' picture to Hogg's is the attack on narrow single-mindedness, and it is an attitude not difficult to find very widely.

The discussion of literary importance also hinges on flexibility of vision. Perhaps two excerpts will introduce the point. The first comes from a weak collection of Scottish 'typical' stories, *Scottish Life and Character in Anecdote and Story* by W J Harvey (Stirling and Toronto, n.d.), in the section entitled 'Gown and Bands' (pp 33f):

> An old divinity professor never ventured to alter a single word of the prayer with which he opened his class every morning. This circumstance was once pointed out to him by a student—'Would it not be better, sir, to occasionally alter your prayer, according to the wants of the times and the periods of the session?' 'Na, na!' sharply answered the professor, 'I've said that prayer every College day for forty years withoot ony change, an' it wad be naething sort [sic] o' sacrilege to alter't noo, to please your whims'.

The other, much more substantial, comes from chapter 29 of Galt's *Annals of the Parish* (1821). Finding that the radical weavers who had moved into the parish 'did not like my manner of preaching, and on that account absented themselves from public worship', the minister calls them in to the manse for rebuke:

> but they confounded me with their objections, and used my arguments, which were the old and orthodox proven opinions of the Divinity Hall, as if they had been the light sayings of a vain man.

And this from the man who introduces chapter 30 of his *Annals*, covering the year 1789, 'This I have always reflected upon as one of our blessed years. It was not remarkable for any extraordinary occurence . . ..'

The difference between these extracts illuminates much of the particular challenges of writing about religion in Scotland. The first is an essentially passive anecdote, told (in English) to a wider audience to illustrate the charm of a narrow way of life, where a professor who has aged gracefully rebukes (significantly, in Scots) beardless youth for suggesting an innovation which would seem perfectly reasonable to the wider audience. By itself the story is witty, pleasant, lightweight—if casting doubt on the up-to-dateness of Divinity training at the time. Even the language levels are significant, for by phrasing the professor's reply in out-of-date Scots, and the student's question in up-to-date English, the teller frames the old religionist in a halo of out-of-date sanctity, which defuses possible criticism. Where stories like these cease to be merely pleasant pastimes is when they become the staple of bestselling collections, and grow by gentle stages to represent the norm of Scottish religious life. When all Scottish kirks are full of white-haired ministers (who seem never to have been young, while their juniors are mocked for trying to hasten change) and worthy elders and beadles, the pews packed with attentive and solemn peasant faces, when even Free Kirk and Established Kirk are both packed and working together in charity, then something has gone wrong with Scotland's image in literature. Assembling *Scottish Life and Character*, Harvey remarked in his preface on the success of Ramsay's 'evergreen and unexcelled "Reminiscences"', which prompted him to record:

> the shrewdness, the wit, the humour of the nation [which] will form a not-altogether-valueless contribution to the literature of anecdote and story that pertains to the Land o' Cakes, and will afford pleasure as well to the Scot at home as to the Scot abroad.

The book, significantly, is dedicated 'to Ilka Scot', and sales of such volumes amply attest to their popularity over the world.

Writing 15 years after the first publication of his *Reminiscences*, Dean Ramsay prefaced his twenty-second edition with a claim that he had tried to 'depict a phase of national manners which was fast passing away', but that 'I make use of anecdotes not for the purpose of telling a good story, but solely in the way of *illustration*' (pp 2–3). Certainly Ramsay's is a better-constructed book than Harvey's, yet reading it is to be almost exhausted by the quantity of anecdote tending to confirm the picture of Scottish religious life as worthy, pawky, shrewd, pleasant, much given to the put-down and the independent line of thought. Ramsay's Episcopalian mind saw some good in the 'increased facilities of communication between the two countries' giving access to 'English books upon religious subjects' to 'minds trained in the strictest school of Calvinistic theology' (pp 65–66). But above all, Ramsay brought out 'the quaint and original humour of the old Scottish minister' (p 80) and his hearers.

The market was a large one in Ramsay's shadow: one other example must suffice, *The Kirk & its Worthies*, an enormously popular collection by Nicholas Dickson (Edinburgh, 1912) which completely devotes itself to anecdote of what is typical—and often delightful—about Scottish country Christianity. On Psalms, for instance, Dickson is at pains to extol the old Psalm tunes, making the interesting point that congregational habit and preference will last much longer in memory than national.

Sweet and tender and touching as most of the hymns are that are used in public worship now, yet to those of us who were brought up under the old dispensation in the days when the precentor reigned in the desk, the psalms can never lose their grip.

Old World and New

What of the Galt example from *Annals of the Parish*? Nostalgia and the change from the past are obviously the immediate subject of the minister's baffled experiences as he reasons with the weaver lads in Dalmailing who laugh at his old, seasoned Glasgow Divinity Hall ideas. In a collection such as Ramsay's, or Harvey's, or Dickson's, such resistance to white-haired sanctity would merit a passing sigh or a short rebuke, but the artistic focus would soon swing back to those pleasant days when weaver lads knew their place, and worked at the hand-loom in the parish cottages and did not imbibe their ideas in factories and new industrial districts far from the kirk building.

Annals of the Parish is a considerable book because, like much of Galt's output, it resists the temptation to flee to the past even in the very laudable aim of preserving a vanishing past. In *The Provost*, in *The Ayrshire Legatees*, in *The Last of the Lairds*, Galt asks repeatedly what it is like to be part of a Scotland that is changing almost too fast to be understood. In *The Ayrshire Legatees* the answer is for the minister set in his old ways to get out, thanks to a fortunate inheritance which allows him to give way to a younger and more flexible man in tune with the times. *Annals of the Parish* takes a more painful course, by examining what happens when the minister has no wish to get out.

The paradox at the heart of Galt's *Annals* is one which the collections of wit and wisdom from the kirk can never penetrate. Balwhidder, Galt's narrator in the *Annals*, has a long and worthy 50 years' pastorate in Dalmailing and retires full of years and honour, a white-haired patriarch. But, as the meeting with the weaver lads makes abundantly clear, he has no way of keeping up with the times—and what times, for Galt chooses to set the novel in the period 1760–1810. Balwhidder's intense conservatism is part of a ministerial strategy which includes hard-working pastoral visiting, hard-working preaching, and an agonised concern for the well-being of his parish. But almost unnoticed by him—though not by the reader—the world changes out of recognition. At the start of his ministry Scotland was a place of intrusion (his own induction was marred by anti-intrusion riots) where kirks were full even of those who resented intrusion by the laird of an unpopular minister, but who still felt the need to attend public worship. Lord Eaglesham was the undisputed laird, and things (it seemed) would never change. A diarist to whom 1789, the year of the French Revolution, was a blessed year of quiet, would hardly have his finger on the pulse of world events, yet he is slow indeed not to see that he has another world in his own parish, a world of weaver lads who need to be kept up with (they, not he, frequent the bookshop and read the London papers), and younger parishioners who will not think much of Glasgow Divinity Hall and its ways.

The end of *Annals of the Parish* is an extraordinarily clever piece of writing, invoking as it does the ambiguous feelings towards the Church of Burns or of Hogg, yet through quite different means. Theirs were ambiguities towards Christians in name but not in practice; Galt's ambiguity is towards one whose private practice and private life are blameless and whose ministry has been characterised throughout by hard work and good intentions. Yet his kirk is empty, his dwindling congregation an elderly one, and the industrial world of the other side of his parish has its own ministers and (it is strongly hinted) a large non-church going proletarian workforce. What has happened to them? The novel chooses not to tell, but rather to remain in the comfortable world of the established long-sanctioned practice in the Auld Kirk.

Where Galt is writing challengingly about religion in Scotland is that he is inviting the reader to see for himself the narrowness of a view which takes no account of change, but lives in the pawky and the pleasant. There are hints aplenty in the *Annals* of the new strident materialistic world beyond the kirk gates, but the narrator himself is too slow and inflexible to enter that world, and the novel functions by calculated ambiguity and hint, much more powerfully than it would by crude and direct attack. Indeed, the novel cleverly ends with the minister's retirement, the people (long settled in another parish or simply long since ceasing to attend worship) coming back for one last service, a packed church, a white-haired old minister saying a long farewell. In weaker, anecdotal hands the scene would be made much of as typical: Galt's success is to make it all too clear that this is not typical; most of those present no longer go to church except on those special occasions, or worship elsewhere. It was good to be part of this old, warm, Scottish Christianity, but the author winds up that part of Scotland as firmly as Grassic Gibbon was to wind up the rustic community of Kinraddie a century later at the end of *Sunset Song*, for both authors shared the insight that to shelter in endless recreations of the past, religious or secular, is to invite cultural atrophy.

Carlyle's Nostalgia

The Church in Scotland is an ever-present temptation to weak writers to indulge in frozen-time atrophy. The Church, the Psalms, the patriarchs of one's youth are comfortable symbols of a past Scotland, but they are dangerous if taken passively. Far more intelligent, and therefore far more incisive, is Thomas Carlyle's memory of his father's Burgher Church background in Ecclefechan:

> He was Religious with the consent of his whole faculties: without Reason he would have been nothing; indeed his habit of intellect was thoroughly free and even incredulous, and strongly enough did the daily example of this work afterwards on me. . . . But he was in Annandale, and it was above fifty years ago; and a Gospel was still preached there to the heart of a man, in the tones of a man.

There is abundant nostalgia here, in a tribute written in 1832 on the death of a much-feared and much-admired pious Christian by a son who never completely outgrew his father's influence. The plangent nostalgia is very visible:

> *He* was never visited with Doubt; the old Theorem of the Universe was sufficient for him . . .[3]

But that was Ecclefechan, and that was 50 years ago. Even writing a day or two after his father's death, Carlyle was clear-sighted enough to record, with that pitiless sharpness of focus which makes him such a powerful commentator on Scotland, the passing of a generation as well as of a father.

Much later, remembering Edward Irving, he created in prose a marvellously vivid picture of a real Scotland of the small congregation and the pious elder and minister:

Men so like what one might call antique 'Evangelists in modern vesture, and Poor Scholars and Gentlemen of Christ', I have nowhere met with in Monasteries or Churches, among Protestant or Papal Clergy, in any country of the world.

This is a Scotland to be proud of. Yet again Carlyle is too honest to take refuge in this Scotland:

All this is altered utterly at present, I grieve to say; and gone to as good as nothing or worse. It began to alter just about that period, on the death of those old hoary Heads; and has gone on with increasing velocity ever since. Irving and I were probably among the last products it delivered before gliding off . . .[4]

This is the outsider's view, from a man who had grown up in a narrow sphere and worked his way out of it—but it is even more interesting for the insight it offers into the mind of the man who had never grown away from Ecclefechan. A rigid church-goer and practitioner of family worship, scrupulous, unsmiling, the type of the grim Calvinist of hostile imagination, Carlyle's father was (we learn) incredulous, freethinking, free. Carlyle himself learned to be free in this way, gradually adjusting his conversation with his pious mother to gloss over his own internal questionings, gently leading her to the impression that his faith was more unshaken than it must have been. A lifelong gentle pusher-aside of questions which would have involved a personal *credo*, Carlyle remained convinced of the value of continuity in Christianity, in church, in public reverence. He might have agreed, in public or in private, with Sir Archibald Geikie's summing-up of his own generation that:

many of the articles of the Christian faith retain a firm hold on minds which, if questioned on the subject, would probably express doubt or denial of them, such as the doctrine of a material heaven and hell, of a system of future rewards and punishments, of a personal devil intent on man's ruin, and of the sinfulness of Sunday work.[5]

Quite so—Carlyle would have retained a private position on all this list, without question. Yet the impact of his father's example was one he was to prolong, to incalculably wider effect, a generation later in the 1840s with the impact of *Heroes and Hero Worship*, and a whole body of social and ethical writing which stressed the value of reverence and public worship.

Healthy Ambiguity

Surely this is healthy ambiguity rather than hypocrisy or double-standard. In the peroration to his great *God and the Poets*, David Daiches recalls the elderly Jewish men of his youth chanting rapidly the Psalms as a holy exercise, without possibly understanding or even thinking of the words, 'as though the Psalms consisted of magic formulas that were to be recited as such', rather than listened to as words. For himself, he goes on, 'I discovered the haunting beauty of Psalm 126 years after I ceased singing it as a religious exercise'.[6]

A healthy ambiguity of literary practice is one which can enrich religious writing in all sorts of ways—Professor Daiches mentions absorbing one of the misunderstood passages of the Bible (see his chapter on Job) which have passed into current use—the sort of misunderstanding which can make a great church hymn out of Blake's 'Jerusalem' while doing some violence to the author's intention. To see beauty in biblical literature after ceasing to use it for worship is as ambiguous as to see beauty in a religious sociological description without necessarily giving assent to the activities of the minister at the heart of the picture of Scotland, or to the author's intention or apparent attitude to religion. Millions have responded to James Thomson's *City of Dreadful Night* without sharing the author's deeply-felt pessimism.

But Carlyle's is a very interesting case in a Scotland torn by the increasing Church pressures of the nineteenth century, pressures which included the Disruption of 1843, the controversies over science and belief, and the total redistribution of the population of a country under the ravages of industrialisation, urbanisation and the Clearances. Carlyle—alert as few others to the undercurrents of his time— made the significant choice to settle in London in 1834 when he had the choice between London and Edinburgh: events were shortly to prove him far-sighted. From Chelsea he wrote to conquer many of the world's English-speaking readers, but I would highlight two features of his practice relevant to this discussion. One is the essentially destructive method of much of his rhetoric: he had, in his *Reminiscences*, paid tribute to his father's power of ridicule and sarcasm, and admitted he had inherited it in full measure; but in later years he confided something to David Masson which shows a keen self-awareness as well as an awareness of his times.

As we sauntered to and fro on the grass, the sole human beings peripatetic, where but a few hours before there had been the roar of the carriages in stream . . . it was the stars and the silence that seemed to work upon him and to suggest his theme. From the mystery and the splendour of physical infinitude he passed to what ought to be the rule of human behaviour, the conduct of one's own spirit, in a world framed so majestically and so divinely. There was too much jesting in it, he said, too much of mere irony and of laughter at the absurd, too little of calm religiousness and serious walk with God. In speaking of the over-prevalence of the habit of irony, sarcasm, and jesting, he used a sudden phrase of self-humiliation which I have never forgotten. 'Ah! and I have given far too much in to that myself—*sniggering at things*': these are the exact words.[7]

A retrospective moment of self-doubt—but an important insight into the methodology of one of Scotland's most influential writers. Carlyle, ever since *Sartor Resartus* (in Hector MacPherson's words) 'brought into Scottish literature an order of thought and emotions which by their revolutionary nature were calculated to break down the commonplace creed of the Jeffreys, the Macaulays',[8] had powerfully fermented thought on religious and moral issues in Scotland—to say nothing of his wider audience. The images of *Sartor* are revolutionary, images of fire and destruction, change and rebirth, the tearing-off of old clothes and the infinitely difficult task of perceiving and tailoring the new clothes which a new age imperiously demands. An outsider to so much of what constituted order and establishment in his generation, Carlyle had an outsider's vision and an outsider's destructive tongue— the Ecclefechan put-down and sarcasm enormously amplified by his reading and wider experience.

Heroes

He had another Ecclefechan habit which he widely disseminated and enlarged—the cult of the single venerated figure ('hero') as focus for description for the abstract and the tenuous. John Stuart Blackie has preserved a vivid memory of visiting Chelsea and hearing a night of this:

> Scottish and English Universities, British Houses of Parliament, ortho-dox theologies, railroads, and free trade, were all shaken out and sifted under the category of Sham; while Oliver Cromwell and his Iron-sides and the old Covenanters who sang psalms and handled pikes on Dunse Moor, were held up to admiration as the only heroes in this country for the last two hundred years.[9]

A Carlyle who can describe Mahomet and Cromwell as 'the two sincerest men the world has seen'[10] has obviously gone far along the road to gathering together difficult abstract ideas and concretising them in the form of a person—not here, but in the past. And the result was seen at its clearest in the hugely successful *Heroes and Hero Worship* of 1841, a book reprinted times without number and reaching (through cheap editions) an enormous cross-section of society. To cast down the 'sham' and embody the alternatives in the heroes of history (chosen according to strictly subjective criteria, but including Jesus Christ and John Knox as well as Cromwell) is to make a religious message intelligible, and also to put it firmly in the regions of ambiguity, since it is well known (if not notorious) that no hero of Carlyle's own lifetime ever arose to match Carlyle's demanding standards. James Carlyle who died in 1832 obviously came close, but that was in Annandale, and 50 years back. It is to Carlyle's credit that he resisted the temptation, as all major writers of his century did, to take refuge in that far-off religious paradise, with all its hardship and hard living. Yet the impetus of his literary and ethical practice was to make it easier for people to handle the ambiguous and the difficult in the personality of a past hero.

John Howie's *The Scots Worthies* (1775) is a very early example of this focussing of feeling on past worthies: the nineteenth century, with its diversity of churches and intentions, of beliefs and practice, was to find the habit a useful one and above all in Scotland to focus on the central characters of literary and religious writing—on 'Christopher North' (John Wilson) and John Stuart Blackie in writing, on the great philosophers such as Sir William Hamilton and James F Ferrier (about whose controversial careers George Elder Davie has written illuminatingly), and in religion on Thomas Chalmers, a man so venerated that (David Masson again) 'Merely to look at him day after day was a liberal education'.[11] William Robertson Nicoll was to write in 1922 to A W Blaikie: 'My own father had no room for pictures, every inch of the space in his little manse being occupied by books, but he found places for three different portraits of Dr Chalmers. So you see I have been well brought up . . . !'[12]

Robertson Nicoll in his turn was to be the centre of a group of literary heroes, and to foster the three most successful writers of his time from Scotland: J M Barrie, S R Crockett and Ian Maclaren. Stevenson grew to heroic stature in his short lifetime, and became a greater hero when his scandal-prone life was safely over and the work of biography and hagiography could commence. Indeed, the nineteenth century in Scotland, overshadowed by the Disruption and so much social change, became for many a battleground of writing in which only great names made any useful sense in trying to understand philosophical and religious controversy, or to understand writing which analysed a country in rapid change—Mrs Oliphant and George MacDonald in England, Stevenson in far-off Samoa.

Perhaps it is now clear why George Douglas Brown chose to leave out the ministers from Barbie in *The House with the Green Shutters*. To concentrate on a single character would simply be to continue a tradition honestly and brilliantly employed by a Carlyle, often sloppily and unthinkingly perpetuated by the creators of kailyard villages populated by saintly stereotypes, but now as out of date as Galt's Balwhidder, pottering amiably around a manse literally and figuratively at the wrong end of a developing community. The twentieth century in Scottish writing has chosen rather to move from the personality of kirk and beadle to that calculated and valuable ambiguity which has always been at the heart of religious writing in this country, whether in satire or in analysis of change, whether in finding publicly acceptable formulations for a publicly acceptable piety when private faith is more ambiguous, or whether in seeking to find poetic and super-rational words to express the infinite.

Anti-Kirk and Anti-Christian

Clearly, some of the potent forces in modern Scottish writing have been anti-Kirk: MacDiarmid, anti-Scottish establishment and anti-Christian, found it easy in *A Drunk Man* to speak of kirks that had done with Christianity, and Grassic Gibbon in a thoughtful essay in *Scottish Scene* does much to analyse in prose what he suggests in the fiction of *Cloud Howe*, a much underestimated book which looks at the life of the manse in the 1920s instead of the 1780s. Grassic Gibbon had never lived in a manse, but he had good friends who had: Robert Colquohoun in *Cloud Howe* seeks to reconcile good Scottish pastoral ministry with an intensely-felt socialist philosophy in a community dreadfully split between a conservative church-going minority and a post-Christian socialist majority. In the circumstances, Robert produces his famous description of a contemporary Christianity:

> a stark, sure creed that will cut like a knife, a surgeon's knife through the doubt and disease—men with unclouded eyes may yet find it, and far off yet in the times to be.[13]

But significantly the character of Robert in *Cloud Howe* does not live to find it, any more than Chris (the central character of the whole *A Scots Quair* trilogy) finds it. The battle between freedom and God at the end of *Grey Granite* is an unreconciled one— deliberately, as the author has the two main surviving characters go their separate ways, to the Scottish countryside (the older generation, to die) and to England (the Marxist, younger generation to work for future justice). Such a dialectic, ongoing and unresolved, is the only honest end the author could find to a wide-ranging picture of his country between 1911 and 1934: what is remarkable about *Cloud Howe*, coming as it does from a convinced anti-Christian and Marxist, is the sympathy it feels for the character of the minister trapped in a social matrix where his personal convictions cannot adequately be transmitted to a community increasingly polarised between haves and have-nots, where distrust is added to generations-old lack of contact and interest, and the inheritance of Galt's picture in the 1820s is fully realised. Grassic Gibbon could be dismissive of the institution—

> Religion for the Scot was essentially a means of assuring himself life in the next world, health in this, prosperity, wealth, fruitful wombs and harvests[14]—

but the people who went, and above all the people who ministered, retained the fascination they had obviously had for him in boyhood Arbuthnott. He knew that the 'kirkwards trickle of folk' persisted, but he felt 'the old fires and the old fears are gone', and he turned the spotlight on the younger ministers—

> (the most of them) free-hearted and liberal, mild socialists, men with pleasant wives who blush over the books of such writers as myself, but read them nevertheless and say pleasant things about the pleasant passages—

and makes one such the centrepiece of *Cloud Howe*.

In life Grassic Gibbon enjoyed the company of some younger ministers—but his fiction exemplifies one of the ways in which modern Scottish writing can treat the question of religion. Assuming a falling-away in church-going and in personal belief, such writing can look at the Church as an ongoing institution seen in public terms from the outside: the plight of the individual whose ministry is in such a kirk, made for powerful writing as far back as 1822 with Lockhart's *Adam Blair*, and continues to exert such a fascination in works such as Fionn MacColla's *The Ministers* and George Mackay Brown's *Greenvoe*.

Often such a view of the Church entails a political stance: Grassic Gibbon linked the Church in Scotland inextricably with questions of national identity and self-vision, and confidently looks ahead to a more politically secure future where 'One sees rise ultimately . . . in place of Religion—Nothing. . . . One does not seek to replace a fever by an attack of jaundice'. Such a nirvana of personal and mental freedom still lies a good deal ahead for the authors of *Scottish Scene*: for Compton Mackenzie, too, writing on *Catholicism and Scotland* at Grassic Gibbon's invitation for the 'Voice of Scotland' series, the question of politics and religion is unhappily very closely linked:

> Even national independence can be achieved at too dear a price if such independence is to mean a recession along the dim and tortuous paths of religious bigotry.[15]

The answer for such writers is often prefaced in Brown's stance in *The House with the Green Shutters*. The minister is acknowledged as a central figure of the community, but his church and the church building alike are simply to be ignored as anachronisms, and organic change will no doubt bring an adjustment in due course. Dickens, writing of his distaste for the clanging of bells and the activities of insensitive evangelists among the urban poor of the nineteenth century, prefigured much of this—the memorable scene in *Hard Times* where the bells rang but the chapels of Coketown seemed strangely empty— certainly of the working class who lounged in wonder at all the church and chapel-going. A century later in *The Uses of Literacy*, Richard Hoggart was to remark on the simple irrelevance of a church connection to many in their self-image of working class in the 1940s and 1950s: the updating of the Scottish stereotype in literature includes a strong move to push the Kirk aside, to relegate it to something not actively to be fought against, but simply disregarded as irrelevant.

Supernatural Experience

An alternative model does exist in modern Scottish writing. While many have recorded resistance to the oppressive and the downputting in the Presbyterian Kirk (George Mackay Brown, Iain Crichton Smith, Fionn MacColla, George MacDougall Hay), others have made a strong case for the survival of religious or supernatural experience as essential. The nature of that extra-normal experience is of course diverse: the Gaelic forces in the poetry of Sorley MacLean; the rejection of blank materialism implicit in much of Edwin Morgan's

Glasgow poetry; the search for a workable aesthetic (or indeed a workable philosophy for living) in contemporary Glasgow fiction; perhaps most popularly successful in the extraordinary experiments in fiction by George Mackay Brown, in short story (typically, *A Time to Keep*) and longer fiction (typically, *Greenvoe*). Brown's formula, which seems capable of extensive reworking and experimentation, and shows no signs of diminishing through repetition, is one which combines a deeply-felt personal faith in Roman Catholicism with a supersensitive awareness of a mythological past and the continuing miracle of season and cycle. Thus Scandinavian, particularly Norse mythology is important in the everyday of his Orkney pictures, as are the Christian year, the survival of oral music and tradition, and the inevitable encroachments of modernity, oil, NATO, Hollywood, television, rationalism. The real achievement of George Mackay Brown is, through a diversity of genre, to show that these diversities are co-existent in a modern mind, admittedly one a little removed from the urban everyday, yet little different save in sensitivity and open-mindedness from the norm of the reader. Many of his Presbyterian preachers are among the most dismissive of that open-mindedness which often resides in tinkers and outsiders. Yet the paradoxical, personal vision of Mackay Brown is translated into one visible and accessible to the metropolitan reader.

And so really this essay comes full circle back to the openness which makes Scott such a remarkable chronicler of a time of change, Brown such a challenging redefiner of a Scotland sunk in stereotype, Galt's narrator in *Annals* such a brilliant half-understander of a complex changing world. Writing about religion in those parts of Scottish literature discussed here has been above all a matter of discerning change: from the Reformation on, the continuity of the Presbyterian Church has been achieved by change and adjustment, stubborn resistance and timely co-operation, and a literature which, in depicting an everyday Scotland, necessarily incorporates that Presbyterian Church at every turn, catching most characteristically that adjustment and change. It has been suggested that openness to change and ambiguity is a sign of positive quality: it has been suggested that negative and satirical writing has most frequently attacked characters in their inflexibility and their negativity in a world of change. In Hogg's *Confessions*, the devil is at his most persuasive when he seems like a good Scottish religionist, and he easily fools the 'justified sinner' at the heart of the narrative. Denying to his parents that he had been talking with the devil (despite his obviously disturbed face and manner), the sinner says:

'. . . I have been conversant this day with one stranger only, whom I took rather than an angel of light.'
'It is one of the devil's most profound wiles to appear like one,' said my mother.
'Woman, hold thy peace!' said my reverend father: 'thou pretendest to teach what thou knowest not'.[16]

But poor Mrs Wringhim, whose fate at the devil's hands is to be a miserable one, does know what she is speaking about, and it is the minister of the Kirk, the flaming predestinarian, who is the devil's greatest dupe in his inflexible arrogance. If Wringhim had listened to his mother he might have avoided hell, but Scottish literature would have lost one of its greatest plots. The devil of disguise requires an alert intelligence and a flexible set of attitudes to circumvent. To many, writing about Scotland has been as difficult as telling good from evil, as the country has changed so rapidly as to make definitive description almost impossible. Clearly, the successful way to write on religion has been by indirection, and the variety of ways in which authors have tackled their subject gives some indication of its centrality to any attempt to describe Scotland's inner workings.

The Bible has not of itself been mentioned much in this study. But the Bible is always there, in the background if not the foreground, known and known well by all the authors and frequently quoted or alluded to by their conservative and radical characters alike, by one side to uphold the old ways, by the other to criticise these ways and to point a new way ahead. Its powerful if partly hidden presence supplies a dimension to Scottish literature which, though often remarked upon, has not received the scholarly attention it merits.

IAN CAMPBELL

Notes

1   J De L Ferguson and G Ross Roy (eds), *The Letters of Robert Burns*, 2 vols (Oxford, 1985), II, p 269-70 and I, p 204.
2   J Carey (ed), J Hogg, *Private Memoirs and Confessions of a Justified Sinner* (London, 1969), p 2.
3   T Carlyle, *Reminiscences* (London, 1972), pp 9–10, 4.
4   Ibid., p 177.
5   Sir A Geikie, *Scottish Reminiscences* (Glasgow, 1904), p 102.
6   David Daiches, *God and the Poets* (Oxford, 1984), pp 210–11.
7   David Masson, *Memories of London in the 'Forties* (Edinburgh and London, 1908), pp 82–3.
8   Hector MacPherson, *The Intellectual Development of Scotland* (London, [1912]), p 194.
9   A M Stodart, *John Stuart Blackie, A Biography* (3rd edition) (Edinburgh and London, 1895), I, p 242.
10   Ian Campbell, 'Conversations with Carlyle: The Monckton Milnes Diaries', *Prose Studies* 8:1 (May 1985), p 54.
11   David Masson, *Memories of Two Cities* (Edinburgh and London, 1911), p 81.
12   T H Darlow, *William Robertson Nicoll, Life and Letters* (London, 1925), p 246.
13   (London, 1933), p 284.
14   L G Gibbon and Hugh MacDiarmid, *Scottish Scene* (London, 1934), from Gibbon's essay on 'Religion', pp 313–27.
15   Compton Mackenzie, *Catholicism and Scotland* (London, 1936), p 187.
16   Op.cit. (Note 2 above), p 121.

Further Reading

Ian Campbell (ed), 'Carlyle's Religion: the Scottish Sources', in J Clubbe (ed) *Carlyle and His Contemporaries: Essays in Honor of Charles Richard Sanders* (Durham, North Carolina, 1976), pp 3–20.

Campbell, 'Non-Fictional Prose', in D Gifford (ed), *History of Scottish Literature*, vol III, *Nineteenth Century* (Aberdeen, 1988).

David Craig, *Scottish Literature and the Scottish People, 1680–1830* (London, 1961).

David Daiches, *God and the Poets* (Oxford, 1984).

David Daiches (ed), *A Companion to Scottish Culture* (London, 1981).

Trevor Royle, *The Macmillan Companion to Scottish Literature* (London, 1983).

III

The Bible
in Scottish Life

9

The Bible in Early Iona

The centrality of the Bible in the life of the Celtic Church is well established. In the monastic schools which were so prominent in Celtic Christianity, Scripture was the chief subject of study, while copies of the books of Holy Writ formed the major part of the output of monastic scribes. Ecclesiastical documents of all kinds, from the legislative to the hagiographical, are imbued with biblical learning. A striking amount of exegetical biblical material survives from the seventh century onward. Yet while the broad picture emerges clearly, many details remain to be filled in. Few monastic texts reveal the names of their compilers, or the locations in which they were compiled. We are particularly fortunate, then, to have texts which are specifically associated with the monastery of Iona, texts which cast much light on the role of the Bible in Scotland's most illustrious foundation.

Columba and the Psalms

In fact, our evidence regarding the place of the Bible in Iona's monastic life is traceable back to the founder's own time. St Columba left Ireland about the year AD 563, and spent most of his remaining 34 years as an 'island soldier' on his monastic outpost off the Scottish coast. Iona's founder is unique among his saintly contemporaries in that his career is well-documented in literary records composed close to the period of his lifetime. The earliest of these records is probably the *Amra* or eulogy, composed in Ireland around the time of Columba's death in the year 597. While praising many aspects of the saint's life of Christian endeavour, the *Amra* makes special mention of his study of the Psalms, as well as more general reference to his reading of the mysteries of Scripture.[1] We are able to amplify these brief

131

allusions, moreover, by turning to our other major early source on Columba, the *Vita Columbae* (*VC—Life of Columba*) compiled in Iona by his successor, Adomnán. The latter, writing about a century after Columba's death, had available an Iona account of the saint, now lost, compiled within living memory of his abbacy. Thus the *Life of Columba* very likely embodies details about Columba derived from the testimonies of those who had been his contemporaries.[2]

Indeed, it is particularly noteworthy that the *Amra* reference to Columba's interest in the Psalms is echoed in Adomnán's text. We must, of course, take account of the hagiographical purpose of the narratives in the *Life* when we read that Columba's Psalm-singing in Iona was miraculously heard over a great distance, or that the saint's recital of the forty-fourth Psalm (*ie* our Ps. 45) outside the fortress of the Pictish king, Brude, raised Columba's voice like a terrible peal of thunder to strike terror into his pagan opponents (*VC* i:37). What we may deduce factually is the evident interest both in the recital and in the copying of the Psalms on Iona. Columba is seen to oversee the process of collation of a newly-copied Psalter in one episode (*VC* i:23), while elsewhere we learn of the existence of books written in his hand (*VC* ii:8, 9). Indeed, the earliest Irish manuscript copy of the Psalms, the *Cathach*, was for long believed to be the work of Columba.[3] At the very least, the tradition affirms the testimony of the written sources that the saint linked his praise of God with that of his biblical forbears. Indeed, the *Life of Columba* strikingly encapsulates this view of the holy man as it relates that Columba's final task on earth was that of transcribing a Psalter:

> And when he came to that verse of the thirty-third Psalm [*ie* Ps. 34] where it is written 'But they that seek the Lord shall not want for anything that is good,' he said, 'Here at the end of the page, I must stop. Let Baithene write what follows'.[4]

Columba's valedictory words obviously stand as a testament to his followers. As Adomnán says, the following Psalm verse 'Come, my sons, hear me, I will teach you fear of the Lord' (Psalm 33:11 = 34:11), is 'fittingly adapted to the successor, the father of spiritual sons, a teacher, who, as his predecessor enjoined, succeeded him not in teaching only but in writing also' (*VC* iii: 23). While the overt reference here is to Baithene, Columba's immediate successor in Iona, it is evident that Adomnán is articulating also his own understanding of the legacy of Columba. Indeed, as we shall now see, the ninth abbot is himself the pre-eminent witness to the manner in which the successors of Columba in Iona promoted, in teaching and in writing, the values of their patron.

The Holy Places of Scripture

The work which most clearly illuminates the continuing significance of the Bible in Iona monastic scholarship was compiled by Adomnán in the early period of his abbacy. *De Locis Sanctis* (*DLS*) is an account of *The Holy Places* of Christianity, which had its genesis in the arrival in Iona of a Gaulish bishop named Arculf, who was en route home from a pilgrimage to Jerusalem and the sacred sites of the east.[5] Arculf's presence on the island offered Adomnán a unique opportunity of obtaining first-hand information about all the places hitherto familiar only through scriptural study. In his own words the abbot expresses his eager reception of this new-found source of knowledge. Though he was, as he says, 'daily beset by laborious and almost insupportable ecclesiastical business from every quarter', he set about making 'careful enquiries' of his informant, and keeping a 'faithful and accurate' record of all that he learned.[6]

The whole of *The Holy Places* is informed by Adomnán's own knowledge of, and interest in, the biblical narratives. He follows the returned pilgrim around the various places associated with the life and death of Christ, referring all the time to the Gospel narratives, yet also linking the Old and New Testaments. He speaks, for instance, of the destruction of Jericho when telling of the Saviour's visitation of the city raised in its place (*DLS* ii:13; Josh. 6, Luke 19:1–10). He echoes John in referring to the well of Jacob, as well as to the Lord's encounter with the Samarian woman at the same well (*DLS* ii:21; John 4:5–30). At times, Adomnán uses Arculf's testimony to clarify particular details in the biblical narratives. Thus, citing the evangelist's words concerning John the Baptist—'His food was locusts and wild honey' (Matt. 3:4)— he relates that Arculf did, indeed, discover, in the solitude where John lived, a type of easily-captured locust and certain edible leaves which constituted the wild honey mentioned in the gospel (*DLS* ii:23). Adomnán the scholar also checks details provided by Arculf against those in a reference-book which he had available in Iona, the *Onomasticon* of Jerome, in which the fourth-century Latin church father had revised the church historian Eusebius' annotated list of all the place-names in the Bible.[7] Thus, he asks precise questions of his informant about such matters as the site of the burial of Rachel (*DLS* ii:7; Gen. 35:19), and the present state of the oak of Mambre, under which Abraham had entertained angels (*DLS* ii:11; Gen. 18:1–15). Moreover, Adomnán's concern extends, not merely to the location and physical descriptions of the Holy Places, but also to the manner in which their sacred character is maintained by the building of churches. He speaks, for example, of the three churches on Mount Tabor:

> . . . according to the number of the tabernacles, concerning which Peter on the same holy mount, rejoicing in the heavenly vision and greatly fearing, said to the Lord, 'It is good for us to be here, and let us make three tabernacles, one for thee and one for Moses and one for Elias'.
> (*DLS* ii:27; Luke 9:33).

He devotes particular attention to describing the church of the sepulchre at Jerusalem (i:2), and the round church of the Mount of Olivet (i:23). On occasion, exegesis takes over from description. Thus, mention of a church founded on the spot on Mount Olivet where Jesus discoursed with his disciples leads to a discussion of the manner in which the incident is related by Matthew and by Mark (*DLS* i:27; Matt. 24:3–44, Mark 13:3–37). Moreover, describing the site of the sepulchres of the patriarchs, he says of Adam:

> He does not rest, like other honoured men of his seed, in a stone sepulchre hollowed out in the rock above the earth's surface; but is buried in the earth, covered by the turf, and dust that he is, to dust returned. (Gen. 3:19). And thus is fulfilled the divine sentence about him pronounced to himself.

Spiritual Pilgrimage

It is evident throughout, in fact, that Adomnán writes as preacher and teacher. He goes beyond mere geographical corroboration of biblical data to stress the ever-living relevance of the story of salvation for those of the present age. He calls attention to visible signs of divine power. On Mount Olivet:

> . . . so lasting is the proof that the dust was trodden by God that the imprints of the feet are visible; and, though crowds of the faithful daily plunder the earth trodden by the Lord, still the spot suffers no perceptible damage, and the ground goes on keeping the semblance, as it were, of footprints.
> (*DLS* i:23)

As regards the rock over which was poured the water of Christ's first washing, Adomnán tells us that this water formed an ever-flowing channel, so that the Saviour from the day of his nativity performed the miracle of which the prophet sings: 'Who brought forth water from the rock' (Psalm 77:16 = 78:16). Moreover, 'it is the same power and wisdom of God which brought forth water from the rock of Bethlehem which always keeps its channel filled with water (*DLS* ii:3).

Adomnán is evidently keenly aware of the spiritual opportunities offered by pilgrimage to the Holy Places. He tells how Arculf was able to view a chalice used by the Lord and the soldier's lance which pierced his side (*DLS* i:7, 8). He recounts what the bishop had learned about the vicissitudes of the relic of the holy shroud, and stresses that Arculf had seen the shroud in its present resting-place in Jerusalem, 'and in the crowded church kissed it himself amongst the multitude of people who were kissing it' (*DLS* i:9). The possibility of seeing and touching such sacred relics was a remote one for Adomnán and his followers on a small island off the Scottish coast. Yet it would seem that the abbot believed that to follow in Arculf's footsteps by writing and reading about the Holy Places was in itself a kind of pilgrimage. Thus, he intends his illumination of the world of the Bible to function like the illumination seen by Arculf on Mount Olivet, which 'pours into the hearts of the faithful greater eagerness for divine love and imbues them with a sense of awe coupled with great interior compunction' (*DLS* i:23).

Iona and Christendom

The fortuitous arrival of the Gaulish bishop during Adomnán's abbacy had linked Iona in a special way with the far-off biblical lands. Yet there was also a continuous, permanent link through shared Christian belief. In his life and writings, Adomnán seems to have been especially conscious of the question of Iona's relationship with the wide world of Christendom. After visits to Northumbria in the years 686 and 688, he adopted the usage of the universal Church in the observance of Easter, though others of his Iona brethren still clung to the traditional custom of Columba.[8] Adomnán's stance on the contemporary question of whether the Celtic Churches should unite in observance with the generality of Christendom may be discerned further in the second of his surviving literary works, the *Life of Columba*. We have noted already that this work incorporates important early material about

Columba. We shall focus now on the manner in which it also reflects the outlook of its compiler.

In the first place, we see that in this work Adomnán views the subject's deeds not from the perspective of the sceptical historian, but from the perspective of one who believes that through divine power all things are possible to the saint. The abbot's own experiences of Columba's wonder-working affirm for him the credibility of miracles recounted by others (*VC* ii:45). Moreover, Adomnán believes, in regard to Columba, that though the saint had lived 'in this small and remote island of the Britannic ocean', nevertheless, he merited that his name should be 'illustriously renowned' as far as Rome itself (*VC* iii:23). To Adomnán's mind, his patron was of equal stature in holiness with the great figures of Scripture and hagiography. Thus, as *The Holy Places* forges a bond between Iona and the Bible lands, so too the *Life of Columba* stresses the connection between the deeds of Iona's founder and the deeds of the prophets and apostles, and of Christ himself.

The *Life* begins, in fact, by pointing out, in the manner of biblical exegesis, that Columba's very name betokens 'divine dispensation', as it recalls the Holy Spirit's assumption of the form of a dove and Christ's admonition to his disciples 'to have within them the simplicity implanted in the pure heart of doves' (Matt. 10:16).[9] Thereafter, Adomnán sets himself the task of combining specific Iona recollections of the founder with narratives which illustrate the universal character of Columba's sanctity. A parallel is strikingly drawn by Adomnán in the opening chapter of Book ii of the *Life*. The saint's first miracle, performed while he was still a student, involved the changing of water into wine.

> And so Christ the Lord manifested through his disciple, as a first evidence of power, this that he had performed through himself in Cana of Galilee, when he made the same thing the beginning of his signs.

Columba and the Biblical World

The remainder of Adomnán's account of Columba is likewise imbued with wide-ranging echoes of biblical themes and language. The saint stills a storm at sea when his fellow-sailors are in fear of drowning (*VC* ii:12; Matt. 8:23–27, Mark 4:35–41, Luke 8:22–25). The sick are cured even by touching the hem of his cloak (*VC* ii:6; Matt. 9:18–26, Mark 5:21–43, Luke 8:43–48). Like Moses, Columba obtains water from a rock (*VC* ii:10; Exod. 17:1–7). In his struggle with demons he takes to himself 'the armour of the apostle Paul' (*VC* iii:8; recalling Eph. 6:11–17). Likewise, just as Paul wrote of his own vision, 'I know a man, caught up to the third heaven' (2 Cor. 12:2), so too Columba spoke indirectly of heavenly manifestations revealed to him (*VC* i:43).

Adomnán draws very explicit scriptural analogies when he speaks of the most spectacular of Columba's miracles, those involving matters of life and death. We are told that through the intervention of Columba the murderer of a girl fell dead on the spot, 'like Ananias before Peter' (*VC* ii:25; Acts 5:5). And having recounted the major miracle of Columba's raising from the dead the son of a newly-converted Pictish layman (*VC* ii:32), Adomnán says:

> Let this miracle of power, in the raising of the dead, be attributed to our Columba, in common with the prophets Elijah and Elisha; and a like share of honour with the apostles Peter and Paul and John; and a glorious place in the heavenly land, among both the companies, namely of prophets and apostles, as a man prophetic and apostolic: with Christ, who reigns with the Father in the unity of the Holy Spirit, through all the ages of the ages.[10]

We see, therefore, that Adomnán wishes to make clear that, though Columba belonged in a special way to Iona, he belonged also to the great communion of holy men of the Old and New Testaments. While this is attested most evidently by the miraculous powers divinely conferred on the saint, it is attested also by his devotion and teaching. One particular episode in the *Life of Columba* relates a heavenly visitation of Columba when 'the grace of the Holy Spirit was poured out upon him', and in this illumination 'everything that in the sacred Scriptures is dark and most difficult became plain' (*VC* iii:18). We are told further of the saint's regret that his foster-son, Baithene, was not there, in order to write down these 'very many mysteries', and 'a number of interpretations of the sacred books'. In this narrative, Adomnán not only points to Columba's own interiorisation of biblical thought, but also stresses again the saint's concern that his followers should have similarly close links with the fount of their belief.

In recounting Columba's career therefore, Adomnán apparently seeks to influence those in seventh-century Iona who opposed change to universal Church custom, on the grounds that this implied abandonment of Columba's teaching.[11] In Adomnán's view, Columba himself was a symbol of unity, a saint whose life and deeds made him at one with those whose lives and deeds were the common currency of all Christians who read and studied Scripture. Iona should look outward to the heritage which it shared with the rest of Christendom rather than remaining introverted and concerned with its own particularities.

The writings of Adomnán thus illuminate for us in a unique way the manner in which the Bible was a guiding star in the teaching and thinking of Iona's ninth abbot. Indeed, his vision of the participation of his remote island community in the great Christian enterprise still reveals itself clearly to us today when we look on Iona's surviving stone crosses.[12] In their representations of scenes such as Abraham's sacrifice of Isaac, Daniel in the lion's den, and the Virgin and Child, they proclaim, as they have proclaimed through many ages, the teachings of the Old and New Testaments, the heritage first brought by Columba to the far west of Scotland in the sixth century.

MÁIRE HERBERT

Notes

1   The most complete edition and translation of this work is that of Whitley Stokes, 'The Bodleian Amra Choluimb Chille', *Revue Celtique* 20 (1899), pp 31–55, 132–83, 248–89, 400–37. Note especially sections 54, 60.
2   The edition and translation used here is that of A O and M O Anderson, *Adomnan's Life of Columba* (Edinburgh, 1961). All following textual references are to this edition, prefixed *VC*. My general remarks on the *Vita* are elaborated further in my book, *Iona, Kells and Derry: The History and Hagiography of the Monastic Familia of Columba* (Oxford University Press, 1988).
3   The manuscript is preserved in the Royal Irish Academy, Dublin. See especially H J Lawlor, 'The Cathach of St Columba', *Proceedings of the Royal Irish Academy* 33 C (1916), pp 241–443.
4   *VC* iii: 23 (Anderson, p 525).
5   The text has been edited and translated by Denis Meehan, *Adamnan's De Locis Sanctis* (Dublin, 1958), hereafter abbreviated as *DLS*. Information about the date and sources is taken from Meehan's work.
6   *DLS*, Introduction (pp 36–7); iii: 6 (pp 120–1).
7   Meehan, pp 15–18.
8   See Anderson, *VC* p 94.
9   *VC*, Second Preface.
10   *VC* ii: 32, echoing Gregory the Great in his *Dialogues*, ii 8.
11   I have discussed this matter in detail in *Iona, Kells and Derry*, pp 142–8.

12   Most recently described in detail in the volume of the Royal Commission on the Ancient and Historical Monuments of Scotland, *Argyll: An Inventory of the Monuments*, vol IV: *Iona* (Edinburgh, HMSO, 1982). An attractive booklet based on the material in this volume was published in 1983: *Iona*, by John G Dunbar and Ian Fisher (for the Royal Commission; Edinburgh, HMSO).

Further Reading

A O and M O Anderson (editors and translators), *Adomnan's Life of Columba* (Edinburgh, 1961).
There are other translations of the *Life*, by W Reeves (Edinburgh, 1874), J T Fowler (London, 1895) and W Huysne (London, 1905).
D Meehan (editor and translator), *Adamnan's De Locis Sanctis* (Dublin, 1958).
M Herbert, *Iona, Kells and Derry: The History and Hagiography of the Monastic Familia of Columba* (Oxford, 1988).
M McNamara (ed), *Biblical Studies: The Medieval Irish Contribution* (Dublin, 1976).
Id., 'Psalter Text and Psalter Study in the Early Irish Church (AD 600– 1200)', in *Proceedings of the Royal Irish Academy* 73 C, 7 (1973), pp 201–98.

10

Sung Psalms in Scottish Worship

Sung Psalms have always been a backbone of Scottish worship. Until the latter part of the nineteenth century they were almost the only item of praise that was sung in Presbyterian churches, although the Independents and Episcopalians introduced hymns a century earlier. Biblically-based *Paraphrases*, published in 1745, were approved for use in 1768 and gradually found acceptance, together with a growing number of hymns (often themselves paraphrases of the Psalms) which achieved popularity as the nineteenth century progressed.

Since the Reformation the people have always sung the Psalms as a congregation. It was largely to facilitate the people's participation that a vernacular metrical Psalter was devised, although its adoption was much encouraged by the 'anti-papist' reaction to the use of plainchant.

From the Early Church to the Reformation

However, Psalms were sung to plainsong in Scotland for at least a thousand years.[1] The Roman rite was used (with the inevitable regional variations) and in mediaeval and monastic Scotland this meant a sung mass and sung Psalms to plainchant. In the 1290s the poet Blind Harry referred to 'Roman buikis and Salysbery oys'.[2]

Although Gregory the Great is apocryphally credited with codifying plainchant in the early seventh century, Psalms were sung in the early Christian Church to a system of chants that can be shown to have Jewish and Middle-Eastern antecedents. The Christian Church assumed the traditions of synagogue worship (far more than those of the temple, which was destroyed in AD 70 and in any case had been the preserve of the Levites) in which sung Psalms formed part of the liturgy. A great deal of other Scripture was sung in a 'cantillation' practice, in which singing was tantamount to speech.[3] This singing was accompanied by instruments, lyres and kitharas being the most usual, but trumpets, cymbals and percussion were also used.[4] The cantillations provided opportunities for improvisation, but only within a chant, which had set rules and set modes. The system of eight modes seems to have been common to Jewish, Roman, Byzantine, Syrian and Armenian chant, but not to Greek. Mostly they were chanted in a solo and responsorial manner. Similarities between Jewish chant and plainsong can be detected, but because such a long period elapsed before notation was first attempted in the eighth century (and even then it was often unclear or ambiguous), the circumstantial evidence as well as contemporary reports become important.

The emerging Christian Church's links with Judaism lasted for several generations after the apostolic age—in fact, until the first synthesis of patristic theology in the fourth century. Very little contemporary documentary evidence has survived about music in the first Hellenistic communities evangelised by St Paul. In AD 112 Pliny wrote in a letter to the Emperor Trajan, that 'they [the Christians] sang in alternate verses a hymn to Christ'. Tertullian reports that Psalm 133 was sung at the Christian *agapai* ('love-feasts').[5] However, the distinction between hymns and psalms seems not clear-cut at this period. Paul mentions 'hymns' in 1 Corinthians 14:26 and 'psalms, hymns and spiritual songs' (*psalmoi, hymnoi, ōdai pneumatikai*) in Ephesians 5:19 and Colossians 3:16, but these references mainly provide comprehensive reinforcement. Instruments receive mention in the New Testament only in connection with secular customs.[6] There seems little doubt that while psalm-singing was praised, instrumental music and accompaniment were proscribed in the early Church.[7]

One major difficulty in transferring Jewish chant to Christian worship was of course the language, since Christian worship was in Greek until about AD 300. As well as the language, the metre and accents changed. In Hebrew the Psalms have a parallelistic structure and are mainly either in iambic rhythm (based on the short-long metrical foot) or anapaestic (short-short-long), whereas Greek song used mostly cretic rhythm (long-short-long). However, the fact that Paul expressed no surprise at the chant system, when Socrates and Pliny did, would point to its not being of Greek origin. Whilst based on Jewish usage, Christian plainchant is likely to have been a distillation of various styles. The oral tradition constantly varied, and no transmission of music and text together survives until the era of Ambrose in the late fourth century.

Hymns were used from the earliest days, but many were considered heretical since they were not biblically-based. The second Synod of Antioch condemned all non-biblical hymns in AD 272 (although the *Sanctus* survived, from Rev. 4:8), but they returned with support from St Ambrose. Exactly what a hymn was still remained variable: for Ambrose in Milan it meant a metrical composition, while in the Eastern Church it denoted a prose text. Ambrosian chant could be metrically simple (the 'three beats' mentioned by St Augustine) or embellished and elaborated with a melismatic treatment, that is, one in which few syllables of text were set to many notes.

Plainsong

Gregorian chant started to appear soon after 600. Processional psalmody developed, leading towards the 'gradual'—a Psalm with a specific liturgical position. The essential characteristics of Gregorian chant are that the verses are sung to a reciting note (the 'tenor'), to which are attached a number of short inflections, called 'intonation', 'flex', 'mediation' and 'cadence'. The intonation is only used for the first verse and the doxology, the flex only for longer verses, and most verses use solely the mediation and cadence. This system was completely codified, with different tones and endings, by the end of the seventh century, and remains essentially unchanged today. It was designed as a simple system in which the congregation could join. In fact they rarely participated, and had decreasing opportunity to do so as monastic orders and choirs undertook all singing in the services.

Settings of the mass became increasingly complex in the mediaeval Church. Following the introduction of polyphony (*ie*, the combination in counterpoint of different melodies or parts) during the eleventh and twelfth centuries, the plainsong base often remained as a *cantus firmus* (literally, 'fixed song', *ie*, basic melody) with embellished patterns woven around it of considerable length and freedom. These developments ran concurrently with the continued use of simple plainchant until the Council of Trent (1545–47) ordered a reform of music so that 'the whole plan of singing in musical modes should be constituted not to give empty pleasure to the ear, but in such a way that the words may be understood by all'.[8] This meant restricting the music to settings of one syllable or more to one note, rather than many notes to one syllable.

Plainchant has several distinct advantages. Being purely melodic and of limited range, it is easy to sing. It has great flexibility because there are no enforced accents, no barlines. Its rhythm is that of free speech and it moves forward almost as quickly as speech.

However, these qualities were not much admired in Scotland by the time of the Reformation, by a people who had had little chance to sing the Psalms even in Latin. The chance of maintaining the tradition was lost with the arrival of a vernacular translation in a metrically rhythmic setting.

After the Reformation

The Reformation brought the metrical Psalter to Scotland. As precious as the metrical Psalter may have become, it is not at all indigenous. The earliest-known metrical Psalm settings come from Apollinaris in fourth-century Rome. Metrical Psalms were introduced to Scotland by English Puritans and thence taken up by the Scottish Reformers. The Council of Trent coincided with the publication in Scotland of the Wedderburn brothers' *Ane Compendius Buik of Godlie Psalms and Spirituall Sangis* (1542–6). Calvin's Psalter, started in 1539, led to the appearance of the first Scottish Psalter in 1564. These Psalters were in the vernacular (Calvin's in French).

Between 1342 and 1545 there were 38 collegiate churches in Scotland, many maintaining choral foundations. Most of them suffered dissolution at the Reformation, although not all choir schools were disbanded. One of the reasons for dissolution was simply financial. George Hay has commented:

> It is well to recall that the economic status of the Reformed kirk did not permit of great patronage of the arts. Of the vast wealth of the mediaeval kirk, much had been alienated by churchmen before the Reformation to subsidise their relatives and allies, their own progeny and that of kings and princes. What remained was largely pilfered by crown and aristocracy and at the end of the scramble the kirk was left virtually unendowed. . . . It remained beholden to heritors and magistrates for minimum provisions in the matters of stipends and buildings, a responsibility which they fulfilled in the main in the most niggardly manner.[9]

The Wedderburns' publication contained no music. The first manuscript collection of psalm-tune settings was Thomas Wode's (Wood's) in St Andrews in 1562. Some of these settings are harmonised or in a simple polyphonic but syllabic style. At the Reformation the Prior of St Andrews, the young Lord James Stuart (later Regent Moray), commissioned David Peebles to set Psalms for four (or more) voices in simple style. Much as Peebles appears only reluctantly to have carried out the commission, his work reflects the diversity of style in the settings by Louis Bourgeois and Claude Goudimel in the 1561 French Psalter. Wode's Psalter was completed, with harmonisations, in 1566.

Seven Scottish Psalters were published between 1564 and 1666. The tunes found in the first (1564) had an international currency; most can be traced to English, French or German sources. Scottish composers arranged them for several voices. The latter five Psalters all had common-metre tunes, harmonised, while the sixth Psalter, by Edward Millar in 1635, had 'proper' tunes set for four voices. Some settings derive from Thomas Este's English Psalter of 1592, some from Thomas Ravenscroft's Psalter of 1621, but most were the work of Scottish composers.

Some hangover from the pre-Reformation tradition was still apparent: Andro Blackhall's setting of Psalm 43, 'Judge and revenge my cause', written for Lord Regent Morton and precisely dated 1578, has a *cantus firmus* based on the *Miserere*, ie, Psalm 51, one of the penitential Psalms.[10]

Edward Millar's Psalter of 1635 is in some ways a kind of musical pudding; analysis of some of the music shows that he performed a 'mix and match' with various tunes to make up composites (*eg*, two lines of Kemp followed by two lines of Peebles, *etc*).[11]

John Knox did not use the Scottish translation in his Psalter of 1561, preferring the English version of 1549 by Thomas Sternhold. About 50 Psalm tunes are not traceable to other sources and may therefore be of Scottish origin. There are more than 200 settings of Psalms and Canticles for three, four or five voices together with a small handful of anthems for four or five voices set to psalm-texts. It is worth noting that the metrication of both Scottish and English Psalters was far more rigid and inflexible than was Clément Marot's and Theodore Beza's work for Calvin's Psalter, which used many more diverse metres.[12] Most of these tunes were written in the late sixteenth century while about half (27/50) of the common-metre tunes found in Scottish sources are seventeenth-century in origin.

The Psalter of 1650

The 1635 Psalter, good as it was, had but a short life and was probably not widely used. It was almost certainly conceived for the Chapel

Royal and choral use. The Church authorities had not sanctioned it and it had to contend with the 1631 Psalter, the latter supposedly based on King James VI's own translations, but in fact thoroughly revised by Sir William Alexander of Menstrie. On the death of King Charles I, the 'Royal' Psalter fell from favour. It had in any case been accused of 'poeticall conceits', and its fate was sealed when it was printed with the 1637 Prayer Book. The Westminster Assembly of 1644 wanted a translation closer to the Hebrew. Francis Rous, a Cornishman, offered a new translation, but it did not find ready acceptance in Scotland. After no fewer than six revisions passing to and fro between Westminster and the General Assembly in Edinburgh, *The Psalms of David in Meeter* was approved for use in the Church of Scotland on 1 May 1650.

This Psalter contained no music. Perhaps it was not surprising, for singing the Psalms had stopped in 1645 (at least in the Synod of Lothian) and was not resumed until after the Restoration in 1661. However, it was this 1650 Psalter which was to last in Scotland, whereas in England it was Nahum Tate's and Nicholas Brady's version of 1696 (also without music) which eventually achieved popularity.[13]

In England, metrical singing of Psalms had been permitted by Elizabeth's injunction of 1559 and metrical settings were used both in cathedral and parish churches. She called them 'Genevan jigs'. Sternhold's metrical Psalter, which had first appeared in 1549, was revised by John Hopkins, so that it became known as 'Sternhold and Hopkins', and was published in 1562 by John Day. This Psalter was in use for nearly a century, indeed until the Westminster Assembly of 1644 which also radically affected Scottish worship. The first music for Sternhold and Hopkins' Psalter came from the Genevan edition of 1556, with 'proper' tunes for every Psalm.

Most of the tunes were set in common metre and were far less varied and tuneful than those in the French Psalter. In fact these rather austere and graceless melodies aptly expressed the mood of the English Puritans of the time. The people soon rectified this and began using popular ballads to sing metrical Psalms, even though many of the tunes had dubious associations.

It is difficult to detect a clear Scottish style in the tunes found in the Scottish Psalters, although one excellent tune from the 1633 Aberdeen Psalter is of likely Scottish origin. This is 'Martyrs', although it is worth noting that the tune is not pentatonic (*ie*, in a five-note scale) but in the simple mode known as Dorian from its ancient Greek form. Like most tunes, the melody, or 'people's part', lies in the tenor. However, not all tunes had the melody in the tenor part: this is a popular misconception perpetuated as late as the Church of Scotland 1929 *Psalter*.

The first part-music to be printed appeared in the 1625 Psalter. In the 1635 Psalter some more elaborate settings, derived from *fauxbourdon* practice and called 'psalms in reports' (French *rapporter*, 'carry back') were given. For instance, Blackhall's setting of Psalm 137, 'When as we sat in Babylon', is a skilful piece involving much imitative part-writing.[14]

In 1666 a collection of tunes for use with the new 1650 Psalter was published in Aberdeen. This work, a far cry from the 1635 Psalter with its 35 tunes, contained only 12 tunes taken from the 1615 Psalter. These were: 'Abbey', 'Dundee', 'Dunfermline', 'Duke's', 'Elgin', 'English', 'French', 'King's', 'London' (London New), 'Martyrs', 'Old Common', 'Stilt' (or 'York')—with 'Bon Accord' (in reports) added for local interest. These 12 tunes were to form the staple, and in many instances the only, diet of Psalm tunes in Scotland for the next 200 years. Even worse, most 'uptakers' of the tune (later called 'precentors') knew only two or three of the 12. The 1666 collection of tunes was republished in 1714 and 1723. It was in use at least until 1820.

Meanwhile, the first 50 Psalms, *An Ceud Chaogad Do Shalmaibh Dhaibhidh*, had been issued in Gaelic by the Synod of Argyll in 1659 in alien metre and without music. Not until 1694 were all the Psalms published in Gaelic by the Church (although the translation had been completed ten years earlier).[15] Only six tunes were given in the Gaelic Psalter: 'Dundee', 'Elgin', 'French', 'London', 'Martyrs', and 'Stilt' set in long-metre.

Psalmody in Need of Reform

Although the tunes were taken from earlier Psalters it was the treatment of them that differed: a Highland development of Lowland style. This different treatment seems first to have appeared in the north-east (not in the west), which was an old Catholic and Episcopal stronghold. Maybe there was a harkback to a pre-Reformation melismatic approach to the psalm-tones. Linked with 'giving the line' or 'lining out' (the precentor sang the first line, then the congregation joined in), first prescribed in the 1645 Westminster *Directory for Public Worship* (but probably already in use since the loss of choirs), it was designed to lead the illiterate (English) in the congregation. The Scots neither wanted nor needed it. But after a heated debate, it was ordered to be used both in England and Scotland. However, whereas it had disappeared from

England well before 1800, in Scotland it can still be found in some places today.

One effect was to produce slower and slower singing which led to improvised embellishments to fill up the gaps or long notes, but the difference between Gaelic or Highland embellishments of the long-metre tunes and those used in common- or short-metre tunes should be noted. A written-out sample of the latter may be found in *A New and Easie Method to Learn to Sing by Book*, published in 1686. Another effect was considerably to shorten the portion of the Psalm sung.

The General Assembly of 1746 tried unsuccessfully to stop the practice of 'lining-out', but it had become quite entrenched in Scotland. A contemporary musician commented:

> Had these nonsensical graces been the same everywhere it would have been the less matter, but every congregation, nay every individual, had different graces to the same note which were dragged by many to such immoderate length that one corner of the church, or the people in one seat, had sung out the line before another half had done.[16]

By the 1790s Rowland Hill could report that 'some have supposed that *snuffling, bellowing* and *groaning* have added to their devotions in prayer . . . in favour of this most barbarous way of singing', and that 'the Scotch folk took so long to sing the 100th Psalm that one could travel from Edinburgh to London by the *old* conveyance before it was finished'.[17]

In the mid-nineteenth century Thomas L Hately tried to notate the Gaelic way of singing Psalms, and the German immigrant Joseph Mainzer also made a (rather poor) attempt at it. Since the technique is largely contingent on extempore choice, there seems little point in trying to notate something which can now be recorded, but whose essence and spirit are improvisatory.

Although the General Assembly had registered concern about the state of psalmody, the first move to improve the situation came from an individual's attempt at reform. In 1753 in Monymusk, Thomas Channon, an English army officer and a Methodist, started to form a choir to sing the Psalms in their unadorned form. Sir Archibald Grant was behind this action, which may have been motivated at least in part by his desire to discourage increasing numbers of people from moving over to Episcopalianism.

As an addition to the diet of sung Psalms, the *Paraphrases* of Scripture passages were approved for use in 1768 and endorsed in 1781. Perhaps it is remarkable that no New Testament passages had been sung in the Reformed Kirk before that (apart from the metrical version of the canticles from the Nativity narratives in the Gospels).

Choirs increased in size and new accommodation (usually choir lofts) had to be provided for them. Once the choir had become established it fulfilled two functions: leading the praise, which could mean introducing a new tune to the congregation, and singing anthems, many of which were based on biblical texts. More new psalm-tunes appeared in 1755 and 1761, published in Glasgow as *The Psalm Singer's Divine Companion*.

In Edinburgh, Robert Smith published *Sacred Harmony* in 1825, including tunes such as 'Invocation', 'St George's West' and 'Selma'. While some of these tunes were frankly not as good as the earlier ones, they contained an innovation: no longer were they strictly syllabic, but, often because they were written in triple-time, they might have two or three notes to one syllable. They also contained repetitive sections where both words and tune were repeated.

By the turn of the century the influence of the English Nonconformists or Independents was felt, and hymns (which fall outwith the scope of this essay) began to appear, many of which were in fact paraphrases of the Psalms.

Many additional tunes were published for the metrical Psalms in the nineteenth century, such as Joseph Mainzer's *Standard Psalmody of Scotland* (1845), *The National Psalmody* (1848) and *Psalm Versions, Paraphrases and Hymns* (1873). These came together in the *Psalter* published with the *Revised Church Hymnary* in 1929, following the Union of the United Free Church with the Church of Scotland. By this time, some of the versification seemed distinctly old-fashioned, and those Psalms then considered still suitable for singing in a metrical version were asterisked. However, no attempt was made to revise the verses or to render them in more modern English.

The Last Hundred Years

As a method of singing the Psalms, Anglican chant did not find any acceptance in Scotland before the influence of the Oxford (or Tractarian) movement which gained momentum in the 1830s and 1840s. Espoused first by the Episcopalians, the movement was taken up by the High Church Presbyterian element and particularly by Dr Robert Lee at Greyfriars Kirk in Edinburgh, who was concerned that Presbyterian worship was in need of reform and should show 'good taste, decency, propriety and solemnity', an example of which he set out in *The Order of Public Worship*, published for use in Greyfriars in 1864.[18] He was also worried that Episcopalian traditions were drawing members away from Presbyterian worship. As well as a more formalised liturgy, the Episcopalians accompanied their singing with an organ, and sang Psalms to Anglican chant, both of which Lee introduced at Greyfriars. His introduction of the organ opened the floodgates once the storms of the General Assembly had been weathered.[19] Within ten years or so (by the Free Church from 1883), organs were once more being accepted and installed. Henceforward the precentor's position waned and it was the presence of the organ to lead the praise, more than any other reason, which led finally to the abandonment of the practice of 'giving out the line' in the psalm-tunes.

Anglican chant as a method of psalm-singing had become firmly established in England in the years following the Restoration of the monarchy.[20] The 1662 *Book of Common Prayer* encouraged antiphonal singing or reading of the Psalms. The Psalter had previously only been printed as an appendix to the Prayer Book, but now the Prayer Book was printed 'together with the Psalter or Psalms of David, pointed as they are to be sung or said in churches'. This pointing, however, amounted to no more than a colon dividing each verse into two halves.

Anglican chant has its roots in plainsong, but in a simplified and harmonised version. The two sections of the chant, paralleling the bipartite structure of the verse of the psalm or canticle, were preserved from the plainsong. The simplest Sarum tones were used for the music. The fourth ending of the first tone has a two-note mediation in the first half, followed by a four-note mediation on the second half. This was to form the pattern for all Anglican psalm-chants, whether single or double.

The earliest source for such chants is Thomas Morley's *Plain and Easie Introduction to Practicall Musick* (1597), but it was not until the Restoration that the melody shifted away from the tenor part to the top part, in the publication of John Barnard's *First Book of Selected Church Music* (1641), James Clifford's *Divine Services* (1664), and John Playford's *Introduction to the Skill of Musick* (1673 and 1730). The first printed collection of chants dates from the mid-eighteenth century: *Fifty Double and Single Chants, being the Most Favourite, as Performed in Most of the Cathedrals of England.*

By 1771, John Alcock's *Six and Twenty Select Anthems* contained ornamented and elaborated chants which had written grace-notes akin to the effect of embellished metrical chants. The inadequate pointing and its musical results had been commented on by Arthur Bedford in

The Temple Musick as early as 1706,[21] but not until 1837 did the first fully-pointed Psalter appear in print, at Ely Cathedral.[22] Even then, the chanting had a metricality and rigid angularity about it far removed from the principles of speech-rhythm applied today.

Robert Lee included fully-pointed prose Psalms in his 1864 *Order*, but he used the more florid King James Version (AV) rather than the terseness of Miles Coverdale's earlier translation (1539–40) preferred by the English.[23] The *Scottish Prose Psalter* of 1929 held to the King James Version and did not follow the increasing number of English Psalters (*Oxford* in 1929, *Parish* in 1930, *etc*) which used Coverdale. The new translation used in the Anglican *Alternative Service Book* (1975) still appears to rely more on expressions used in Coverdale than in the KJV/AV.

Anglican chant was mostly found only in cathedrals and major parish churches in England until the middle of the nineteenth century, when the Oxford movement made its influence felt. In most churches in England the Psalms would still have been sung metrically. In Scotland, Anglican chant has never managed to oust the metrical Psalter, and its use has been even more restricted to the major churches than in England.

One of the influences of the Scottish Episcopalians and Non-conformists in the nineteenth century was hymn-singing. From 1781 collections of hymns appeared in ever-increasing numbers (and quantity per volume), until by the turn of the century almost every denomination had its own hymnary. The Church of Scotland published the *Church Hymnary and Psalter* in 1899.

Some hymnaries included metrical psalm-tunes from the Genevan Psalters of 1542–62, such as the *English Hymnal* in 1906 (which had a seminal influence on others), but with the appearance in Scotland of the 1929 *Revised Church Hymnary and Psalter* the two were combined. This metrical *Psalter* had the advantage of being split across the page, so that, although 'proper' tunes were recommended, it was easy to match any tune of the correct metre with the Psalm in question. It had the disadvantage that the metrication was still that of the 1650 *Psalter*, but with 'recommended' portions for use.

Psalm-Singing at Risk

The Church Hymnary (Third Edition, commonly known as *CH3*), published in 1973 and now widely in use, was not combined with a complete Psalter. Of the Psalms it contains mostly only excerpts. Of 57 portions, all but nine are from the 1650 *Psalter*. Two come from the *Irish Presbyterian Psalter* (1880) and seven are composite. Some textual revision was undertaken, but without significant change. Rather its compilers chose to widen the scope of musical psalm-settings by including a majority of metrical versions and also examples of Psalms set to plainsong, Anglican chant (to both AV and Coverdale's translations), together with three settings by Joseph Gelineau and two by John Currie.[24] Although the latter two types appear not to be widely used in Scotland, Gelineau's musical solution to singing the Psalms may turn out to be significant, and it has been much used in France. In 1956 Gelineau published a new translation of the Psalter in French, strictly following the Hebrew speech-rhythm and developed as a reaction to the traditional system of singing plainsong promoted in modern times by the monks of the Abbey of Solesmes.[25]

Gelineau took a simple principle. He constructed a melody where the change of note coincided with the strong beat of the verbal rhythm, instead of the plainsong method of a chant which inflected only on the end of the phrase. A regular four-beat bar was then used to cater for syllables falling between the main beats. This method, of course, runs contrary to the speech-rhythm of Anglican chanting. Its regularity of stresses within the bar is the opposite of the extension or compression of the bar necessary in Anglican chant to allow for the rhythm of the English translation. Designed to be used with antiphons and definitely intended for congregational participation, these settings can be remarkably effective. The chants themselves generally have a modal flavour, but the harmonisations can at times be surprisingly chromatic and colourful.

John Currie's settings in *CH3* are based on a single chant which follows a pointed plainsong method. The chant merely consists of a series of chords which do not correspond to the plainsong formulae but which allow a natural speech-rhythm to be used. The simplicity of these chants (and other similar ones) has made this type of psalm-singing popular in the Roman Catholic Church as an alternative to the Gelineau settings. Two newly-metricised Psalms from the New English Bible by Ian Pitt-Watson introduced a diversity of metre, albeit the same for both Psalms.

Psalm-singing in Scotland in the latter part of the twentieth century has to a considerable extent been ousted by hymn-singing. Most congregations no longer have access to a complete Psalter or

can choose freely from it, and the number of Psalms available in
CH3 has restricted the choice even for regular Sunday use to the
point where the inadequate repertoire soon becomes apparent
(and reflects on the lack of liturgically-appointed Psalms for the
day). Well-known metrical Psalms continue to be retained, but
they are increasingly regarded simply as hymns. Many of the
translations of the 1650 version of the metrical Psalter (the
translation still in use today) now seem old-fashioned and very
awkward. The new version by the Free Church of Scotland,
Scottish Psalmody, may therefore find ready acceptance. However,
perhaps what is most needed is a wider-based collection containing various types of chant set to a Psalter whose translation reflects
present use of language and whose expression is more unified
and felicitous. Whilst some of the texts in each style of psalm-
setting will no doubt remain dear and of enduring value, it
is nevertheless a long way from Coverdale's translation to
Gelineau's.

Such a move may halt the increasing trend nowadays to avoid
both metrical and musical complications by only reading the
Psalms in the more recent prose versions. This trend denies many
of the Psalms much of their original purpose as sung praise to the
Lord.

MICHAEL CHIBBETT

Notes

1   W O E Oesterley, *A Fresh Approach to the Psalms* (London, 1937), p
    181.
2   Quoted in J Galbraith, 'The Middle Ages', D B Forrester and D
    Murray (eds). *Studies in the History of Worship in Scotland*
    (Edinburgh, 1984), p 18.
3   E Werner, *The Sacred Bridge* (London and New York, 1959), p 110.
4   Oesterley, op.cit., p 118.
5   O Cullmann, *Early Christian Worship* (London, 1953), p 22, note. 3.
6   NT references to instruments: Matthew 9:23 and 11:17; Luke 7:32;
    Revelation 18:22. Metaphorical references: Matthew 6:2; 1 Corinthians
    13:1 and 14:7–8; Revelation 14:2.
7   Werner, op.cit., p 317, and 'The Attitude of the Early Church Fathers
    to Hebrew Psalmody', *Review of Religion* (New York, May 1943), p
    343.
8   Quoted in full in G Reese, *Music in the Renaissance* (London, 1954), p
    449.

9   G Hay, 'An Introduction to Scottish Post-Reformation Churches', *Transactions of the Scottish Ecclesiological Society* 14:3 (1951), p 8.

10   Discussed in K Elliott, 'Scottish Music of the Early Reformed Church', *Transactions of the Scottish Ecclesiological Society* 15:2 (1961), p 18.

11   Elliott, art.cit., p 28.

12   W D Maxwell, *John Knox's Genevan Service Book* (Edinburgh, 1931), p 63.

13   Discussed further in M Patrick, *Four Centuries of Scottish Psalmody* (London, 1949), ch 9.

14   K Elliott, *Fourteen Psalm Settings of the Early Reformed Church in Scotland* (reprinted) (London, 1960), p 22.

15   E A MacLean, 'Gaelic Psalm-Singing and the Lowland Connection', *Liturgical Review* 3 (1973), p 54. See also Chapter 1 of this volume.

16   R Bremner, *Rudiments of Music* (Edinburgh, 1756), p xiii.

17   R Hill, *Journal of a Tour through the North of England and Parts of Scotland* (London, 1799), p 175.

18   R Lee, *The Reform of the Church of Scotland* (Edinburgh, 1864), Part 1, p 45.

19   The 'Pirie' argument is outlined in D Murray, 'Disruption to Union', *Studies in the History of Worship in Scotland*, p 84.

20   C Dearnley, *English Church Music* (London, 1970), p 104.

21   A Bedford, *The Temple Musick* (London, 1706), ch 9.

22   The Work of R Janes (London, 1837), 'Carefully marked and pointed to enable the voices of a choir to keep exactly together by singing the same syllables to the same note'.

23   Miles Coverdale, *Goostly Psalms and Spirituall Songs* (London, 1540), whose translation was used in the first *Book of Common Prayer* of 1549; discussed in N Livingston, *The Scottish Metrical Psalter of 1635* (Glasgow, 1864).

24   R S Louden, 'Psalmody in the Church', and I Pitt-Watson, 'The Music', in *Handbook to the Church Hymnary Third Edition*, J Barkley (ed) (London, 1979), pp 34 and 68 respectively.

25   An English version, *The Psalms. Translated from the Hebrew and Arranged for Singing . . .* , was published in Fontana Books in London, 1963.

Further Reading

G Dix, *The Shape of the Liturgy* (London, 1945).

D B Forrester and D Murray (eds), *Studies in the History of Worship in Scotland* (Edinburgh, 1984).

M Frost, *English and Scottish Psalm and Hymn Tunes c. 1543–1677* (London, 1953).

F

W McMillan, *The Worship of the Scottish Reformed Church 1550–1638* (London, 1931).

W D Maxwell, *A History of Worship in the Church of Scotland* (London, 1955).

M Patrick, *Four Centuries of Scottish Psalmody* (London, 1949).

E Werner, *The Sacred Bridge* (London and New York, 1959).

11

'The Commoun Buke of the Kirke':
The Bible in the Scottish Reformation

The sixteenth-century Reformation was all about the Bible. Its most creative instigator, Martin Luther, believed so:

> All I have done is to put forth, preach and write the Word of God, and apart from this I have done nothing. While I have been sleeping, or drinking Wittenberg beer . . . , it is the Word that has done great things . . . I have done nothing; the Word has done and achieved everything.[1]

An eminent Reformation historian fully agrees: 'If there is a single thread running through the whole story of the Reformation, it is the explosive and renovating and often disintegrating effect of the Bible'.[2]
    The Scottish Reformation was no exception. Indeed, the 'scriptural principle' was applied more rigorously to the purification of Church life in Scotland than in most areas of Reformation Europe. Yet the Bible's role in the Reformation in Scotland is in some ways a paradoxical one.[3] The most forceful Scottish champion of free access to the vernacular Bible himself wrote nothing in English, let alone Scots. The Scottish Reformers relied on English translations, and made no attempt to provide a Scots version. Nor did they succeed in having an English Bible (or New Testament) produced in Scotland until 1579, in a reprinting of the Geneva Bible with not the slightest attempt at adaptation in vocabulary or spelling for a Scots readership. Its Dedicatory Epistle rejoices that 'almaist in euerie priuate house the buike of Gods lawe is red and understand in oure vulgaire language', apparently overlooking the differences between English and Scots. No further printing occurred until 1610, when the Edinburgh printer, Andrew Hart, issued a more Calvinist revision of the same Geneva Bible. These two earliest editions were pulpit-size folio Bibles, and not until 1633 was a Bible in a manageable octavo format produced in

Scotland. The 90 years following Parliament's authorisation in 1543 of the possession and study of the Bible in the language of the people saw only three printings of the Bible in Scotland. A pocket Bible was finally issued in 1638. English New Testaments for Scottish use were still being printed in the Netherlands in the early seventeenth century.

Early Renderings in Scots

In the new age of the printing press, English Bible translation was expertly pioneered by the scholarly Reformer, William Tyndale (d. 1536). His New Testament, translated from the Greek text and first published in Germany in 1526, had found its way into Scotland by early 1527. It was in Germany or the Low Countries that a Scot by the name of Murdoch Nisbet made the first known attempt around 1520 to Scotticise the New Testament. Nisbet's roots probably lay among the so-called Lollards attested in Kyle in Ayrshire from the late fifteenth century. The Lollards were the followers of John Wyclif, the fourteenth-century English reformer, and Nisbet used the Wycliffite English version when he 'took a copy of the New Testament in writ'. Although it is often referred to as a translation into Scots, and was eventually published early this century as *The New Testament in Scots*, it is little more than a transcript into Scots.[4] Nisbet worked from the revision attributed to John Purvey of the original Wycliffite version (itself inspired, but not executed, by Wyclif). Apart from adapting it to Scottish orthography, he changed little of its vocabulary, and then as often in the direction of the Wycliffite original as in favour of Scotticisms. Furthermore, his text circulated only in manuscript samizdat form.

A full linguistic examination of Nisbet's text remains to be done. It is not easy to see why he made some changes—such as 'mirk' for 'derk', 'ire' for 'wraththe'—and not others. Scotticisms like 'speir' (ask) are absent, but 'follow' replaces 'sue', 'called' replaces 'clepid', 'nowk' or 'newk' replaces 'cornere', and 'tolbuth' replaces of 'moot halle' (Acts 23:35). His preference for '[e]vangel' over 'gospel' reflects the Latin influence in the Scots of his day.[5] Indeed, Nisbet could not avoid inheriting the defects of the Latin Vulgate (the established Bible of the Catholic Church for over a millennium) from which the Wycliffite versions were made. Hence, although his prologue was largely a translation of Luther's preface to his German New Testament, Nisbet still has to 'do pennance' (Matthew 3:2, *etc*). The rejection of this rendering of the Latin in favour of the Greek (English: 'repent') was a milestone in Luther's biblical awakening.

The limitations of Nisbet's revision are evident when compared with biblical quotations in other Scots writings of the time. To John Gau's *The Richt Vay to the Kingdom of Heuine* (1533) belongs the distinction of being the first exposition of the reformed faith to appear in the Scottish tongue, but the paradoxical element noted above persists. Gau's work was published in Malmö in Sweden, and was not only a translation of a Danish treatise (itself largely translated from a German Lutheran original) but in its language strongly coloured by Gau's familiarity with Danish and German. It quotes the Bible extensively but rarely *verbatim*. 'Repent' now stands in Matthew 3:2. The linguistic flavour can be gauged from this abridged citation of Job 19:25–27:

> I vait that my redemer liffis and that i sal risz vp apone the later day of the zeird and i sal se god my saluiour in my flesch quhome i sal se and na oder (for me) and my eyne sal behald hime.[6]

This rendering may be compared with another, complete and more truly indigenous, of some 20 years later:

> I ken that my redemar is on lyfe, and that in the last day I sall ryse up out of the erd, and agane I salbe cled with my awin skein, and in my awin flesch, I shall se God, quhom my awin self sal se and my awin eyne sal behald him, and nane uthir in my stede for me.[7]

This comes from the *Catechism* produced under the auspices of John Hamilton, the reform-minded Archbishop of St Andrews, in 1552. Its tempered Catholicism betrays the influence of Protestant writers, including Gau, but the hour for moderation had passed and it made little impression. It nevertheless retains its interest as an original vernacular composition and a rare monument of Catholic piety in late mediaeval Scotland.

The many biblical verses of the *Catechism* are normally given first in Latin and then in Scots. Its retention of 'pen[n]ance' is symptomatic of its close adherence to the Vulgate. Its version of the Lord's Prayer may be set beside those of Nisbet, Gau and *The Gude and Godlie Ballatis*:[8]

Nisbet	Gau	Hamilton ('in Inglis')	Ballatis
Our fader	Our fader	O our Father	Our Father
that art	thow quhilk is	quhilk is	that art
in heuenis,	in ye heuine	in Hevinnis	in heuin,
hallewit be thi name.	thy nayme mot be hallowit	Thy name mot be hallowit	hallowit be thy Name
Thi Kingdom come to.	thy kingdom mot cum (to vsz)	Thy kyngdome mot cum.	Thy Kingdome cum.
Thi will be done in erde, as in heuen Gefe to vs this day our breid ouer vthir substance.	thy wil mot be dwne in ye zeird as it is in the heuine giff wsz this day our dailie breid	Thy wyll mot be done in erd, as it is in hevin. Geve us this day, our daylie breid.	Thy will be done in eirth as it is in heuin Giue vs this day our daylie breid.
And forgif to vs our dettis	and forgiff wsz our dettis	And forgyff us our dettis	Forgiue vs our trespassis,
as we forgef to our dettouris	as we forgiff our dettours	as we forgyfe our dettouris	as we forgiue them that trespas aganis vs.
And leid vs nocht into temptatioun,	and leid vsz notht in temptatione	And lede us nocht in temptatioun	And leid vs not into temptatioun.
bot deliuer vs fra evile	bot deliuer vsz fra ewil	Bot delyver us fra evyl.	Bot deliuer vs from evill.
Amen	Amen	Sa be it.	For thine is the Kingdome the power, and the glorie for ever. Amen.

It is illuminating to compare biblical quotations in Nisbet, Gau, Hamilton and similar works, such as *Ane Compendius Tractiue* (1558) by Quintin Kennedy, abbot of Crossraguel in Ayrshire and one of Knox's opponents, with William Lorimer's recent Scots version of the New Testament, especially in the light of the comment that Lorimer 'set out to recreate Scots prose, very little of which had been published since the late sixteenth century'.[9] Between ancient and modern yawns a gulf akin to that between the Authorised Version (AV) and the Bible Societies' Today's English Version or Good News Bible. Hamilton's 'Quhat hais thow, quhilk thow hais nocht resaivit?' and Lorimer's 'War ye no gíen onie fore at ye hae?' both translate 1 Corinthians 4:7. Less of a contrast is seen in Matthew 10:28: 'Feir nocht thame that slais your body and may nocht slay your saulis' (Hamilton), and 'Binna ye frichtit for them at kills the bodie, but canna kill the saul' (Lorimer).

Quintin Kennedy appealed to the Jerusalem 'council' of Acts 15 in arguing that the Kirk is judge of the true understanding of Scripture. His rendering of its decree (vv 28–29)[10] may be compared with Lorimer's:

Kennedy	Lorimer
It hes plesit	It hes seemed guid
the Haly Gaist and ws,	til the Halie Spírit, an til us,
to putt na uther	tae lay nae
burdyng on zow,	birns on your backs,
	binna thir necessar things—
bot tyil abstayne fra	at ye haud atowre frae
the filthynes of	mait offert til ídols,
ydols blude,	flesh wi the bluid in it,
it that is worreit,	the flesh o wirriet beass,
and fornicatioun,	an hurin.
fra the quhilk	Hae nocht adae wi
ze kepand zow,	thir things,
ze do weill;	an ye will be daein richt.
and weill fair ze.	Fareweill.

Lorimer is often snappier than the sixteenth-century texts, but not invariably, as Acts 3:8–9, after the healing of the cripple at the Beautiful Gate ('Bonnie Yett': Lorimer), illustrates:

Nisbet	Lorimer
And he lap,	an he banged up
and stude,	an stuid steive on his feet,
and yede.	an syne begoud
	traivlin about.
And he entrit with	Than he gaed intil
thame in to the tempile,	the Temple wi them
and yede,	gangin on his feet,
and lap,	spangin,
and louit God.	an ruisin God.
And al the pepile	Aa the fowk
saw him gangand,	saw him gangin on his feet
and louand God.	an ruisin God.

This passage has the added interest that Nisbet made more changes to Purvey's text than usual: 'lap' for 'lippide', 'yede' for 'wandride', and 'gangand' for 'walkinge'.

The Bible in English

English, not Scots, was the language of the vernacular Bibles that fostered religious reform in Scotland. However, the decisive differences between the two in the sixteenth century lay more in speech than in writing. 'English' and 'Scots' could be used interchangeably of the 'vulgar tongue' of Lowland Scotland, not least in reference to vernacular Scripture.[11] Scottish Protestants adopted the Geneva Bible of 1560 as their favoured version. It was the work of English-speaking exiles in Geneva under the lead of William Whittingham. Knox may have had some part in it prior to leaving Geneva in 1559, but his command of Hebrew and Greek was limited.

Between Tyndale's New Testament and the Geneva Bible, English biblical translation had continued almost unbroken. Tyndale's Pentateuch (1530) was followed by his revised New Testament at Antwerp in 1534–5. The first complete English Bible in 1535 was the achievement of Miles Coverdale, who incorporated Tyndale's translations, and for the rest worked from Latin and German. Two years later came 'Matthew's' Bible, based on Coverdale and Tyndale, including the latter's manuscript version of the Old Testament historical books. 'Thomas Matthew' was John Rogers, the first Protestant martyr under Mary in England. The 'Great Bible' of 1539 (extensively revised in 1540) was Coverdale's revision of 'Matthew's', and was ordered to be set up in every parish church in England. The Geneva translators in turn used the 'Great Bible', but also for the first time checked the Hebrew for the parts of the Old Testament not translated by Tyndale.

Most, if not all, of these English versions must have circulated in Scotland. Tyndale's Testament is more readily identifiable in the records than any of the complete Bibles,[12] but basic research in this field has yet to be attempted.

The first Bible to be printed in Scotland is commonly known as the Bassendyne Bible, although it was finally produced in Edinburgh in 1579 by Alexander Arbuthnot, printer to James VI. His associate, Thomas Bassendyne, died in 1577 after preparing the New Testament, whose title page bears his name and the date 1576. This Bible was a straight reprint of the 1562 edition of the Geneva Bible. The considerable merits of this translation, to which the Authorised Version was much indebted, are often forgotten. In C S Lewis' judgement, the Genevan translators, with Tyndale, stand head and shoulders above other early creators of the English Bible tradition.[13]

Scholars have been overly fascinated with Geneva's extensive annotations, which inculcated a strongly Reformed or Calvinist reading of Scripture. This does not prevent them springing some surprises—in commending, for example, the perpetual virginity of Mary. More predictable (but scarcely the sole preserve of Reformed Protestants) is the discernment of the papacy in the Revelation of John. The 'noysome and grieuous sore' of Revelation 16:2 is likened to the sixth plague of Egypt of sores, boils or pox, 'and this reigneth communly among Canons, monkes, friars, nonnes, Priestes and suche filthie vermin, which beare the marke of the beast'. 'It is the Lord's Passeouer' (Exod. 12:11) is the occasion for corrective teaching: 'The lambe was not the Passeouer, but signified it: as sacraments are not the thing it selfe, which thei do represent, but signifie it'.

The attitude of Knox and others to ungodly rulers finds expression at several points. Asa deposed his mother (2 Chron. 15:16), but 'herein he shewed that he lacked zeale: for she oght to haue dyed . . .'. But the vast majority of the notes are useful or necessary explanations or clarifications, often occasioned by the closely literal style of the translation. Nevertheless, the Geneva Bible, with its battery of readers' aids, served to stiffen the Reformed and Puritan ethos of the Kirk after 1560.

The Bassendyne Bible bore an address to James VI from the General Assembly which alerted him to his duties. A copy of it should be kept in every parish kirk 'to be called the commoun buke of the kirke . . . to be made patent to all the people of euerie congregation'. Within a few months an Act of Parliament commanded every householder, yeoman or burgess of substance to have a copy of the Bible and Psalter, on pain of a fine. By this Act the fortunes of the vernacular Bible in Scotland had finally come full circle.

Earlier in the century the possession or study of the Scriptures in the common tongue frequently evoked a charge of heresy. A translated Bible became the commonest demand of the clamour for reform, and derided 'New Testamentars' formed the nucleus of an awakened Church. Chief among the charges against Patrick Hamilton, the proto-martyr of the Scottish Reformation in 1528, was his insistence that it was lawful for everyone to read the Word of God, especially the New Testament. Among those condemned under an Act of 1536 banning the English Bible was Thomas Forret, vicar of Dollar, who was burned before the Castle in Edinburgh in 1539. Forret's regular preaching on the Epistle and the Gospel had provoked George Crichton, the bishop of Dunkeld, to declare: 'I thanke God, that I never knew quhat the Old and New Testament was!'—an utterance that deservedly set a proverbial standard for ignorance.

Some of the exchanges at Forret's trial are worth reproducing[14]:

> *Accuser*: 'Thow fals Heretick! Thow learned all thy parochiners to say ye Pater noster, ye Creed and ye Ten Commandments in Englisch, which is contrare to oure actis, that thay sould knaw what they say'.
>
> *Forret*: 'Brother, my people are so roode and ignorant they vnderstand no Latine. . . . The Apostle Paule sayeth in his doctrine to ye Corinthians, that he haid rather speak fyve words to the understanding and edefeing of his people, then ten thowsand in a strainge tongue whilk they understand not'.
>
> *A*: 'Where finds thow that?'
>
> *F*: 'In my books, heir in my sleife'.
>
> *A*: (grabbing the book): 'Behold, Sirs, he has the booke (of Heresie) in his sleiffe, that makes all the din and play in our Kirk!'
>
> *F*: 'God forgive yow! Ye could say better, if ye pleased, nor to call the book of the Evangell of Jesus Chryst the booke of Heresie!'
>
> *A*: 'Knowes thow not, Heretick, that it is contrare to our acts and expresse commands, to have a New Testament or Byble in Englische, quhilk is eneugh to burne the for?'
>
> Then the counsall of the Clargie gave sentence on him to be Burnt, for the vseing of the same buik—the New Testament in Inglis.

Alexander Alesius: Advocate for the Vernacular Scriptures

An earlier ban by the Scottish bishops provoked a letter of protest to James V from Alexander Alesius, a native of Edinburgh won to Lutheran convictions at St Andrews in 1528. His complaint was published in 1533 somewhere on the continent, whither he had fled from a Scottish prison. His ship had put in at Malmö, where John Gau, likewise an alumnus of St Andrews, may well have been among the Protestants who welcomed him.

Alesius' letter, although written in Latin, is the first known defence of the Scottish people's right to the Word of God in their mother tongue.[15] He accused the bishops (unknown to the King, he is sure) of doing the work of anti-Christian nations like the Turks in keeping the oracles of Christ under wraps. The open availability of the Bible is of a piece with the incarnation itself, which revealed 'mysteries unknown to the world' that God wishes 'to have a high profile, to be seen and handled. . . . To bury or obscure the knowledge of such important matters is more damaging than removing the sun from the cosmos'.

The enemies of a common-language Bible claim to dread that people reading without understanding and without the aid of the professional, will lapse into error. Why not also ban food and wine and money, which some abuse to their injury? There were heresies enough in the early days when the apostles gave instructions for the corporate study of Scripture (an allusion to Colossians 3:16). Peace will ensue in the churches not by suppression but by cultivating godly, learned and wise teachers. In reality, it is not the alleged obscurity of the Scriptures that agitates the bishops, but their crystal clarity, which they know to threaten their own perverse opinions. Divine judgement awaits those who rob the people of God of the teaching of God. Recent celestial phenomena have startled the world, but there is no more awful portent than this law against the sacred writings.

Alesius' plea was speedily countered by another treatise addressed to James V, *Is It Expedient for the Laity to Read the Books of the New Testament in the Vernacular?*,[16] by an inveterate opponent of Lutheranism and Tyndale's New Testament, John Cochlaeus or Dobneck ('he was not fortunate in names', comments C S Lewis). He admits that his is a hapless task—to deny Christian people 'the bread of life and the food of the soul'. But if only the King knew what havoc the vernacular Scriptures had wrought in Germany! Enormous sums of money have been wasted on 'so many hundreds of thousand of copies', to the neglect of family livelihood. Peasant tumult can be expected in

Scotland. Above all, Luther's New Testament (which Cochlaeus mistakenly believed Tyndale had translated into English) is not Holy Scripture. But even an accurate and reliable translation would foster unimaginable evil, and wise shepherds will drive their sheep away from 'pasture so noxious and deadly'. Customs officers must guard against the infiltration of this paper poison.

Alesius' *Reply to the Calumnies of Cochlaeus* (1534) had first to address personal allegations. In any case, the cause of the common Bible needs no extended advocacy. Even if preachers taught purely and faithfully, scriptural study at home would still be necessary for the instruction of the young, among whom Luther's translation has had signal success in Germany. 'Scotland's need for books in the vernacular is greater than Germany's, so deep is the darkness among the Scots.' Alesius' task is not to defend Luther's version: 'I speak of the Scottish, or whatever way it may have been translated by any learned bishop or monk'. Neither of these has ever assailed the fidelity of 'that version which now, for some time past, has existed in the country' (which can only be Tyndale's). 'I have heard even our leading preachers declare that this version gave them far more light than numerous commentaries.' All peoples are dependent on translations: biblical Hebrew and Greek are no longer the vernacular of Jews and Greeks. Nor is our knowledge of these languages so insecure that translation is a hazardous undertaking.

Alesius rests his case at the bar of experience:

> Anyone who brings a serious mind to the Scriptures will realise that not only in the sublimity and sweetness of their teaching but also in their clarity they far excel the rhapsodies of modern divines. The impression of their statements is such that they inflame their readers more than ice-cool disputations, and leave in their minds stings more poignant than even the thunderous and flashing eloquence of Pericles. It has frequently been my experience that when I read over again however well known a passage, I come away from the reading a new person. Either the meaning is made plainer and my attention is caught by something I had not noticed before, or I am profoundly moved in my spirit.

Cochlaeus returned to the fray the same year, charging Philip Melanchthon with being the real author of Alesius' writings. But even if, as is not improbable, Alesius had enlisted Melanchthon's aid, it would not detract one whit from the Scotsman's doughty championship of his countrymen's Bible.

The Campaign in Popular Verse

Although preaching was perhaps the most significant medium of communication of the new biblical gospel, very few sermons of the Scottish Reformers have survived. Nor did they leave behind any body of biblical commentary. We must note another paradox, that in a Reformation frequently lambasted today as the harbinger of a raw philistinism in Scottish culture, drama and verse were powerful carriers of the rediscovered teaching of the Bible.[17] They, rather than Alesius' Latin treatises, took up the hue and cry for the open Bible in the marketplace.

Throughout *The Gude and Godlie Ballatis*, first issued in some form in the mid-1540s by the Wedderburn brothers of Dundee, there runs like a refrain the appeal to Scripture: 'As witnes beiris the trew Scripture', 'As we may reid in Scripture plaine', 'that quhilk Scripture hes exprest'. God is the lord and giver of Scripture: 'I haif spoken in my Scripture', 'As schawis my Scripture'. In 'Remember Man', 'testament' bears an extended meaning:

My New Testament, plaine and gude,
For quhilk I sched my precious blude,
Zour onlie hope and Saulis fude,
    Thay hald for Heresie . . ..
Thair tryflis all ar maid be men,
Quhilk my Gospell did neuer ken,
My law and my Commandementis ten,
Thay hid from mennis eine.
My New Testament thay wald keip downe,
Quhilk suld be preicheit fra towne to towne,
Cause it wald cut thair long taillit gowne,
And schaw thair lyues vnclene.[18]

Another song, 'Of the Greit Louing and Blyithnes of Goddis Word', sounds a note of release, perhaps suggesting a date after the Act of 1543 (see below):

Lord God thy face, and word of grace,
Hes lang bene hid be craft of men,
Quhill at the last, the nycht is past,
And we full weill thair falset ken:
We knaw perfyte, the halie writ,
Thairfoir be gloir and pryse to thé:
Quhilk did vs geue, this tyme to leue,
Thy word trew preichit for to sé.

Sir David Lindsay's *Ane Pleasant Satyre of the Thrie Estaits* was first performed about 1535–40. The conflict over Tyndale's New Testament is felt throughout. The 'Pardoner' (*ie*, seller of pardons or indulgences) laments:

> Of all credence, now I am quyte,
> For, ilk man halds me at dispyte,
> That reids the New Test'ment . . ..

He will have none of it:

> I give to the Devill, with gude intent,
> This unsell wickit New Testament,
> With thame that it translaitit . . ..
> By Him, that buir the crowne of thorne,
> I wald Sanct Paul had never bene borne,
> And als, I wald his buiks,
> War never red in the kirk,
> Bot among freirs, into the mirk,
> or riven among ruiks.[19]

Lindsay's *The Monarchie* was published in 1554. It includes an extended plea for vernacular Scripture, in the form of 'Ane Exclamatioun to the Redar, Twycheyng the Wrytting of Vulgare and Maternall Language'.[20] God did not give Moses the law in Greek or Latin:

> He wrait the Law, in Tablis hard of stone,
> In thare awin vulgare language of Hebrew,
> That all the bairnis of Israell, every one,
> Mycht knaw the Law, and so the same ensew.
> Had he done wryt in Latyne or in Grew,
> It had to thame bene bot ane sawrles jest:
> Ye may weill wytt God wrocht all for the best.

Before the building of Babel, the human race spoke but one tongue, but now 'thre score and twelf'. Christ's sending of the Spirit 'in toungis of fyre' was a sign to his disciples to teach his faith to everyone 'in thare awin leid [language]'. And so Jerome turned Hebrew and Greek 'in Latyne plane', but

> Had Sanct Jerome bene borne in tyll Argyle,
> In to Yrische toung his bukis had done compyle.

Nuns who recite the office without understanding what they are saying are

> . . . lyke one Stirlyng or ane Papingay [parrot],
> Quhilk leirnit ar to speik be lang usage:
> Thame I compair to byrdis in ane cage.

Lindsay's concern extends also to the laws of the realm. Scholars, scientists and even poets may display their skills in Greek or Latin as they please:

> Bot lat us haif the Bukis necessare
>   To Commoun weill and our Salvatioun
> Justlye translatit in our toung Vulgare.

Protestant versifiers did not lay down their pens with the Reformation settlement of 1560. James Anderson, 'minister of the Evangile' at Collessie in Fife, composed around 1580 *The Winter Night*, 'Showing plainly the blindness wherein were misled of in Popery'. It even celebrated the work of Immanuel Tremellius, a converted Italian Jew whose services to the Reformation included new Latin versions from the Hebrew and Syriac. Attitudes to the Bible define the Church:

> That is the true Catholick Kirk,
> Of Gods own word that doth not irk,
> But thereto frames all that they work,
>   Both Faith and fact alswa.[21]

In March 1543, the opposition of the clerical estate notwithstanding, the Scottish Parliament passed an Act making it 'free to all man and woman to reid the Scriptures in thair awin toung, or in the Engliss toung'.[22] 'This was no small victorie of Christ Jesus', was Knox's comment. He may be forgiven a degree of exaggeration:

> Then mycht have bene sein the Byble lying almaist upoun everie gentilmanis table. The New Testament was borne about in many manis handes. . . . Thairby did the knowledge of God wonderouslie increase, and God geve his Holy Spreit to sempill men in great aboundance.

This Act stemmed from the pro-English policy of the early regency of the Earl of Arran, which he soon abandoned. Nevertheless, the Act was never repealed, although its proviso, 'unto such tyme as the Prelattis and Kirk men should geue and sett furth . . . ane translatioun more correct', was never fulfilled. The Scottish bishops in 1546 defiantly ruled that only the Vulgate was to be read and no interpretation given contrary to the teaching of the Church. Possessing a Bible or Testament, or engaging in public dispute about Scripture, might still expose a person to danger, for Cardinal David Beaton

> . . . purposit tyll put to gret torment,
> All favoraris of the Auld and New Testament.[23]

But the swelling lay demand was increasingly satisfied by a deliberate English programme of Bible smuggling across the border. The Bible became one of the bestsellers of the age. Archbishop Hamilton's reformism offered too little, too late. David Panter, bishop of Ross, urged the clergy to avoid argument. Otherwise (as Knox reports it)

> thei will call yow to your compt booke, and that is to the Bible; and by it ye will no more be found the men that ye ar called, then the Devill wilbe approvin to be God. And therefor, yf ye love your selfis, enter never in disputatioun; . . . or ellis all is lost.
>
> (Volume I, p 267)

Knox had the *mot juste*, as ever: even Caiaphas could not have done better.

The Bible in the Reformation Settlement

The uncompromising centrality of Scripture in the foundation documents of the Reformed Church—the Scots Confession of 1560, the *First Book of Discipline* of the same year, and the *Forme of Prayers* or *Book of Common Order* first authorised in 1562—needs only brief illustration. The Confession was approved by Parliament, according to its extended title, 'as Hailsome and Sound Doctrine, Groundit upoun the Infallable Trewth of Godis Word'. Its Preface guarantees to anyone who notes 'any article or sentence repugning to Godis holie word, . . . satisfactioun fra the mouth of God (that is, fra his holy Scriptures), or ellis reformatioun of that quhilk he sall prove to be amyss'. It is a mark of the true Kirk that it 'alwayis heareth and obeyeth the voice of hir awin Spouse and Pastour' in Scripture, whose authority depends on neither Kirk nor angels, but on God. Much of the Confession itself consists of a mosaic of biblical phrases or quotations, taken mostly from the translations of Tyndale or Coverdale, although other influences can be detected. It has also been shown that the Confession illustrates 'how Biblical English, having been *pronounced* as Scots, is then *written*, partly at least, in a restrictedly Scots option by the Scottish scribe or printer'.[24]

The *Forme of Prayers* deals first with the election of ministers. A candidate shall be examined:

> First, as towchying their doctrine, whether he . . . have good and sownde knowlage in the Holy Scriptures, and fitte and apte giftes to communicate the same to the edification of the people. For the triall wherof, they propose hym a theme or text to be treated privatly, wherby his habilitie may the more manifestlie appeare unto them.

'The Order of Public Worship' is arranged around the sermon, and a note 'To the Reader' at the end of 'The Maner of the Lordes Supper', assures the scrupulous that 'without his [Christ's] worde and warrant, there is nothing in this holie action attempted'.[25]

But it is the *First Book of Discipline*[26] which demonstrates how rigorously scriptural the Reformed Church of Scotland would be, in the style of Zurich and Geneva rather than Wittenberg or Lambeth. The Preface, the First Head and the Conclusion frame the *Book* in a reiterated commitment to require only what God requires. The test is 'by Gods plaine Scriptures', 'the expressed commandment of Gods word', which entails that 'all honouring of God, not conteined in his holy word' is idolatry. It is essential for every kirk to have the Bible in English, and for the people to be 'commanded to convene and heare the plaine reading and interpretation of the Scripture'. This was best accomplished by following through, in lection and sermon, one book of the Bible after another from beginning to end, eschewing the 'skipping and divagation from place to place of Scripture' of the old lectionary.

Every week in each town the ministers and elders are to assemble for a corporate Bible study called, from 1 Corinthians 14:29–32, 'prophesying', designed to advance the understanding of Scripture. It is strictly laid down that 'the Interpreter in this exercise may not take to himself the liberty of a publick Preacher . . . but he must bind himselfe to his text. . . .[and] be short, that the time may be spent in opening the minde of the Holy Ghost in that place; following the sequele and dependance of the text'. Such prophesying had its home in Zurich and Geneva. One of its presuppositions is the Confession's assertion that the interpretation of Scripture 'neather apperteaneth to privat nor publict persone'. No one is sufficient of himself to plumb the depths of Scripture.

John Knox: Language and Bible

The major draughtsman of these official manifestoes of the Reformed Church was John Knox. Critics from his own day onwards have lamented his influential neglect of the Scots tongue.[27] None of his writings is in pure Scots, but then we have no evidence of his language prior to his English period. All his works display some measure of Anglicisation, from the almost complete Englishness of his controversial treatises, such as the *First Blast of the Trumpet against the Monstrous Regiment of Women*, to the Scots-English mixture in his later *History of the Reformation of Religion within the Realm of Scotland*. Even after his final return to Scotland, he apparently made no attempt to re-Scotticise his language. One of his Catholic opponents, Ninian Winzet, reproached him in 1563:

> Gif ze, throw curiositie of nouationis, hes forzet our auld plane Scottish quhilk zour mother lerit zou, in tymes cuming I sall wryte to zou my mind in Latin, for I am nocht acquyntit with zour Southeroun.[28]

Basic research still has far to go in this territory, and a critical edition of Knox's works is sorely needed. In particular, the contribution of transcribers, editors and printers to the published texts requires careful evaluation.

Knox saw himself, particularly in the task of expounding the Bible, as chiefly called to teach 'by tong and livelye voyce' rather than 'to compose bokes for the age to come', as he put it in the preface to his sermon on Isaiah 26:13–21 (Volume VI, p 229). The reader should not be surprised 'that of al my studye and travayle within the Scriptures of God these twentye yeares, I have set forth nothing in exponing anye portion of Scripture, except this onely rude and indigest Sermon. That I did not in writ communicat my judgement upon the Scriptures, I have ever thought and yet thinke my selfe to have most just reason'. In fact, some of Knox's other writings are based more or less directly on the spoken word, and oral techniques are easily recognisable in controversial treatises and pastoral letters alike.

Although Knox presumably used the Geneva Bible as soon as it became available, no study has been attempted of his use of earlier English versions.[29] A cursory examination of a few works suggests that he rarely cited *verbatim* from a single translation. Even his 1565 sermon on Isaiah 26, although never far from the Geneva Bible's text, introduces several minor variations. A thorough investigation of Knox's Bible prior to 1560 might cast new light on his methods as a writer and scholar, although it will be at least as difficult as tracing the development of his language. Editors and printers may have thought it entirely proper to assimilate Knox's earlier biblical texts to the Genevan version.

Even the most superficial perusal of Knox's works cannot overlook his unrivalled regard for the Bible. He is forever talking about 'submitting' to the 'plain, expresse, simple, evident, manifest, native' meaning of the Scriptures. They are, he told Queen Mary, 'the tuichstone to try the rycht from the wrang'. The old religion, especially the mass, must be 'laid to the squair-reull of Goddis worde'. It would allow no equivocation:

> In religioun thair is no middis: either it is the religioun of God, and that in everie thing that is done it must have the assurance of his awn Word, and than is his Majestie trewlie honourit, or els it is the religioun of the Divill.

> (Volume IV, p 232)

Nor was Knox daunted when Mary taxed him with the difficulty of choosing between divergent interpretations:

> Ye shall beleve God, that planelie speaketh in his word: and farther than the word teaches you, ye neather shall beleve the ane or the other. The word of God is plane in the self; and yf thair appear any obscuritie in one place, the Holy Ghost, whiche is never contrariouse to him self, explanes the same more clearlie in other places.

> (Volume II, p 284)

'The Commoun Buke of the Kirke'

The indispensability of the Bible meant that, when preaching was still fettered, ways had to be found to give it voice. In *A Letter of Wholesome Counsel* (Volume IV, pp 129–40), written shortly before he left Scotland in 1556, Knox advised his countrymen

> touchinge the exercise of God's mooste sacred and holy Woorde, without which, neither shal knowledge encrease, godlines appeare, nor fervencye contynewe amongest you.

Taking his cue from Deuteronomy 6:6–9, he exhorts them to 'Let no daye slyppe or want some comfort receyved from the mouth of God'. The head of the house should recognise that 'your wyfe, chyldren, servauntes, and familye are youre bishopryke and charge . . . ye must make them partakers in readyng, exhorting, and in makyng common prayers, which I would in every house wer used once a day at least'. Furthermore, 'I thynke it necessary for the conference of Scriptures, assemblies of brethren be had', for which the pattern was set by 1 Corinthians 14:265ff:

> Hereof I doubt not but greate profet shall shortly ensue: for, first, by hearing, readyng, and conferryng the Scriptures in the assemblie, the hole body of the Scriptures of God shall become familiar, the judgements and sprites of men shall bee tryed, their pacience and modesty shalbe knowen; and, finally their gifts and utterance shall appeare.

'Multiplication of wordes, prolixet interpretaciouns, and wilfulnese in reasoning' must be strictly avoided. Knox is aware of the temptation that 'within the simple Scriptures of God the perpetuall repetition of one thinge is fashious and werysome'. He adds some practical guidance, for example, in studying books of both Testaments, in order 'to heire that harmony and weill-tuned song of the Holie Sprite speiking in oure fartheris frome the begynnyng'. Insoluble difficulties are to be recorded, and addressed to an available 'interpreter' in person or by letter, to such as Knox himself:

> I wyll more gladly spende xv. houres in communicatyng my judgemente with yow, in explanyng as God pleases to open to me any place of Scripture, then halfe ane houre in any matter besyd.

The *Forme of Prayers* envisages a similar practice of corporate Bible study:

> Everie weeke once, the Congregation assemble to heare some place of the Scriptures orderly expounded. At which tyme, it is lawfull for every man to speake or enquire, as God shall move his harte, and the text minister occasion.[30]

Should a contentious issue arise, it was to be referred to the ministers or elders. The Lords of Congregation had similarly resolved in 1558 that:

> It is thought necessare, that doctrin, preacheing, and intepretatioun of Scriptures be had and used privatlie in qwyet houssis, without great conventionis of the people tharto, whill afterward that God move the Prince to grant publict preacheing be faithfull and trew ministeris.
>
> (Volume I, pp 275f)

Many impulses of religious renewal in Scotland combined to promote the shared unfolding of the Scriptures in the home and in informal assemblies, whether or not minister or elder could be present. From the 'New Testamentars' and Alesius to Knox's *Letter of Wholesome Counsel* and the *Forme of Prayers*, the Scottish reform evinced an inexorable demand that the Bible be 'the commoun buke of the kirke'. The vernacular Bible had to be not merely read but actively explained and expounded. The *First Book of Discipline* declared preaching of the Word to be 'utterly necessarie' but reading merely 'profitable'. 'The reading of the Word ceased to be a distinct devotional act. It was absorbed into the pulpit and, as every form of worship took on the pulpit tone, the Bible underwent a subtle process of fermentation.'[31] The Scottish Reformation rediscovered the Bible not for liturgical recitation, but for common apprehension of its mind and message. Undergirding this pursuit was the conviction, writ large throughout the writings of John Knox, that the meaning of Scripture was plain and simple.

Those who took Knox's *Wholesome Counsel* to heart would not be unaware of the risks. In 1550 Adam Wallace, 'a sempill man, without great learnyng', was burned for heresy (Volume I, pp 237ff, 545). At his trial in Edinburgh it was charged 'That he took upoun him to preach'. The exchange continued as follows:

> He answered, 'That he never judged himself worthy of sa excellent a vocatioun, and tharefoir he never took upoun him to preach; but he would not deny, butt sometymes at the table, and sometymes in other prevey places, he wald reid, and had red the Scriptures . . ..'
>
> 'Knave (quod ane), what have ye to do to medle with Scriptures?'
>
> 'I think (said he) it is the dewitie of everie Christiane to seak the will of his God, and the assurance of his salvatioun, whare it is to be found, and that is within his Old and New Testament.'
>
> 'What then (said ane other), shall we leave to the Bischoppis and Kirkmen to do, yf everie man shalbe a babler upoun the Byble?'

It is worth noting that Wallace had 'a Bible at his belte, in French, Dutch, and English'—but not Scots! Two years after Knox's *Letter*, Walter Myln, a priest 'of decrepite age' in his early eighties, was likewise martyred. Among the allegations he faced was, 'Thou preachest quietly and priuatly in houses and openly in the fields', to which Myln replied, 'Yea man, and on the sea also sailyng in shyp'. He had been apprehended 'in ane poore womans house in Dysart . . . teichand hir the commandis of god to hir and hir bairnes and leirand hir how scho sould instruct hir house to bring wpe hir bairnes in the feir of god'.[32] His prayer that he would be the last to suffer death for such a cause in Scotland was indeed to be answered.

Knox the Prophetic Expositor

John Knox has been frequently depicted as a man of the Old Testament—recently by contrast with New Testament Reformers like Erskine of Dun. He believed that God 'made my tong a trumpet, to forwarne realmes and nations, yea, certaine great personages, of translations and chaunges, when no such thinges were feared, nor yet was appearing' (Volume VI, p 229). He saw himself as a prophet and the struggle for pure religion as 'the drama of the Old Testament re-enacted in Scotland, with himself as Moses, Joshua, Isaiah, Jeremiah, Ezekiel and Daniel rolled into one'.[33] It followed, of course, that he cast some of his contemporaries as other Old Testament characters. Mary, Queen of Scots was none other than Jezebel and Athaliah, Ahab's daughter. God would 'eyther destroy that hoore in hir hurdome, or ellis he shall putt it in the harttis of a multitude, to tak the same vengeance upoun hir, that hes bein tane of Jesabell and Athalia' (Volume I, p 218).

The application of biblical precedents could be keenly contested. Against William Maitland of Lethington, Knox argued that Jehu, who was anointed to wreak divine vengeance on Ahab's house (2 Kings 9:1–10), was at the time 'ane meir subject' and no king (Volume II, pp 445ff). Nor was Jehu's action strictly inimitable, for God's unalterable law requires the death of the idolater. Hence:

> whair the exampill aggreis with the law, and is, as it wer, the executioun of Godis jugementis expressit in the same, I say, that the exampill approved of God standis to us in place of a commandiment.

If it is objected that the apostles did not treat idolatrous Gentiles as Jehu did the house of Ahab, Knox counters that once the Gentiles embraced Christ they became bound to the same obedience exacted of Israel. The case of Deborah, on the other hand, did not justify 'the monstrous regiment [rule] of women', for no example can establish a law.

Knox did not always have to make the historical equation explicit. His sermon on Isaiah 26 was attended by Mary's new husband, now King—Lord Darnley. When he touched on Ahab's punishment for failing to bring to order 'that harlot Jezabel', Darnley made the connection himself. Coupled with the inordinate length of the sermon, it quite put him off his food, and he had to go a-hawking to work off his anger. Knox was banned from preaching for a couple of weeks.

But if Knox (and the Geneva Bible) took their political theology from the Old Testament, the New Testament came into its own in other contexts, especially of a pastoral kind. In particular, it provided guidance for the demeanour of the godly under persecution. *A Faythfull Admonition . . . unto the professours of Gods truthe in England* applies Jesus' stilling of the storm (Matthew 8:23–27) directly to the plight of the faithful in England under their Queen Mary in 1554 (Volume III, pp 274, 294f):

> Consider and marke, beloved in the Lord, what we reade here to have chaunsed, to Christes disciples, and to their poore bote; and you shal wel perceave, that the same thynge hath chaunsed, dothe, and shal chaunse, to the true churche and congregation of Christe (whiche is nothing els in this miserable lyfe but a poore bote) travelyng in the seas of this unstable and troublesome world, towarde the heavenly porte and haven of eternal felicite.

Knox makes delightful play with contemporary depictions of Mary as 'Ladye Marye', 'Mary the virgine', 'most blessed Virgine'. 'Let her be your virgine, and a goddes mete to maintaine such idolatrers.' Even Jezebel 'never erected halfe so many gallowes in al Israel as myschevous Mary hath done within London alone'.

Knox's language is shot through with biblical phrases and echoes, with an almost unconscious impregnation. Pierre Janton illustrates this from a passage in *A Brief Exhortation to England for the Spedie Imbrasing of Christs Gospel* (1558):[34]

> I neither looked, nor could beleve, that the Lord Jesus wolde so suddainly knocke at thy gate, or call upon thee in thy open stretes, offring himself to pardon thy iniquitie: yea, to enter into thy house, and so to abyde and make his habitation with thee, who so inobediently had rejected his yoke, so disdainfully had troden under fote the bloode of the testament, and so cruelly had murthered those that were sent to call thee to repentance.

This is almost wholly a mosaic of expressions and allusions from, in succession, Revelation 3:20, Proverbs 1:20, John 14:23 and Revelation 3:20, Matthew 11:29, Hebrews 10:29 and Luke 11:47–48.

What begins in Knox's writings is that intensive informing of the common language of Scotland with the language of the Bible. It was admittedly the Bible in English and not in Scots. If blame there be on such a score, the Reformers cannot escape from their failure to give Scotland a truly vernacular Bible. Nevertheless, they set the Bible, in a sufficiently vulgar tongue, on its way to become 'the commoun buke' not only of the Kirk but also of the people of Scotland. 'The Bible seems to have attained almost at once, in a dramatic resurgence, a quite unique hold on the Scots imagination and mind'.[35]

DAVID F WRIGHT

Notes

1   In a sermon on 10 March 1552: *Luther's Works*, J Pelikan and H T Lehmann (eds), vol 51 (translated by J W Doberstein; Philadelphia, 1959), pp 77–8.

2   G R Elton, *Reformation Europe 1517–1559* (London, 1963), p 52.

3   See especially John Lee, *Memorial for the Bible Societies in Scotland* (Edinburgh, 1824) and *Additional Memorial on Printing and Importing Bibles* (Edinburgh, 1826); Christopher Anderson, *The Annals of the English Bible*, vol 2 (London, 1845).

4   T G Law (ed), *The New Testament in Scots*, 3 vols (Scottish Text Society, Edinburgh, 1901–5). Cf. T M Lindsay, 'A Literary Relic of Scottish Lollardy', *Scottish Historical Review* 1 (1904), pp 260–73.

5   M Robinson, 'Language Choice in the Reformation: The Scots Confession of 1560', in J D McClure (ed), *Scotland and the Lowland Tongue. Studies . . . in Honour of David M. Murison* (Aberdeen, 1983), p 61.

6   A F Mitchell (ed), *The Richt Vay to the Kingdom of Heuine* (Scott. Text Society, Edinburgh, 1888), p 67.

7   T G Law (ed), *The Catechism of John Hamilton Archbishop of St. Andrews 1552* (Oxford, 1884), pp 174–5.

8   Ibid., p 249 (Hamilton); op.cit. (note 4 above), vol 1, p 34 (Nisbet); op.cit. (note 6 above), p 82 (Gau); A F Mitchell (ed), *A Compendious Book of Godly and Spiritual Songs Commonly Known as 'The Gude and Godlie Ballatis'* (Scottish Text Society, Edinburgh, 1897), p 4.

9   *The New Testament in Scots*, tr W L Lorimer (revised edition) (Harmondsworth, 1985), p i.

10   D Laing (ed), *The Miscellany of the Wodrow Society*, vol 1 (Edinburgh, 1844), pp 95–174, at p 106.

11   Robinson, art.cit. (note 5 above), pp 59%f.

12   Only the OT section of 'Matthew's' Bible (1551 printing) is recorded in

J Durkan and A Ross, *Early Scottish Libraries* (Glasgow, 1961), p 158. This work lists only extant books.

13 There is a facsimile of the 1560 edition, L E Berry (ed) (Madison, 1969). Cf. B Hall, *The Genevan Version of the English Bible* (London, 1957); G Hammond, *The Making of the English Bible* (New York, 1983); C S Lewis, *English Literature in the Sixteenth Century* (Oxford, 1954), pp 210f.

14 R Pitcairn, *Ancient Criminal Trials in Scotland* (Bannatyne Club, Edinburgh), vol I:1 (1833), pp *210–*215.

15 Translated extracts in Anderson, op.cit. (note 3 above), vol 2, pp 430–7. On Alesius, A F Mitchell, *The Scottish Reformation* (Edinburgh, 1900).

16 Anderson, op.cit., vol 2, pp 438–41, and, for the subsequent exchanges, pp 444–65 and 465–7.

17 See the chapter in this volume by Sarah Carpenter.

18 Op.cit. (note 8 above), pp 200, 202. The next quotation is from p 55.

19 D Laing (ed), *The Poetical Works of Sir David Lindsay*, 3 vols (Edinburgh, 1879), vol 2, pp 106–7 (lines 2069–71, 2054–6, 2078–83).

20 Ibid., vol 2, pp 246–51. The quotations are from lines 559–65, 593, 603, 607, 624, 627–8, 612–4, 678–80.

21 J Anderson, *The Winter Night* (Glasgow, 1713), pp 21, 16.

22 D Laing (ed), *The Works of John Knox*, 6 vols (Edinburgh, 1846–64), vol I, pp 100f. Subsequent references, in text or notes, by volume and page alone, are to this edition.

23 Lindsay, *The Tragedie of the . . . Cardinall*, D Laing (ed) (note 19 above), vol 1, p 147 (lines 216–7).

24 Robinson, art.cit., pp 61f. Quotations from edition in vol II, pp 93, 96, 111f. W I P Hazlitt, 'The Scots Confession 1560: Context, Complexion and Critique', *Archiv für Reformationsgeschichte* 78 (1987), pp 299f.

25 *The Liturgy of John Knox* (Glasgow, 1886), pp 17, 146. This edition refrains from modernising the spelling.

26 J K Cameron (ed), *The First Book of Discipline* (Edinburgh, 1972), pp 86, 88, 208, 95, 185f., 187–91.

27 J H Millar, *A Literary History of Scotland* (London, 1903), pp 133–45; M A Bald, 'The Pioneers of Anglicized Speech in Scotland', *Scott.Hist.Rev.* 24 (1926–7), pp 182–4; D M Murison, *Knox the Writer* (Edinburgh, 1975) – also in D Shaw (ed), *John Knox: A Quatercentenary Reappraisal* (Edinburgh, 1975).

28 *Certain Tractates . . .* , J K Hewison (ed), (Scottish Text Society, Edinburgh), vol 1 (1888), p 138.

29 As has been done for John Erskine of Dun by F D Bargett, *Faith, Families and Factions : The Scottish Reformation in Angus and the Mearns* (PhD thesis, University of Edinburgh, 1987), pp 310–4.

30 *The Liturgy of John Knox*, pp 22f.

31 Lord Eustace Percy, *John Knox* (2nd edition) (London, 1964), p 165.

32 Vol I, pp 308, 553: Robert Lindesay of Piscottie, *The Historie and Chronicles of Scotland*, A J G Mackay (ed) (Scottish Text Society, Edinburgh, 1899), vol II, p 130.

33   Murison, op.cit. (note 27 above), p 11.
34   Vol V, p 503, P Janton, *John Knox (ca.1513–1572), L'homme et l'oeuvre* (Paris, n.d.), pp 481–3.
35   G Johnston, 'Scripture in the Scottish Reformation', *Canadian Journal of Theology* 8 (1962), p 250.

Further Reading

C Anderson, *The Annals of the English Bible*, vol 2 (London, 1845).

G Christie, *The Influence of Letters on the Scottish Reformation* (Edinburgh, 1908).

W T Dobson, *History of the Bassendyne Bible* (Edinburgh, 1887).

G D Henderson, 'The Exercise', *Records of the Scottish Church History Society* 7 (1941), pp 13–29.

G D Henderson, 'John Knox and the Bible', *Records of the Scottish Church History Society* 9 (1946), pp 97–110.

G Johnston, 'Scripture in the Scottish Reformation', *Canadian Journal of Theology* 8 (1962), pp 249–57, and 9 (1963), pp 40–49.

R G Kyle, *The Mind of John Knox*, (Lawrence, Kansas, 1984).

12

The Bible and Social Change in the
Nineteenth-Century Highlands

In 1801 the translation of the Bible into Scottish Gaelic was brought to completion. This important literary achievement stands at the beginning of a century of great significance for the Highland people. In the course of the century, many Highlanders emigrated, as famine and clearance cut through the fabric of traditional society, and the bonds which once linked them to their leaders were severed by commercial landlordism. Not all Highlanders had to face the horror of enforced clearance; some were enticed to leave the Highlands by the brighter prospects which were offered by the New World of Canada and the more remote continent of Australia, to which many ventured after 1836. Those who remained in the Highlands were, however, able to witness a resurgence of Highland spirit towards the end of the century, when the tensions and frustrations which had been created before 1870 issued in the campaign for crofters' rights commonly known as the 'land agitation'.[1]

Into this world of change the Gaelic Bible brought a new religious enthusiasm. The nineteenth century was undoubtedly the period when the Gaelic Bible entered the deepest consciousness of Highland people. It did so primarily through two channels. The first of these was the Gaelic school movement, which aimed to make the Highlanders sufficiently literate to read the Bible in their own tongue. The second channel was the preaching of Evangelical ministers and roving evangelists, whose spiritual emphasis lay on personal accountability before God. Through the schools and the preachers, deep spiritual movements or 'awakenings' broke out in different parts of the Highlands until the end of the century. Mass gatherings of Highlanders attended open-air celebrations of the Lord's Supper, as happened in Skye in 1842. In that year a major awakening occurred throughout the island in the prelude to the Disruption of 1843, when the majority of

Highlanders left the Established Church of Scotland and joined the Free Church.[2]

For the Highland people, however, the Bible was not only the book which laid bare their hearts before God; it was also the book in which they could read about a chosen people whose history could be seen to be parallel to their own, in spiritual, social and even political terms. The Old Testament contained an account of God's people, Israel, who came to occupy Canaan initially in the time of the patriarchs. Their subsequent bondage in Egypt was relieved by the exodus and their re-entry into the promised land of Canaan. At a later stage these same people were carried into bondage in Babylon, and only a remnant were allowed to return to Jerusalem. The impending distress of the nation in exile was the message of prophets such as Isaiah and Jeremiah, whose strong words condemned the excesses of earthly rulers and the breaking of God's covenant by his people. The New Testament offered the Highland people the means of becoming, through Christ's sacrifice, a part of God's continuing remnant, the spiritual Israel, whose existence was not confined to Canaan.

The Promised Land

The Bible provided a model by which Highland history could be interpreted, and it offered a guide by which devout Highlanders could respond to the changing society to which they belonged. This can be seen in several ways. For some Highlanders, the challenge of moving from the Highlands to the New World could be envisaged in terms of the exodus, in which Moses led the Israelites to the promised land. The Highlands, as a land of oppression, were comparable with Egypt, and the leaders of emigrant groups could be compared with Moses. The evidence indicates that such equations were being made in the Highlands even before 1800, and not only in Protestant circles. One of the earliest instances of such parallelism occurs in a Gaelic poem composed in honour of a priest, Father Alexander ('Scotus') MacDonell, who led a group of Knoydart emigrants to Glengarry County, Ontario, in 1786. The poetess, Anna Gillis, describes him thus:

> Maighstir Alasdair òg,
> Mac Fear Scotais na sròil,
> Sagart beannaicht' bha mór le éibhneas.

Dh'fhalbh e leinne mar naomh
Gus ar beatha bhi saor,
Mar dh'fhalbh iad le Maois o'n Eipheit.

('Young Father Alexander, son of Scotus of the banners, the holy priest,
was full of kindness.
    'Like a saint he brought us out so that we would be free, as were
those who followed Moses out of Egypt.')[3]

The promised land is here identified clearly with bountiful Upper
Canada. The route to this promised land was, however, beset by
danger, not least by the crossing of the Atlantic. Here too the
paradigm of the exodus could be invoked to demonstrate God's power
in removing obstacles and hazards from his people's path. A Strath-
glass poet, Donald Chisholm, who emigrated to Nova Scotia in 1803,
cited the crossing of the Red Sea as an example of God's power, from
which his emigrant group could take heart:

Na biodh eagal oirbh mu'n chuan;
Faicibh mar sgoilt a' Mhuir Ruadh;
Tha cumhachdan an Tì tha shuas
An diugh cho buan 's an ceud là.

('Do not fear the sea; observe how the Red Sea was divided. The powers
of God above are as strong today as on the very first day).'[4]

By the Rivers of Babylon

Like Egypt and the exodus, the exile of the Hebrews in Babylon was
associated with thralldom and oppression. The condition of the
Highland people could therefore be compared with that of the
Hebrews in exile, especially since some Highlanders were compelled
to emigrate. In the 1870s, John Smith of Iarsiadar, Lewis, composed a
major poem entitled 'Spiorad a' Charthannais' ('The Spirit of
Kindliness'), in which he offered an explanation of the plight of the
contemporary Highlands. Smith's viewpoint is strongly influenced by
Christian values, and his main argument is that kindness and
consideration had been replaced by oppression and exploitation.
Matters had reached such a pass that the condition of the Highlanders,
according to Smith, was even worse than that of the exile:

A chionn nach faoidte 'm bàthadh,
Chaidh an sgànradh thar a' chuain;

Bu mhiosa na bruid Bhàbiloin
An càradh sin a fhuair.

('Since they could not be drowned, they were sent fleeing in terror over
the ocean; the predicament which came to them was worse than the
Babylonian captivity).'[5]

The exile in Babylon naturally implied separation from the homeland,
and it is not surprising to find that the parallel could be applied in the
emigrant context, usually by Highlanders remaining in Scotland who
were parted from their relatives because of emigration. A rather
touching and specific example of this is found in a letter sent in 1838 by
Donald MacLean—'An Cùpair' ('The Cooper')—in Tiree, to his
brother, John MacLean, Bard to the Laird of Coll, who had emigrated
to Nova Scotia, and had settled at Barney's River. The Cooper had not
been in touch with his brother for at least two years, but in 1838 he
received a booklet of Gaelic hymns which had been composed by the
Bard. Receipt of the book, he says,

. . . rejoiced us to understand that you are yet living. And more so when
we heard the tuneful sound of your Lyre turned Spiritually. And though
in a foreign land that you could Sing of the Songs of Jehovah. So near the
foreign Streams of Babilon (or at the Streams of Barney).[6]

The reference here is, of course, to Psalm 137: 'By the rivers of
Babylon, there we sat down, yea, we wept, when we remembered
Zion. We hanged our harps upon the willows in the midst thereof. For
there they that carried us away captive required of us a song; and they
that wasted us required of us mirth, saying, Sing us one of the songs of
Zion'.

Hopes of Return

In the scheme of biblical history, the exile in Babylon was followed by
the return of the remnant to Jerusalem. The return is described in the
Old Testament books of Ezra and Nehemiah, and it was the culmination of a prophecy that the Lord would 'turn again the captivity of
Zion'. The fulfilment of this prophecy is commemorated in Psalm 126,
which begins, 'When the Lord turned again the captivity of Zion, we
were like them that dream', and concludes, 'He that goeth forth and
weepeth, bearing precious seed, shall doubtless come again with
rejoicing, bringing his sheaves with him'. This inspired some

Highlanders to prophesy that their fellow Highlanders, now in foreign lands, would return to the Highlands and to a propitious future. Indeed, certain latter-day Highland 'prophets' were prepared to believe that the whole process of social change within the Highlands, including landlords' improvements and emigration itself, were but the preparation for the great day when the Highlanders would return to their homeland. This was the opinion of John Mackintosh, the pastor of Lochgilphead Baptist Church, when he wrote his 1854 dispatch to the Baptist Home Missionary Society for Scotland:

> Some districts of the country, formerly inhabited by hundreds of industrious people, are made a comparative wilderness, under sheep and black cattle, generally occupied by Low-Country tacksmen, or in the hands of the proprietors. In some instances, where proprietors are wealthy and able, great improvements are made on the soil, in draining and cultivating the land, preparing the face of the earth for the glorious days and generations forthcoming, for the captivity of our land [*ie*, those taken captive from our land] will return, and the ruined and waste places will be built and inhabited, more so than in the days of old.[7]

Although Mackintosh was writing in 1854, the possibility that the exiled Highlanders would return to reoccupy their territory remained alive until the end of the century, and may even have been encouraged by the successes which were gained by crofters in the 1880s. In fact, this prophetic view of Highland history finds its fullest expression in the verse of Mary MacPherson—'Màiri Mhór nan Oran' ('Big Mary of the Songs')—who championed the crofters' cause in the 1870s and 1880s. In her poem, 'Fàistneachd agus Beannachd do na Gàidheil' ('A Prophecy and a Blessing for the Gaels'), she expressed herself thus:

'S nuair bhios mise 'sna bòrdaibh,
Bidh mo chòmhradh mar fhàistneachd.

'S tillidh gineal na tuatha
Rinneadh fhuadach thar sàile.

'S bidh na baigearan uasal
Air an ruaig mar bha iadsan.

Am cur is ám buana,
'S ám duais dha na meàirlich.

'S théid na tobhtachan fuara
Thogail suas le ar càirdean.

('When I shall be in coffin-boards, my comments will be like a prophecy.

'The descendants of those who were driven overseas will return.

'And the noble beggars will be routed, just as they [*ie*, the exiled crofters] were.

'There will be a time to sow and a time to reap, and a time to reward the robbers.

'And the cold ruined walls will be rebuilt by our kinsmen).'[8]

Such prognostication represents a remarkable fusion of Judaic and Highland perspectives, and contains an idealistic view of the degree to which the emigrant tide might be reversed. There is little evidence that emigrant Highlanders themselves anticipated a day when they would return to their homeland. Indeed, some went as far as to thank God that he had contrived circumstances conducive to their emigration. Hugh MacCorquodale, an Islayman who emigrated to Grey County, Ontario, about 1850, composed a Gaelic poem in which the following verse occurs:

> Bheir mi nis anns a' chomh-dhùnadh
> Cliù do rìgh nan àirdean,
> A dh'fhosgail dhuinne dùthaich ùr
> 'Us cùisean tha gu'r fàbhar.
> Faodaidh duine cur 'us buain
> Gun uamhas romh na màil orr'
> 'S do'n duine bhochd chan 'eil fo'n ghréin
> 'Ga fheum aon tìr as fheàrr dha.

('Now in conclusion I will give praise to the God above, who opened up for us a new country and circumstances favourable to us. People may sow and reap without dread of rents, and for the poor man there is not under the sun a land better suited to his needs'). [9]

The Journey of Faith

As our earlier discussion of the exodus theme indicates, Highlanders not infrequently left their homeland with the conviction that they were being guided to the promised land. Sometimes, however, their journey to the New World was compared to the foundational expeditions of the Old Testament patriarchs, especially Abraham and Jacob. The patriarchal narratives not only provided comfort for those who may have felt that they were venturing into the unknown, but they also reinforced a sense of the sovereignty of God in the affairs of men. Indeed, sermons which emphasised these points were sometimes preached on board emigrant ships in Highland harbours in the emotionally charged hours before sailing. In his essay, 'Long Mhór nan Eilthireach' ('The Emigrant Ship'), composed in the early 1830s, the Revd Dr Norman MacLeod provides a vivid account of such preaching on board an emigrant ship in Tobermory Bay. The preacher addresses his faint-hearted audience with these questions:

> Am bheil sibh a' dol na's fhaide o Dhia, na bha sibh riamh? . . . Cò 'sheas le Abraham 'n uair a dh' fhàg e 'thìr 's a dhaoine? Cò a thaisbein e féin do Iacob, 'n uair a dh' fhàg e tigh 'athar, 's a chaidil e 'muigh air an raon?

> ('Are you going farther away from God than you have ever been before? . . . Who stood by the side of Abraham when he left his land and his people? Who revealed himself to Jacob when he left his father's house, and slept outside on the plain?')[10]

New Testament texts and themes could also be used in this context. In 1829 a body of people were cleared from Mid Sannox, Arran, to make way for a sheep farm. These people were associated with the Congregational Church in Sannox, whose pastor was Alexander MacKay. Before they left Lamlash on a voyage which was to take them to Megantic County, Quebec, MacKay preached to them on the text, 'Casting all your care upon him; for he careth for you' (1 Peter 5:7).[11] The choice of a text from the First Epistle of Peter is probably significant, since it is addressed to 'the strangers scattered throughout' several parts of the Roman Empire. These 'strangers' were Christian believers, and the 'scattering' of the early Church, frequently through persecution, is a recurrent theme in the New Testament. For Congregationalists and Baptists in the nineteenth-century Highlands, such 'scattering' may have had a particular application in the context of emigration. The texts found on the gravestones of some of those settlers in Canada make it clear that they regarded themselves as 'strangers and pilgrims' (Heb. 11:13) in the New World. It is also apparent that Baptists, and probably Congregationalists, regarded emigration as an opportunity to take the Christian gospel to other lands, and that this consideration was a comfort to Highland pastors whose congregations were seriously weakened by emigration.[12]

In the context of migration and the uncertainties of moving from one land to another, the Bible offered consolation and encouragement to peoples other than Highlanders. English colonists who entered

North America as early as 1609 had, in some instances, a sense of divine destiny which they compared with that of the Old Testament patriarchs.[13] It is also claimed (although sometimes disputed) that the Afrikaners of South Africa regarded themselves as a chosen people; when attempting to escape from British domination of the Cape in the 1830s, they equated their Great Trek northwards with the exodus. From such an equation, it is said, there arose the Afrikaner sense of national superiority.[14] There is no evidence that the espousal of biblical comparisons gave any such sense of superiority to emigrant Highlanders. At most, the evidence might suggest that the Bible strengthened the resolve of Highland emigrants by reinforcing a sense of God's all-pervasive sovereignty, regardless of circumstances. It could therefore be argued that the Bible helped to weaken the Gaelic-speaking communities of the Highlands, at the same time as it helped to build new communities overseas. Yet, there is equally compelling evidence to indicate that the Bible contributed power and confidence to the strong reaction against oppressive landlordism which emerged in the Highlands in the 1870s, and which attempted to halt the emigrant tide. Indeed, it is no exaggeration to claim that the Bible was a key document in the success of the movement for crofters' rights and its culmination in the passing of the Crofters' Holdings (Scotland) Act of 1886.

Out of Bondage

The use of the Bible in attacking the policies of Highland landlords is attested from the early nineteenth century. The Revd Lachlan Mackenzie of Lochcarron, a celebrated Evangelical minister who died in 1819, preached a series of anti-landlord sermons on the text, 'Woe unto them that join house to house, that lay field to field, till there be no place, that they may be placed alone in the midst of the earth!' (Isa. 5:8). In the 1820s dissenting itinerant preachers in Perthshire were alleged to have compared local landlords to 'the taskmasters of Egypt'. It was not, however, until the 1880s that an attempt was made to provide a systematic, but highly selective, anthology of biblical passages and texts which could be used to encourage the crofting people to fight against their landlords. The chief architect of this anthology was apparently John Murdoch, one of the main leaders of the crofters, and the editor of the radical *Highlander* newspaper. Most of the material in Murdoch's pamphlet of 1833, *The Land Question Answered from the Bible*, was derived from the Pentateuch, and it advocated an application of the Mosaic law to the Highlands.

Highlanders, and especially those who were familiar with covenant theology, were generally susceptible to such arguments. The parallel with the children of Israel was attractive, as a crofter from Raasay showed when he gave evidence before the Napier Commission in 1833:

> It is with the view of getting deliverance from bondage that we have come here today. The Israelites before us were in bondage but there is One above who heard the sighing of those in bondage and fixed the time for their deliverance.[15]

The parallel could be pressed to the extreme of urging the removal of the landlord class, or its more rapacious representatives, from the Highlands. The Revd Donald MacCallum, a parish minister successively in Arisaig, Skye, Tiree and Lewis, and the most forceful of the group of clergymen who advocated the crofters' cause, was alleged to have suggested the slaying of the Egyptian by Moses (Exod. 2:11–15) as a parallel for action in the Highlands. One of his speeches is said to have contained the challenge, 'Have you not here Egyptians to deal with—Laird, factors and large farmers?' Such 'strong language' amounted to 'instigation to murder', according to the Revd Donald MacKinnon of Strath, Skye, who did not approve of this use of the Scriptures, and reported MacCallum's word to Sheriff William Ivory in December 1886.[16] The application of the Bible in this manner foreshadows the development of liberation theology in present-day Latin America and South Africa. In the Highlands, as in these countries, it became an influential book in the struggle against social oppression.[17]

A New Culture

If the Bible contributed to the restructuring of Highland society in the nineteenth century by encouraging the seemingly contradictory processes of emigration and radical protest, there were other less obvious, but equally significant, ways in which it helped to modify the nature of society and especially that important ingredient of society called 'culture'. In the course of the nineteenth century the Highlands became increasingly exposed to the languages and values of the outside world. In this the Bible had its part to play, largely through the work of the various Gaelic school societies. The first of these was founded in Edinburgh in 1810. The Edinburgh Gaelic School Society was interdenominational, and brought together representatives of the Established Church and dissenting bodies. The principal founder of the Society was the Revd Christopher Anderson, a Baptist pastor in Edinburgh who became familiar with the Highlands through preaching tours. It was the aim of the Society to teach the people to read the Gaelic Bible, and Anderson tried hard to maintain the primacy of Gaelic in the curriculum of the schools.[18]

Yet the desire to read the Gaelic Bible, and consequent literacy in Gaelic, led to a strong interest in reading English literature. The Gaelic Bible thus paved the way for literacy in English among Highlanders. The Gaelic Bible also introduced Highlanders to 'book culture', in contrast to the predominantly (but not exclusively) oral culture of Gaelic society. Fortunately, however, this stimulated the production of Gaelic tracts, devotional books and periodicals to encourage further reading of Gaelic literature, mainly of a religious kind. A considerable supply of such material was written by ministers like Dr Norman MacLeod, and it helped to lay the foundation of modern Gaelic literature. This development, together with the tradition of powerful preaching which came to be associated with the Gaelic Bible, erected a major bulwark against the erosion of the language, especially in the domain of religion. Even so, it is arguable that the Gaelic Bible, and especially the work of the Gaelic schools, had already placed the Highlands in a wider context through which the influence of English and its associated culture could percolate, as the SSPCK had originally envisaged.[19] Such a context was, however, developing for other reasons; migration to the Lowlands and improved communications, by rail and steamship, were eroding what remained of Highland 'isolation'.[20]

The effect of the work of the Gaelic school societies, together with the revivals which often accompanied their labours, was the elevation of the Bible to a position of pre-eminence among Highlanders. It was the Book of Books, which came to be known as 'An Fhìrinn' ('The Truth'), and the message which it contained presented a challenge to falsehood and error. As far back as 1567, John Carswell, Superintendent of Argyll, had contrasted 'the vain, hurtful, lying, worldly tales' about traditional Gaelic heroes with the truth of Christian doctrine.[21] In the nineteenth century, certain Evangelical preachers undoubtedly viewed particular aspects of Highland secular society as inimical to biblical teaching. The proclamation of this teaching by preachers was seen as the means of dispelling falsehood. Thus Peter Grant, the Baptist pastor at Grantown-on-Spey, composed a poem entitled 'Gearan nan Gàidheal' ('The Complaint of the Highlanders'), in which he asked for more preachers to be sent to the Highlands to continue the work of enlightenment. He portrayed the manner in which the people spent a Sunday before they came to a knowledge of 'The Truth':

> 'S an t-Sàbaid ghlòrmhor bu chòir a naomhach',
> 'S tric chaith sinn faoin i bho cheann gu ceann,
> Le cainnt ro-dhìomhain mu thimchioll Fhianntaibh,
> 'S gach gnothach tìmeil a bhiodh 'nar ceann;
> Air cnuic 's air sléibhtean 'sna taighean céilidh,
> Bhiodh sinn le chéile a' tional ann;
> Cha b'e am Bìobull a bhiodh 'ga leughadh,
> Ach faoin sgeul air nach tigeadh ceann.

('The glorious Sabbath which ought to have been kept holy, we frequently spent frivolously from end to end, with exceedingly idle talk about Fian warriors, and every temporal matter that was in our heads; on hills and moors we used to gather together in the ceilidh-houses; it is not the Bible which would have been declaimed, but a vain tale of endless length'.[22]

Grant is opposed to the misuse of the Sabbath day in what he would regard as levity, and he stresses, by implication, the superiority of the Bible to 'vain tales'. He does not, however, suggest that these tales should be destroyed; rather, people should be 'rescued' from them. The Bible thus set up a polarity between the indigenous hero-tales of the people and the heroic narratives of the Old and New Testaments. It was possible to view the native tradition in different ways, depending on one's position relative to the two poles. Yet even ministers of the deepest Evangelical dye, for whom the Bible brooked no rivals, could accommodate certain aspects of native tradition, and even contribute to their preservation. No less a person than the great itinerant revivalist preacher, the Revd John MacDonald of Ferintosh, 'the Apostle of the North', was a collector of Gaelic heroic ballads.[23]

It is therefore extremely difficult to argue that the Bible, in and of itself, was responsible for the dilution of Gaelic native culture which took place in the nineteenth century and has continued into the twentieth. Nor can it be argued any more plausibly that the Bible led to emigration, or that it was the chief cause of the policy of stout anti-landlord resistance which emerged in the 1880s. Social change was in the air when the Gaelic Bible entered the Highlands. The power of the Book lay in the manner in which preachers, politicians and people applied it to the various processes by which such change was accelerated, accepted or resisted.

DONALD MEEK

H

Notes

1   For general background, see James Hunter, *The Making of the Crofting Community*, (Edinburgh, 1976), and Eric Richards, *A History of the Highland Clearances*, 2 vols (London, 1982-85), vol 2.

2   For the Gaelic school movement, see V.E. Durkacz, *The Decline of the Celtic Languages*, (Edinburgh, 1983), pp 96–153, and C.W. Withers, *Gaelic in Scotland 1698-1981 The Geographical History of a Language*, (Edinburgh, 1984), pp 116–60. For awakenings (or 'revivals'), see Alexander MacRae, *Revivals in the Highlands and Islands in the Nineteenth Century* (Stirling, 1905).

3   Margaret MacDonnell (ed), *The Emigrant Experience: Songs of Highland Emigrants in North America* (Toronto, 1982), pp 136–7.

4   Ibid., pp 66–7.

5   Iain N MacLeòid (ed), *Bàrdachd Leòdhais* (Glasgow, 1933), p 81.

6   A copy of this letter is in the Archives of the School of Scottish Studies, University of Edinburgh. I owe this reference to the kindness of Dr Margaret A Mackay.

7   *Annual Reports of the Baptist Home Missionary Society for Scotland* (Edinburgh, 1854), p 23.

8   D E Meek (ed), *Màiri Mhór nan Oran* (Glasgow, 1977), p 82.

9   MacDonnell, *Emigrant Experience*, pp 144–5.

10   A Clerk (ed), *Caraid nan Gàidheal; Gaelic Writings by Norman MacLeod, D.D.* (Edinburgh, 1910), p 270.

11   D M McKillop, *Annals of Megantic Co., Quebec* (Inverness, Quebec, 1981 edition), p 170.

12   D E Meek, 'Evangelicalism and Emigration: Some Aspects of the Role of Dissenting Evangelicalism and its Preachers in Highland Emigration, especially to Canada, c.1800–c.1850', *Proceedings of the North American Congress of Celtic Studies held in Ottawa 26–30 March 1986* (forthcoming).

13   D S Lovejoy, *Religious Enthusiasm in the New World* (Cambridge, Massachusetts, 1985), p 13.

14   J Leatt, et al. (eds), *Contending Ideologies in South Africa* (Cape Town, 1986), pp 66–7, 79–81.

15   Quoted in I M M MacPhail, 'The Napier Commission', *Transactions of the Gaelic Society of Inverness* 48 (1972–74), p 457.

16   MacKinnon to Ivory, 18 December 1886, in the Ivory Papers, Scottish Record Office GD 1/47 (29). The Keeper of the Records of Scotland has kindly granted permission to use this reference.

17   For further references and discussion of this theme, see D E Meek, ' "The Land Question Answered from the Bible": The Land Issue and the Development of a Highland Theology of Liberation', *The Scottish Geographical Magazine* 103:2 (September 1987), pp 84–9.

18   See note 2 above.

19   For the SSPCK, see Chapter 1 in this volume.
20   D J MacLeod, 'Gaelic Prose', *Transactions of the Gaelic Society of Inverness* 49 (1974–76), pp 200–3; D E Meek, 'Evangelical Missionaries in the Early Nineteenth-Century Highlands', *Scottish Studies* 28 (1987), pp 14–17.
21   R L Thomson (ed), *Foirm na n-Urrnuidheadh* (Edinburgh, 1970), pp 11, 179.
22   Hector MacDougall (ed), *Dàin Spioradail le Pàdruig Grannd* (Glasgow, 1926), p 117.
23   John Kennedy, *The 'Apostle of the North'. The Life and Labours of . . . Dr. McDonald* (London and Edinburgh, 1866), pp 22–4.

Further Reading

J M Bumsted, *The People's Clearance: Highland Emigration to British North America 1770–1815* (Edinburgh, 1982).

V E Durkacz, *The Decline of the Celtic Languages* (Edinburgh, 1983).

I F Grigor, *Mightier than a Lord* (Stornoway, 1979).

James Hunter, *The Making of the Crofting Community* (Edinburgh, 1976).

Eric Richards, *A History of the Highland Clearances*, 2 vols (London, 1982–85).

Don Watson, *Caledonia Australis: Scottish Highlanders on the Frontier of Australia* (Sydney, 1984).

C W Withers, *Gaelic in Scotland 1698–1981: The Geographical History of a Language* (Edinburgh, 1984).

13

The Bible and Change in the Nineteenth Century

Like all their spiritual forbears since the Reformation, Scottish Protestants at the outset of the nineteenth century shared John Knox's conviction that 'Faith hath both her beginning and continuance by the Word of God'.[1] Identifying that Word with the Scriptures of the Old and New Testaments, they regarded the Bible as the supreme rule of faith and life, both personal and national, whose divine authority very few were disposed to question. Sceptical views, together with the tentative beginnings of an interest in the sources and literary methods used by the biblical writers (the so-called 'higher' criticism), had admittedly made their appearance during the age of Enlightenment; but the average minister and his parishioners were unaffected by them, and there is little evidence of their having attracted much attention from the sophisticated urban intelligentsia either. Whether in the Established Church or in the various Dissenting bodies which had hived off from it in the decades after the Revolution Settlement of 1690, the Bible was indeed the *Holy* Bible, and the entire life of the people was profoundly affected by it.

In days when a high proportion of the total population were regular church attenders, a major part of every service of worship was given over to the lection and exposition of the sacred text. The principal object of parish school education was to enable children to read the Bible for themselves, and it seems likely that most of them were more familiar with the history and literature of ancient Israel than with that of their native land. Common speech was shot through with biblical language and biblical allusions, and in many homes the opening and closing of the day found the whole family gathered around the Word. When the youthful Thomas Carlyle left Ecclefechan for Edinburgh University in 1809, his mother gave him a two-volume Bible to keep him company[2]; and on his death-bed in 1832 the great Sir

Walter Scott, when asked what book should be read to him, replied, 'Need you ask? There is but one'—and could be heard, even in delirium, repeating fragments from Job, Isaiah and the Psalms.[3] It would not be a very great exaggeration to say that Scotland, as she stood on the threshold of the Victorian age, was indeed the country of a Book.

Evangelical Conservatism

The reason why her attitude to the sacred volume, and her use of it, was not essentially different in the 1830s from what it had been in the days of Knox, or the Covenanters, or the original Seceders, was due in large measure to the Evangelical Revival and its conservative—not to say reactionary—influence. As the spiritual temperature rose in the years immediately after the Napoleonic Wars, there was a quite conscious return to the things which, in the estimation of Evangelical leaders like Andrew Thomson (minister of St George's, Edinburgh, from 1814 to 1831) and Thomas Chalmers (professor of Divinity at Edinburgh University from 1828 until the Disruption of 1843), had laid the foundations of national greatness; and supreme among these were the Holy Scriptures. But along with the exuberance and ardour of resurgent Evangelicalism went an intransigence and acrimony which ushered in a more embattled age; and the bitter Apocrypha Controversy was one of the earliest manifestations of this.

It began in 1821 when Robert Haldane, an outstanding Evangelical activist of Baptist principles, was horrified to discover that the British and Foreign Bible Society (a body with many subscribers in Scotland) had covertly been distributing Bibles contaminated by the inclusion of the 'Apocryphal' books.[4] He and his numerous supporters agreed with the original leaders of Protestantism—though not with the early Christian Fathers or the authorities of mediaeval and post-Reformation Catholicism—that 1 and 2 Esdras, Ecclesiasticus, 1 and 2 Maccabees and the other 'uncanonical' works associated with them, had no place in the corpus of truly inspired literature, the Christians' Bible. They set about rectifying the situation, and campaigned against the Apocrypha with passion and skill. But their stance did not go unchallenged, even inside the Evangelical camp, and a furious battle raged throughout the 1820s. It saw the emergence of Haldane as 'the founding father of Fundamentalism',[5] and resulted in the large-scale withdrawal of Scottish support from the BFBS. It was also responsible for the introduction of a new edginess into theological debate throughout the English-speaking world. It raised, in more pressing form than ever before, questions about the nature and even the reality of biblical inspiration which were never very far from the centre of religious concern and debate during the remainder of the century. And (of particular importance for the present study) it led to the formulation of what would long remain the typical conservative answer to a whole constellation of biblical problems.

Scrutiny of that answer reveals one outstandingly important feature. While it was worked out in relation to a widely diverse range of antagonists—typical early eighteenth-century rationalists like John Toland and Thomas Woolston; later Socinians like Joseph Priestley; more compromising spirits like Philip Doddridge the eminent English Dissenter, who professed to find different degrees of inspiration within the covers of the Bible; forerunners of modern liberalism like Schleiermacher and Coleridge; and of course the defenders of the Apocrypha —it inclined more and more to opt for the unequivocal, neck-or-nothing assertion of a uniformly divine authorship throughout the sacred volume. The biblical writers were increasingly cast in the role of amanuenses of the Almighty.

This development stands clearly revealed in the work of four influential writers, all from the opening decades of the century: George Hill, professor of Divinity at St Andrews from 1788 to 1819, possibly the most distinguished theological teacher of the reformed Establishment; John Dick, occupant of the only professorial chair in the United Secession Church from 1820–1833; Robert Haldane (1764–1851), a man of great stature in the Evangelical world, whom we have already met; and Thomas Chalmers, who dominated the ecclesiastical scene for a generation before his death in 1847. In all their writings on the subject we can detect the same tendency to make the highest possible claims for Scripture, as well as more or less the same predilection, when speaking of it, for words like 'infallible', 'inerrant', 'perfect' and 'immaculately pure'—words destined to be at the centre of even more intense debate in the later decades of the century.

Degrees of Inspiration

The discussion of biblical authority to be found in these men's writings, and others like them, tended (when not directly concerned with the status of the Apocrypha) to focus upon the question of whether or not different degrees of inspiration could be found in Holy Scripture. Might it be said that at one level—the lowest—God so superintended the minds of the biblical writers as to obviate the possibility of errors occurring in their works; that at another he 'elevated their conceptions beyond the measure of ordinary men'; and that at the highest level he actually suggested the thoughts they were to express and the words they were to employ? Of our four authorities, only George Hill was prepared to give an affirmative answer. Dissenting from those apologists for the faith who held that the highest form of inspiration was at work throughout the Bible, he contended that

> this opinion, which is probably entertained by many well-meaning people, and which has been held by some able defenders of Christianity, is now generally abandoned by those who examine the subject with due care. . . . It is not only unnecessary to suppose that the highest degree of inspiration was extended through all the parts of the New Testament, but the supposition is really inconsistent with many circumstances that occur there.

In so saying, however, he disclaimed any desire to undermine the doctrine that the writers of Holy Scripture were divinely inspired in all things, and their works the infallible standard of Christian truth. 'We do not say,' he averred in his *Lectures in Divinity* (the first edition of which, dealing almost exclusively with the New Testament, was published posthumously in 1821),

> that every thought was put into the mind of the apostles, and every word dictated to their pen, by the Spirit of God. But we say, that by the superintendence of the Spirit they were at all times guarded from error, and were furnished upon every occasion with the measure of inspiration which the nature of the subject required.

He therefore felt able to summarise his conclusions in language which was as assured and even uncompromising as that of his most dogmatic contemporaries:

> His [Jesus'] apostles . . . received . . . such a measure of the visible gifts of the Spirit as attested their commission, and such a measure of internal illumination as render their writings the infallible standard of Christian truth. From hence it follows, that everything which is clearly contained in the gospels and epistles, or which may be fairly deduced from the words there used, is true.[6]

Hill's careful phraseology may have left room for greater flexibility in certain respects than some of his contemporaries would have liked; but his old-style orthodoxy can hardly have been in doubt. Dick, Haldane and Chalmers were much more intransigent. The first of them, whose *Essay on the Inspiration of the Holy Scriptures* was originally published in 1800, would (like Haldane and Chalmers after him) have no truck with the notion of degrees of inspiration:

> Few writers [he lamented] who now undertake to defend the cause of revelation, hold the plenary inspiration of the Scriptures. That idea has become unfashionable . . . and he only is supposed to entertain rational sentiments on the subject, who looks upon the sacred books as partly human and partly divine; as a heterogeneous compound of the oracles of God, and the stories and the sentiments of men. There are even some, by whom this partial inspiration is denied [he was probably thinking of Priestley] and the Scriptures are regarded as the writings of faithful but fallible men, who had nothing to preserve them from error but the accuracy of their information, and the integrity of their hearts. The spirit of infidelity is working among Christians themselves.

Against any such flirting with faithlessness, the old Seceder reminded his public that a supernatural revelation surely requires a supernatural record. After all,

> to those who admit that miracles are wrought to attest revelation, it will not seem incredible that there should have been one miracle more, so obviously necessary, as the inspiration of the persons by whom it was committed to writing.

Yet in the last resort he put his trust not in reasoning but in the Scriptures' own claim to divine authority: 'We appeal to their own testimony, and might produce many passages in which it is explicitly asserted, or plainly implied'.[7]

Free Church Fathers

Haldane, as might have been expected of one never deficient in pugnacity, showed even less inclination to compromise. In his *Evidence and Authority of Divine Revelation* (Volume 1, 1816), he declared that the Holy Scriptures themselves give 'no countenance whatever' to the notion of differing degrees of inspiration. There is but one kind of inspiration, and that is the highest, for God communicated to the biblical writers the very 'ideas and words [sic] which they have engrossed in that sacred book'.[8] Chalmers likewise would have nothing to do with 'superintendence' or 'suggestion'. But in his lectures *On the Inspiration of the Old and New Testaments* (delivered in the 1830s, but republished as late as 1879 during a subsequent phase of the Bible debate) he went his own distinctive way in refusing point-blank to discuss what he called 'the act of inspiration'. For him, all that mattered was 'the product of inspiration': the Bible as we have it, whose language God has made his own, and through which he speaks to us now. Over and above the Scriptures' own claims to divine authority and complete reliability, we must reckon with the unanimous verdict of Christian tradition over many centuries, which has always held that the Bible 'is not a medley of things divine and things human; but is either throughout a fallible composition, or throughout, in all its parts, the rescript of the only wise and true God'. His conclusion, therefore, though reached by a somewhat different route, agreed in all essentials with Haldane's, and even matched it in belligerency:

> We know that the anti-apocryphalists of the day have been accused of too fiercely resenting the encroachments that have been attempted on the canon and inspiration of Scripture, and that on the plea of the encroachments being small ones. We shall say nothing of the resentment; but however slight those encroachments may have been, they could not be too strenuously or too energetically resisted. . . . It is the part of Christians to rise like a wall of fire round the integrity and inspiration of Scripture; and to hold them as intact and inviolable as if a rampart were thrown around them, whose foundations are on earth and whose battlements are in heaven.[9]

The conservatism of pronouncements such as these was only reinforced by the Ten Years' Conflict and the Disruption; and reached its apogee in the mood of the Free Church of Scotland during the first decades of its existence. At the opening in 1850 of New College, the denomination's theological seminary in Edinburgh, lectures were delivered which can be seen as a kind of manifesto for the traditional views; and the same message comes through in subsequent publications by Free Church teachers. 'What are we to understand by the inspiration of the Bible?', asked Dr Robert Candlish, minister of Free St George's, Edinburgh, and Principal of New College (1861–73), in a lecture given in 1851. He answered:

> I hold it to be an infallible divine guidance exercised over those who are commissioned to declare the mind of God, so as to secure that in declaring it they do not err. What they say, or write, under this guidance, is as truly said and written by God, through them, as if their instrumentality were not used at all. God is in the fullest sense responsible for every word of it.

James Bannerman, who taught at New College from 1848 to 1868, brought out his *Inspiration: The Infallible Truth and Divine Authority of the Holy Scriptures* in 1865. Hailed as the definitive defence of orthodox doctrine on the subject, it contained this summary appreciation of the Scriptures:

> In *the first place*, they contain a communication of truth supernaturally given to man; and in *the second place*, they contain that truth supernaturally transferred to human language, and therefore free from all mixture or addition or error.

Supremely formidable was the celebrated William Cunningham, who succeeded Chalmers as Principal of New College in 1847 and taught there from 1843 until his death in 1861. His *Theological Lectures* (not actually published until 1878) probably constitute the ablest— certainly the most learned and subtle—exposition of traditional views by any Scottish theologian in modern times. His arguments cannot be easily summarised, but the following sentence may serve as a not unrepresentative indication of his stance: 'The Holy Spirit not merely superintended the writers [of the Bible] so as to preserve them from error, but suggested to them the words in which the communication was to be conveyed'.[10]

New Stirrings

Alas! for Cunningham and his friends: scarcely had the conservative doctrine of scriptural authority been formulated in such unyielding terms when a very different view began to infiltrate scholarship in Scotland and elsewhere. Within the span of a single lifetime, attitudes were revolutionised; and by the end of the century, still more by 1914, the older approach barely survived in universities and colleges and was visibly in retreat on the parochial front as well. Perhaps the Free Church fathers themselves had something to do with the change. As has been recently pointed out, they not only provided the hard doctrine for their successors to react against, but also accelerated the process they deplored by raising crucial questions without always returning satisfactory answers.[11] Even Evangelicalism's encouragement of Bible reading may have introduced some Scottish believers to inaccuracies and inconsistencies—not to mention scientific or ethical anomalies—in the sacred text of which they would otherwise have been unaware.

Nor did the spirit of reform, abroad during the 1830s, leave the scholarly world untouched: a Royal Commission set up to inquire into the state of the universities drew attention, *inter alia*, to the lamentable provision then made for the study of the biblical languages and text as compared with the resources devoted to systematic theology. 'A system,' remarked one campaigner, 'ought not to supersede the study of the sacred record itself';[12] and in due course the foundation of new chairs of Biblical Criticism redressed the balance a little in favour of textual rather than purely dogmatic study. Account should likewise be taken of the heightened moral sensitivity of the Victorian age, which made it difficult to maintain that every part of the Bible was equally authoritative. A new spirit of tolerance and tentativeness which, along with a growing preference for the apologetic as opposed to the dogmatic spirit, rendered the hard-line orthodoxy of the traditionalists increasingly uncongenial, was also a factor. Most important of all was the scientific revolution associated with the writings of Charles Lyell and Charles Darwin, which provided a picture of man and his environment difficult to reconcile with the statements of Scripture if literally understood.

But there can be no doubt that what really transformed the situation was the emergence, in the wake of Enlightenment and Romanticism, of a new *historical* way of looking at life, and the rapid development of the attitudes and techniques of historical scholarship. Students of the Bible were encouraged thereby to regard it not so much as a quarry of texts easily removable from their peculiar setting, or as a compendium of theological propositions, but as the record of a particular people—its history and its literature—over many centuries: to ask questions about the original context of each narrative or pronouncement as well as about its author's distinctive concerns and purposes, to appreciate the diversity of materials and viewpoints that it contained, to be aware of possible inconsistencies and inaccuracies, to seek the early sources behind the later compilations, and to steer clear, as much as possible, of *a priori* assumptions and harmonisations. They came to recognise that the whole great literature might not everywhere attain a uniformly high moral and religious level. They rejoiced to discover that they were conceivably reviving a view not unknown to the original Reformers: in Robertson Smith's words, 'Just as the principle of a personal faith is the foundation of all the fresh life of the Reformation, so the principle of a historical treatment of Scripture is at bottom the principle of the whole Reformation theology'.[13] And in all their labours they were guided less by the traditions of the Church and the demands of dogmatic theology than by what the text actually said to the well-informed, candid and sensitive mind. There were, of course, some disadvantages in the new approach. It could encourage the view that the Bible was a book for literary and historical experts. It could be vitiated by naturalistic or positivist presuppositions, or represented as coming 'in paper parcels from Germany'.[14] It could reduce 'the impregnable rock of Holy Scripture'[15] to shifting sands. But to those who adopted it there came a sense of liberation and a conviction that the riches of Holy Scripture were being opened up in a way scarcely conceivable under the old ordering of things.

William Robertson Smith

The story of the revolution is inextricably bound up with the career of William Robertson Smith. A pupil of Scotland's first great biblical critic, A B Davidson, Smith completed his studies at New College in 1870, when—such was his precocious distinction—the Free Church appointed him professor of Hebrew and Old Testament at its Aberdeen College. His inaugural lecture bore the title, 'What history teaches us to seek in the Bible', and was in essence a plea for the historical rather than the dogmatic approach. 'We must,' he told his hearers, 'let the Bible speak for itself. Our notion of the origin, the purpose, the character of the scriptural books must be drawn, not from vain traditions but from a historical study of the books themselves.'[16] Smith's pursuit of this ideal soon led him to adopt positions that were unlikely to commend themselves to Free Church traditionalists. An article he contributed to the *Encyclopaedia Britannica* in 1875 assumed that the Scripture narratives we now possess are later, edited versions of accounts dating from various periods in Jewish history; it also assigned the so-called 'Mosaic' legislation to a period hundreds of years after Moses; suggested that most of the Psalms were of non-Davidic origin; eliminated much of the predictive element in the prophets; and denied authorship of the Gospels to the persons whose names they bear.

The horrified conservatives took action in the courts of the Church, accusing Smith of teaching that was 'of a dangerous and unsettling tendency' and constituted (whether by direct contradiction or subtle disparagement) a threat to 'the doctrine of the immediate inspiration, infallible truth, and divine authority of the Holy Scriptures'.[17] In 1881—despite all his learning and his forensic brilliance—he was removed from his chair as unworthy to be trusted with the teaching of candidates for the Free Church ministry. Soon moving to Cambridge, he spent the rest of his tragically brief career as university librarian and professor of Arabic there. His deposition was a major blow to the new scholarship in Scotland. But it is noteworthy that the Free Church General Assembly had contrived to get rid of the heretic without specifying—far less condemning—his heresies; and that on the morrow of the great debate a number of his supporters boldly declared their determination 'to pursue the critical questions raised by Professor W R Smith' and 'to protect any man who pursues these studies deliberately'.[18] No one called them to account, and it soon became evident that the Assembly's action had been powerless to undo Smith's work of educating Scotland in the new views.

Three further 'heresy trials' followed in the course of the next 25 years. In 1890, Professors Marcus Dods and A B Bruce fell foul of the conservatives for their espousal of views not vastly different from Smith's. Dods' inaugural lecture at New College in 1889 revived suspicions aroused as early as 1877 by a sermon of his on 'Inspiration and Revelation'. His offences included speaking of 'mistakes and immoralities' in the Old Testament, as well as asserting that the doctrine of verbal inspiration was 'a theory . . . which is dishonouring to God, and which has turned inquirers into sceptics by the thousand'.[19] But despite the provocation, the Free Church Assembly decided to proceed no further with the case. Most significantly, its leader, Robert Rainy of New College, opined that a man should not be deemed unsuitable for the Christian ministry because he had detected 'inaccuracies' in Holy Writ—so long as he also took it to be everywhere the Word of God.[20] Bruce's errors had been expressed in a book, also published in 1889: *The Kingdom of God: Christ's Preaching According to the Synoptic Gospels*. He was said to have imputed untrustworthiness to the gospel writers, and in the course of his defence he certainly declared that they were not objectively reliable. He was also accused of presenting Christ as a poet, a mystic, even a schemer, rather than a divine figure. But in his very able defence, Bruce argued that (however infelicitous his expressions) he had as an apologist to deal with difficult topics, that he merited indulgence for tackling a new field of study, and—above all—that though his view of inspiration might differ from that of the conservatives, he was, like them, absolutely convinced of the unique, divine character of Holy Scripture.[21] Once again, the case was dropped.

Twelve years later, in 1902, came the last of the great heresy trials. George Adam Smith, Professor of Old Testament in the United Free Church College, Glasgow, had published a volume of lectures, *Modern Criticism and the Preaching of the Old Testament*, which contained assertions that Jewish religion before the eighth century BC was polytheistic in character, that the early chapters of Genesis were unhistorical, and that the lives of the patriarchs had their 'fanciful' elements. The Church's College Committee, however, refused to indict him. Their report agreed with much of what he had written, and contended that to assign a late date to the 'Mosaic' legislation of the Pentateuch was not to cast doubt on the divine inspiration and authority of the Bible. In the end, the Assembly dismissed the case, though Smith's views were neither accepted nor rejected and scholars were warned to be careful what they said.[22] Clearly, the atmosphere had greatly changed since 1881.

Traditional View Marginalised

In the decades immediately before the First World War, the traditional view of Scripture had been driven to the remoter fringes of ecclesiastical and academic life. A host of well-respected scholars was at work applying the new principles and methods to every part and aspect of Holy Scripture, converting ministers and members to agree with them, and publishing a flood of commentaries, translations and dictionary articles. The allegedly 'assured' results of literary and historical criticism were confidently spoken of. A developmental account of Israel's religion was becoming the rule rather than the exception, and the inerrancy of the biblical narratives found fewer and fewer defendants. The kind of assertions for which Robertson Smith was condemned had lost their power to shock. More and more frequently, open acknowledgement was made of the diversity of attitudes found among the New Testament writers; and the 'quest of the historical Jesus' came to be pursued as eagerly in Scottish as in German universities. Yet despite all the activity, and the confidence, biblical scholarship in Scotland seldom manifested unbalanced or excessive enthusiasm for the new ideals. If A B Bruce adopted even more radical views, his colleague James Orr moved steadily in the opposite direction; and James Denney, one of the ablest biblical scholars his country ever produced, pursued a notably middle-of-the-road course. Only the most prescient observer, however, could have foreseen the counter-revolution due to be effected in the 1940s and subsequently by the disciples of Karl Barth and the devotees of American fundamentalism.

The prevailing attitude to Scripture at the close of the period under review may be found conveniently expressed in Marcus Dods'

The Bible: Its Origin and Nature (1905). In it he made the following points. On revelation: 'Those books which form our Bible are all in direct connection with God's historical revelation which culminated in Christ'. Consequently, 'if anyone wishes to know what God is in His revelation to men . . . it is to the Bible appeal must be made. And therefore the Bible may itself legitimately, if loosely, be called the revelation'.[23] On inspiration: all preconceived notions of what it ought to be or accomplish must be rejected. It cannot mean inerrancy, for 'Had verbal accuracy been required for our saving use of the Bible, it would have been secured. It has not been secured, therefore it was not required'. Nor are we to think of it as present in some parts of the Bible and absent from others. What we *can* say is that it is not the *ipsissima verba* of Scripture that were inspired, but the writers themselves. Inspiration 'enables its possessor to see and apprehend God and His will, and to impart to other men what he himself has apprehended'; and if Scripture gives us a trustworthy account of the divine self-revelation (as it does), we have no need to claim that every phrase or word has God's authority behind it.[24] On infallibility: this does not mean inerrancy, for criticism, 'with a virtually unanimous voice', has ruled out that in the case of either Testament. What it does mean is complete reliability in conveying to us 'a sufficient knowledge of Christ ' and of the divine self-revelation which was consummated in him. In the end of the day, therefore, it is Scripture's 'self-evidencing power' which persuades us to accept it as the Word of God—and which enables Dods to assure his readers that 'If it is spiritual guidance . . . man is in search of then you may refer him absolutely to the Bible'.[25]

Criticism and Conviction

Throughout our period, opponents of criticism nearly always linked it with unbelief. In actual fact, however, one of the most arresting facts about Scottish biblical scholarship between, say, 1860 and 1914, was its leaders' success in combining critical practice with a fervently-expressed Christian faith and deep involvement in the life of the Church. Of A B Davidson, criticism's true founding father in Scotland, his biographer tells us that 'he never put Historical Criticism first. To him it was only the handmaid of religion'.[26] The arch-heretic (according to some reckonings) Robertson Smith, was equally affirmative, and in one of his earliest controversial writings stated a conviction from which he never departed:

> I receive Scripture as the Word of God and as the only perfect rule of faith
> · and life . . . because in the Bible alone I find God drawing near to men in
> Christ Jesus and declaring to us in Him His will for our salvation. And this
> record I know to be true by the witness of His Spirit in my heart, whereby
> I am assured that none other than God Himself is able to speak such
> words to my soul.[27]

One of Smith's most enthusiastic supporters, Professor J S Candlish of Glasgow Free Church College, made his standpoint sufficiently clear in the title of a pamphlet he issued during the trial: *The Authority of Scripture Independent of Criticism*. A B Bruce delivered a like message: 'This,' he told the Assembly in 1890, 'is a book by itself, the literature of a very real revelation which God has made to mankind through the Hebrew race. Whatever differences there may be among us . . . we are all at one on the main question'.[28] And Marcus Dods agreed: 'The affirmation of inaccuracy in certain details,' he informed the College Committee in 1905, 'has assuredly a bearing on one's theory of inspiration; but it does not, on my part, involve the slightest hesitation as to the divine authority of Scripture, the pervading influence which makes it God's Word'.[29]

This belief in the compatibility of faith and criticism, which had sustained many Scottish scholars throughout the century of change, remained a dominant influence in the life and work of their immediate successors, as the writings of H R Mackintosh and James Moffatt (to name only two) bear ample witness. The former, Scotland's finest systematic theologian between James Denney and John Baillie, believed, like T M Lindsay before him, that the new approach to Scripture realised some basic insights of early Protestantism; and he transmitted that message with an eloquence which revealed his own heartfelt agreement. Writing in 1924, he recalled how the Reformers, while clearly distinguishing between the Bible and the Word of God, nonetheless 'never lost sight of the cardinal point that it is only in and through the Bible that God's word of mercy and judgment reaches us'. And in the same article he united a commendation of criticism with a summons to faith:

> The whole Reformation view of Christianity is bound up with a historical
> treatment of Scripture. But that is only a half truth. The other half, of still
> greater importance, is that nothing but the Spirit of God in the heart of
> the believer enables him to realise that in very truth it is God, and none
> else, who is seen in the history.[30]

James Moffatt, then probably the world's best-known New

Testament scholar, argued in his *Approach to the New Testament* (1921) that the obvious drawbacks of literary and historical criticism were either 'incidental defects' or 'temporary pains of growth', whereas 'What the historical approach means, is that a truer estimate of the writings is put forward than could be reached so long as they were regarded as equally and verbally inspired'.[31] And in the introduction to his pioneering translation of the whole Bible (1926), after quoting the Preface to the Authorised Version of 1611, he commented: 'These words put nobly the chief end of reading the Bible, and the object of any version' [might he have added, of all critical study as well?]; 'it is to stir and sustain present faith in a living God who spoke and speaks'.[32] With such testimonies this survey of biblical scholarship in Scotland's century of change may be brought to a not inappropriate close.

ALEC CHEYNE

Notes

1 D Laing (ed), *The Works of John Knox*, vol IV (Edinburgh, 1855), p 133.
2 F Kaplan, *Thomas Carlyle: A Biography* (Cambridge, 1983), p 28.
3 E Johnson, *Sir Walter Scott: The Great Unknown*, vol II: *1821–1832* (London, 1970), pp 1266, 1275.
4 A Haldane, *The Lives of Robert Haldane of Airthrey, and of his brother, James Alexander Haldane* (8th edition, London, 1871), pp 484–5. On the Apocrypha controversy, see also Chapter 2 in this volume.
5 A L Drummond and J Bulloch, *The Church in Victorian Scotland, 1843–1874* (Edinburgh, 1975), p 251.
6 G Hill, *Lectures in Divinity*, vol I (Edinburgh, 1821), pp 368–9, 373–4.
7 J Dick, *An Essay on the Inspiration of the Holy Scriptures* (4th edition, Glasgow, 1840), pp x–xi, 236.
8 R Haldane, *The Evidence and Authority of Divine Revelation*, vol I (Edinburgh, 1816), pp 135, 137.
9 T Chalmers, *On the Inspiration of the Old and New Testaments* (Edinburgh, 1879), pp 21, 35–6.
10 Cited by R Riesen, *Criticism and Faith in Late Victorian Scotland: A B Davidson, William Robertson Smith and George Adam Smith* (Lanham and London, 1985), p 61.
11 R Riesen, 'Higher Criticism in the Free Church Fathers', *Records of the Scottish Church History Society* 20:2 (1979), p 120.
12 W M Gunn, *Hints on the Study of Biblical Criticism in Scotland* (Edinburgh, 1838), p 20.

13   Cited by T M Lindsay, 'Professor Robertson Smith's Doctrine of Scripture', *The Expositor*, 4th ser., 10 (1894), pp 241–64.

14   John Kennedy of Dingwall, cited by J S Black and G W Chrystal, *The Life of William Robertson Smith* (London, 1912), p 401.

15   Title of a series of articles by W E Gladstone, published in *Good Words*, March–November 1900.

16   J S Black and G W Chrystal (eds), *Lectures and Essays of William Robertson Smith* (London, 1912), p 233.

17   'The Draft Form of Libel', J S Black and G W Chrystal (eds), *Lectures and Essays*, Appendix B, p 582.

18   Black and Chrystal, *Life*, p 450.

19   M Dods, *Recent Progress in Theology* (Edinburgh, 1889), p 30.

20   *Proceedings and Debates of the General Assembly of the Free Church of Scotland, 1890* (Edinburgh, 1890), pp 111–15.

21   *Proceedings and Debates* (1890), pp 169–73.

22   *Proceedings and Debates of the General Assembly of the United Free Church, 1902* (Edinburgh, 1902), pp 87–118, and College Committee's Special Report XI A, p 9, *Reports to the General Assembly of the United Free Church of Scotland* (Edinburgh, 1902).

23   M Dods, *The Bible: Its Origin and Nature* (Edinburgh, 1905), pp 23, 95–6.

24   Ibid., ch 4, esp. pp 112, 127.

25   Ibid., ch 5, esp. pp 135, 152, 162.

26   J Strahan, *Andrew Bruce Davidson* (London, 1917), p 249.

27   Quoted from 'Answer to the Form of Libel', p 21 in Lindsay, art.cit. (note 13 above), p 250.

28   *Proceedings and Debates* (1890), p 175.

29   Quoted from College Committee's Special Report in H F Henderson, *The Religious Controversies of Scotland* (Edinburgh, 1905), p 239.

30   H R Mackintosh, 'The Reformers' View of Scripture', pp 56–7, in C Gore, *The Doctrine of the Infallible Book* (London, 1924), pp 55–60.

31   J Moffatt, *The Approach to the New Testament* (London, 1921), pp 235, 206.

32   J Moffatt, Introduction to *The Moffatt Translation of the Bible* (London, 1935), p xlv.

Further Reading

J S Black and G W Chrystal, *The Life of William Robertson Smith* (London, 1912).

A C Cheyne, *The Transforming of the Kirk: Victorian Scotland's Religious Revolution* (Edinburgh, 1983).

A L Drummond and J Bulloch, *The Church in Victorian Scotland, 1843–1874* (Edinburgh, 1975); *1874–1900* (Edinburgh, 1978).

S L Greenslade (ed), *The Cambridge History of the Bible: The West from the Reformation to the Present Day* (London, 1963), esp. chapters 7 and 8.

J E McFadyen, *The Approach to the Old Testament* (London, 1926).

J Moffatt, *The Approach to the New Testament* (London, 1921).

R Riesen, *Criticism and Faith in Late Victorian Scotland: A B Davidson, William Robertson Smith and George Adam Smith* (Lanham and London, 1985).

14

The Bible in Scotland Today:
Retrospect and Prospect

There is a paradox at the heart of this Bible Year book. It is that a nation which was thirled more than most to the Scriptures, not only in its ecclesiastical but in its political, literary and private life, never produced a Bible in its own language. Scotland's Gaelic-speaking minority were eventually provided with a version in Scots Gaelic, although it appeared long after there were versions in Irish and Welsh. But the Bible that played so prominent a role in the moulding of Scotland's Reformation and thereafter took over the soul of its Scots-speaking majority was an English Bible: at first the Tyndale and Geneva Bibles and, from about the middle of the seventeenth century onwards, the King James Version. There was a Scots rendering by Murdoch Nisbet of the Wycliffite New Testament as early as 1520, and the appearance of biblical quotations in Scots catechisms, treatises and popular literature of the immediate pre-Reformation period shows that there were those in Scotland prepared to take, at its face value, the Reformation ideal that people should be given access to the Scriptures in their mother tongue. Moreover, the resources of a rich and confident literature from the golden age of Scottish letters in the reigns of James IV and V were to hand. When the Latin Vulgate, the mediaeval Scriptures of Scotland as of all Christendom, was dethroned, a Bible in Scots ought automatically to have come along.

It is not easy to say why it did not. But in a serious book of this kind we ought at least to be able to dispose of the hoary jibe that it was John Knox's fault. We know that he preferred to write, if not to speak, in an English that was only sparsely influenced by the native Scots of his youth. But Knox was not in Scotland for much of the crucial half-century that saw a veritable cascade of English versions—Tyndale, Coverdale, Geneva and the rest—pour from the printing presses south of the border and hardly a corresponding activity north of it. Even the copies of the English Bible that circulated in Scotland were for the most part imported from England or abroad. Many more than a single person were implicated in what to us, looking back, seems a subconscious conspiracy not to have a vernacular Bible. The whole non-Celtic part of the nation, from King to commoner, spoke Scots, so that no social prejudice of the kind that delayed a Scots Gaelic Bible was involved. Could it have been simply that there were not enough scholars with the necessary command of Hebrew and Greek to rise to the challenge? Or was it that reforming zeal came late to Scotland and was more derivative at its core than we today like to think—in other words, was it assumed that Scotland's Bible as well as its ecclesiastical polity must come from outside? Or did a sixth sense tell the Scottish people, although 1603 was still some way off, that unity and peace with England were on the horizon, and that an English Bible was a small price to pay if that end could be achieved?

Paradox, not Tragedy

I leave those who read this book to point the explaining or the accusing finger where they will. And with many of them I shed a silent tear for what might have been; for there is little doubt that a Scots Bible could have worked wonders for the future of Scots language and literature, not to mention Scottish self-esteem. But let us at the same time be realistic; and let us resist the temptation to talk a paradox into a tragedy. In the period of which we are speaking, standard Tudor English was already in process of becoming the *lingua franca* of Great Britain, and was understood in Scotland much better than Stuart Scots was understood in England. Moreover, Scots who could read were well used to books in English and, it seems, did not find it difficult to translate mentally into Scots as they went along. But an English Bible was not just another book for private reading; it was there to be read aloud in public worship, and when it was read with an inevitable Scots pronunciation of the words and a Scots intonation, there can have been few listening who did not follow perfectly well what was being said. Specific Scots vocabulary and grammar would be missed, and no doubt the worshippers found it rather strange to begin with. But no one would be in the dark as to the sense; and as time went on, the cadences of the English Bible in their Scots inflection would feed more and more naturally into Scottish religious rhetoric. We get the flavour of what eventually transpired in the Scots passages of Scott's *Old Mortality* or *The Heart of Midlothian* or Hogg's *Confessions of a Justified Sinner* or

Stevenson's *Weir of Hermiston*: a rather unique amalgam of pure Scots interspersed with stretches of Scotticised English as biblical quotations and allusions were woven in. Once taken over, both Calvinist ecclesiology and English Bible became thoroughly at home on the Scottish scene.

Thus the English Bible may have dented the Scottishness of the Scots language, but it did no deep or lasting damage. The substantive cause of the decline of Scots, or at any rate of its being shunted off the visible stage occupied by the socially respectable and influential, should not be looked for in the language spoken in the Scottish kirk, which must have remained as heavily Scots-flavoured, and for similar cantankerous reasons, as did the language of the Scottish bar and bench until the nineteenth century. Scottish humanism as represented by the Edinburgh Enlightenment was in fact much quicker to sell the pass; and to it, far more than to Scottish Calvinism and its King James Bible, should be traced that split in the Scottish linguistic psyche which is still seen today in an educational system that—some contrary voices apart—insists on standard English being taught in the classrooms and banishes the mother tongue of our children to the playground.

Scots Revived

As things worked out, then, there was no demand, or indeed need, for a Scots Bible during the long and indubitably Scottish hegemony of Presbyterianism in Scotland. It should not surprise us, therefore, that renderings of the Bible into Scots appear only in the romantic revival of Scots in the nineteenth century, by which time Church and Law had both surrendered to the Enlightenment and become genteel, and in the sturdier renaissance of Scots letters in the present century, when the Church was becoming more and more middle-class and fast losing any hold it once had on those who still regularly spoke some Scots. P Hately Waddell's not unattractive, but rather pawky and sentimental, semi-paraphrases of the Hebrew in his translations of the Psalms and the Book of Isaiah belong to the first of these phases. W L Lorimer's recent vigorous and stirring and sometimes lyrical *The New Testament in Scots* belongs to the second. Both, in their generations, are laments for the loss of Scottishness in Kirk and wider society. Waddell flourished for a short while before passing into oblivion (though his *The Psalms Frae Hebrew Intil Scottis* has recently been reissued in the wake of the interest engendered by Lorimer). How will the Lorimer translation fare? Scottish ears will tingle with pleasure at many a striking word or phrase, but it is idle to pretend that Scottish congregations today will be able to make much of it, except in small doses. Most home readers of it will not get far without *The Concise Scots Dictionary* by their side. It is too literary a production, and it has come too late to be a genuinely religious or even popular event.

I could wish that it may find a welcome in Scottish worship, and not only in Presbyterian worship, but (now that Rome is keen on vernacular liturgies) in Catholic worship too; but it has really no chance beyond an occasional airing by way of light relief or a special treat. Lorimer's real role in the future will be to serve the aforesaid Scots literary renaissance pioneered by Hugh MacDiarmid, a most exciting but as yet largely contrived phenomenon only lightly touching the common life of the nation. It should remind those taking part in that renaissance of a Christian Scotland they so easily forget, and do something to prevent the movement being hijacked by MacDiarmid's relentless and sometimes vindictive secularism—and that is good reason to rejoice at Lorimer's work. But where that renaissance will lead, and whether it will effect a rapprochement with the still surviving dialects of the Scottish regions and go on from there to achieve authentic success and a revival of Scotland's brightness—and, if it does, where along the line religious Scotland will join in—only time will tell.

Which Modern Version?

The pressing problem of the moment for those in this land who still care about the Bible is not to make room at last for a worthy Scots version but, more realistically, to know which English version to employ. For Lorimer has arrived on the scene just as the Authorised Version is departing it; and that departure is real reason for Scots—and for many beyond Scotland—to cry 'Ichabod!' (cf. 1 Samuel 4:21). Its sonorous seventeenth-century English is (so we are told, though I am not completely convinced) becoming as incomprehensible to the majority of present-day Scots as Lorimer's Scots; and soon its memorable phrases will fade from the collective Scots consciousness as a congeries of very diverse English Bibles compete to take its place. These range from the partially traditionalist like the Revised Standard Version (or Common Bible) and the New International Version which try to retain links with the King James Bible and concentrate on removing archaisms and inaccuracies, to the overtly populist like the Good News Bible (or Today's English Version) which sets its face against the past and is replete with modern idioms, racy paraphrases and not a little shameless oversimplification. Somewhere between these two extremes come the New English Bible and the Jerusalem Bible, both of which aim at a dignified modern standard English, but in both of which the dominating desire seems to be to bring the translation into line with the findings—including some of the more controversial findings—of modern biblical criticism.

All of these modern versions have something going for them, if only in the shocks they deliver as sacred phrases, long since part and parcel of the English and Scots languages, come out offendingly or intriguingly different; their iconoclasm at least gets you thinking about the subject matter. But as long as the incomparable magic of the King James Version still weaves a lingering spell, it is their defects which will obtrude. Certainly, none of them has paid anything like sufficient attention to liturgical usefulness or literary taste. It is also noteworthy that the first three of them originate in the United States, reflecting the growing influence of that country in cultural as in political affairs, and that four of the five (the Jerusalem with its French Catholic parentage is the exception) are, or claim to be, ecumenical or interdenominational projects (though that does not mean that they do not also, like the Jerusalem Bible, have partisan objectives).

An obvious state of flux confronts us, and it will be a long time before one of these versions, or a revision of one of them, or indeed some as yet unplanned version, remotely approaches the status, in Scotland or elsewhere, once enjoyed by the Authorised Version. We cannot but be apprehensive as a rock of religious language and metaphor gives way to shifting sands and the Bible adds its own uncertain voice to all the other uncertain voices that confuse the modern believer. But let us not surrender to despair. It should be remembered that the King James Version itself stood at the end of a century of many versions and did not become *the* Bible, either in England or Scotland, until several decades after 1611. Numerous criticisms, no whit less crabbed than those now being directed against today's versions, had to be silenced before it mounted the throne of English-speaking Protestantism, brought a real measure of unity to its otherwise bitterly squabbling factions, and beyond that insinuated itself into the very marrow of all the variants, Scots included, of the English tongue.

Prescription for Scotland

My own prognosis (for what it is worth) is that in Great Britain the New

English Bible ought eventually to triumph, though not as it now is and only after extensive revision which takes honestly to heart the substantial faults which have been laid at its door. It is by far the solidest scholarly achievement of the five versions I have mentioned; and it is the least denominationally biased: all the British Churches, including (belatedly) the Roman Catholic, have had a hand in it. But of special interest to the readers of this book, Scotland's investment in it has been very considerable. It was an overture from the Presbytery of Stirling and Dunblane to the General Assembly of 1946 that led to its getting off the ground; and several distinguished Scottish academics have served on its panel of translators and are still serving as its first major revision nears completion. I would like to think that the Scottish contribution can be maintained and also that there can be more input from conservative and from Roman Catholic scholars. In the present state of literary English I am not, however, so sanguine about whether the effects of journalese, or of business or social-science English, or of the British equivalent of what people in Washington call 'federal prose', can be avoided and a more pleasing lyrical style achieved. Meanwhile I would like to see a New American Bible of similar depth and commitment emerging out of (or in spite of) the various extant American versions, a Bible that could do much to define what American English is at its best, and to bring some much-needed sense of common purpose to the fissiparous American religious scene.

For the present, then, my hope is that Great Britain and the United States will each do their own biblical thing, and will do it with all the scholarship and faith and grace and urgency they can severally summon; for the times are out of joint, and a dissipated Word of God is not going to be easily heard. In the meantime, we Scots should cultivate Lorimer as we can, both as a superb example of the speech of our forefathers which we are in danger of losing and as a unique personal interpretation of the New Testament by a formidable Classical scholar. And we should rediscover James Moffatt's once deservedly popular translation of both Testaments, an English translation which has a rich vein of Scots running through it and which is also a masterly scholarly performance; it merits a reprinting. William Barclay's couthier New Testament translation, recently reissued, is also worth acquiring. These three quintessentially Scottish productions should impart a Scottish dimension to our biblical experience as we listen in church to whatever English version our betters think is good for us and as we await a more meritorious replacement of the English Bible our land once knew and loved.

Bible's Influence in the Church

So much, if not for the Scots Bible that might have been but never was, at any rate for Scotland's Bible, past, present and to come! Let us turn now to the other concern of this book, the influence of the Bible on Scottish life and thought, and ask how that may best be retained and furthered in a generation that seems to have little time for the Bible or the faith that issues from it.

There is a lot in this collection of studies to be savoured and learned from. There is, of course, the centrality of the Bible which the Reformation established. But we should be careful how we sloganise about this. There is also the devotion which the Columban and mediaeval Churches lavished on the Latin Scriptures in monastery and private piety, and the allegorising but imaginative and effective manner in which the Bible story and message were passed on to ordinary people through art and drama. It is a travesty of the facts to suggest that mediaeval Scotland neither knew nor cared about the Bible, even in the corrupt times that preceded the Reformation. The Reformation was not so much about the Bible, or even the neglect of the Bible, as about the right of Christians to criticise and suggest changes in the Church on the basis of the Bible. To the mediaeval Catholic mind, pure or corrupt, Church and Bible were so umbilically joined in a rich tapestry of ritual and belief and imagery that it was simply inconceivable that such critical protest could be countenanced. And even today in Catholic thinking the Church's tradition, properly expressed, and the Bible's message, properly understood, are not meant to clash (which does not, in this Protestant writer's view, augur well for the independence of the Bible in that Church).

The Reformation, however, rigorously separated the new Bible in the people's language from the Church and set it above the Church. How ironic, then, that the Bible should again and so soon have become the prisoner of the Church! As all over Europe dissatisfaction mounted with a Church that refused to change, the Bible became the catalyst of reform; now widely available, it was honestly and anxiously consulted to provide light on the way forward in doctrine and Church structure. But once the Reformation took firm hold in northern Europe, whether in an Anglican or a Lutheran or a Calvinist form—once, as it were, biblical truth had been apprehended and applied—the new Churches began to speak less about freedom of interpretation and more about the Bible's authority, even its infallibility. Something remarkably like Catholic tradition began to operate alongside Scripture, and in Scotland that meant that biblical truth and Calvinism were, if not in principle (that would never do), in practice very nearly equated. Theoretically, statements about the authority and inerrancy of the Bible were intended to assure the believer that amid the rough seas of life he had a trusty ark onto which he could climb and feel safe; practically, they were a warning to him not to challenge the new establishment.

Critical Disturbance

Thus, when in the nineteenth century what is known as modern biblical criticism began to produce novel interpretations of Scripture that were as potentially revolutionary in their effect as had been those of the Reformers in their day, the initial reaction of official Presbyterianism was to condemn it as dangerous and heretical. That biblical criticism was not overtly concerned to reform the present Church but rather, using the methods of the new philological and historical disciplines and the resources of archaeology, to uncover what actually went on in biblical times, was neither here nor there; the outcome was to focus attention once again on the gap between then and now and, by implication, to relativise the claims of Presbyterianism—or Catholicism or any other denomination—to represent in its doctrine and organisation the eternal plan of God for his people. So once again, as in the fiercer era of the Reformation, heretical heads rolled in Europe, if this time only metaphorically.

The most notorious Scottish head to roll was that of William Robertson Smith, who was removed from the Chair of Hebrew in the Aberdeen College of the Free Church. His teaching on the nature and growth of the Old Testament writings questioned, for example, the historicity of the biblical narratives of creation and the flood and sat uneasily with the Christian doctrine of man, not to mention the doctrine of the Word of God, as these had traditionally been formulated. In the days of Charles Darwin and his theory of evolution, this was heady and upsetting stuff; and it called for a rethinking of fundamental positions that not many in the Church were yet ready to face. In this regard it is significant that A B Davidson, Smith's teacher, although he cast his vote in Assembly for him, did not speak on his behalf. This suggests that he considered his erstwhile student too headstrong and not sufficiently mindful of the peace of the Church. Be that as it may, Davidson's desire to work within the Church (though without being circumscribed by it) has been a noteworthy feature of Scotland's biblical scholarship in the last century or so; a canny *festina lente* ('hurry slowly') has, on the whole, been its watchword. For this, many in Scotland ought to be more grateful than they are. (As an example of Scottish biblical scholarship at its best, one may cite George Adam Smith's now classic *Historical Geography of the Holy Land*. This is a winsomely evocative description laced with many Scottish touches of the scenery against which, and the people among whom, the Bible took its rise).

But back to our argument. Following the Robertson Smith case a few more heresy hunts were half-heartedly and unsuccessfully pursued, but thereafter the main Presbyterian bodies moved surprisingly quickly to get their priorities right. (The Catholic Church took a lot longer to come to terms with biblical criticism.) A clause enshrining 'liberty of opinion on such points of doctrine as do not enter into the substance of the faith' was attached to the Preamble read out at ordinations when ministers give their assent to the subordinate standard (*ie*, subordinate to the Scriptures) of the *Westminster Confession of Faith* (a high Calvinist document which—alas!—originated in England and in 1647 replaced the *Scots Confession* of 1560). The Preamble as a whole is a rather tortuous statement; but this clause at least makes a brave attempt to retreat from a triumphant Calvinism which saw itself as enshrining all truth, to a more modest Calvinism which defends its own emphases as genuinely biblical, but admits that the Bible was not written with modern Europeans in mind, but for ancient Jews (and Gentiles), and that it strikes other notes which Calvinism has overlooked or neglected. There have been lapses of vision, as when in 1984 the General Assembly, in one of its tetchier moods, flung out without courtesy of a debate the *Motherhood of God* report, refusing even to look at the not inconsiderable evidence which it adduced from Scripture for the presence of a feminine element in the divine nature. On that occasion—and there have been others—a solidly biblical, if daring, argument proved no match for the weight of conservative tradition.

The converse has also sometimes been true, when the Church has compromised itself by taking up positions on ethical or social questions which owed more to the prevailing ethos than to the Bible, and conservative strictures have gone unheeded; homosexuality and abortion may be cases in point. But on the whole my feeling is that the Church of Scotland is, in an age of creeping unbelief, maintaining a reasoned if rather querulous balance between recognising the needs of the society to which it must preach and confronting that society with a message from the biblical past which it is not keen to hear. It is trying its best to relate an ancient book to a modern era, and if it is not at the moment having any conspicuous success, it may be preparing the ground for God's Spirit in God's own good time to fertilise and make fruitful again. At any rate, I would like to think so.

Bible in Society and Culture

But there is more—much more—to the Bible's influence than the attitude to it of the official Church; and it is when the present book explores that wider influence, whether in pre-Presbyterian or Presbyterian times, that it, for me, comes most fully alive. It makes it abundantly clear that the biblical piety of the Scottish people, and the biblical involvement of Scottish writers, have always been more vital and imaginative than the interpretations of Scotland's Kirk or its Divinity Faculties which, as institutional or academic, are as apt to stifle as to encourage free creative interplay with the biblical text.

We can think in this regard of the marvellously colourful pageants of mediaeval Scotland, as at Aberdeen, weaving scenes from the Bible with scenes of Robert the Bruce, and inviting the audience to make the link between God's providence then and God's providence now. We can think of the Covenanting troops, magnificently militant and fresh from a field-conventicle, marching down to the battlefield at Drumclog singing the words of Psalm 76:

> There arrows of the bow he broke,
> The shield, the sword, the war.
> More glorious thou than hills of prey,
> More excellent art far.

We can think of the more peaceful mood of a typical Saturday night when, as Burns recalls for us:

> The cheerfu' Supper done, wi' serious face,
> They, round the ingle, form a circle wide;
> The Sire turns o'er, with patriarchal grace,
> The big ha'-Bible, ance his Father's pride.

There is the motto of my own city of Edinburgh, *Nisi Dominus frustra* (Psalm 127:1), reminding us not only, like my second example above, of the place of the Psalms, particularly in their metrical form, in the worship and witness of Presbyterian Scotland, but of the Latin Psalms chanted in the liturgy as soon as Christianity reached these shores. There is Hogg in the *Confessions*, because he had absorbed Bible and metrical Psalter at his mother's knee and knew a better Calvinist devotion, bitterly lampooning the biblical cant of the Calvinist 'unco guid'.

There is, poignantly, Catholic priest as well as Presbyterian minister, in Gaelic song and sermon, drawing richly on ancient Israel's experience in exodus and exile, to illumine and make bearable the lot of an alienated and emigrating flock. There is General Gordon's courageous last letter from Khartoum, written just before his betrayal and death and ending with the words, 'The angels of God are with me—Mahanaim!' (see Genesis 32:1–2). There is even the Marxist Grassic Gibbon's sympathetic picture of the minister in *Cloud Howe*, as he finds in Scripture a message of social concern which his tiny respectable congregation do not want to hear, and which the big world outside is not there to hear, but 'may yet find it, and far off yet, in the times to be'. And, a final example, there is the Scottish Jew and Professor of English, David Daiches, in his sensitive and (for a volume in so academic a series) wonderfully readable Gifford Lectures *God and the Poets*, analysing the Book of Job or the Psalms as works of literature, and making more of them as religious writings in the best sense than the most painstaking commentaries of biblical scholars—and incidentally bringing forcibly to our attention that the long first part of the Christian Bible, the Old Testament, is not and should never be made an exclusive Christian preserve.

[handwritten margin note: John Cook, my uncle, taught R. Davies, Latin &, Greek in the late 1920's]

The Bible's Power in Scotland

It is when we turn from church formulae and academic treatises to examine the relationship that the Scottish people, in their common life and in their literature, have forged with the words and images and themes and situations of Scripture, that we begin to detect the amazing power of the Bible to move the heart, stir the emotions and prick the conscience of a nation. Narrow and partisan interpretations are of course present, as denominational allegiances are defended and attacked, frequently with panache if too frequently without much sign of the milk of human kindness. But beyond and above that we witness a lighting-up of the human predicament in its ongoing fragility and need, as comfort and challenge and hope are sought and found in the Word of God, and the soiled vanity of human pretensions is alternatively punctured and redeemed by a voice from heaven. Even in these irreligious times in which we live, that voice, though fractured, is not silent; for there are still many professed atheists who, as Yeats said of Shaw, 'tremble in the haunted corridor'.

And there I must stop. The influence of the Bible on Scottish life, sometimes through the agency of the Church, just as often in spite of it, has hitherto been immense. It is now plainly waning; there are no easy recipes for its survival into an era when the sacred is being remorselessly swallowed up in the secular, and the visionary in the mechanical, and God, we are told, is dead. The future of the Bible's cause in this land will depend much on whether the Church is honestly listening to it and not simply talking about it or, worse, manipulating it. It will depend even more on whether a wide enough spectrum of our children are introduced to it in school. It will depend on the maintenance of Hebrew and Greek learning in our universities. It will depend beyond that on how long it takes Scottish society to realise that without the Bible its spirit is being starved and its imagination atrophied. Above all, it will depend on how long before the God who speaks in its pages and who is supposed to be dead, wakes up and gets things moving in his direction again. May it be soon!

> What shall I cry? All flesh is grass, and all the goodliness thereof is as the flower of the field: the grass withereth, the flower fadeth: because the spirit of the Lord bloweth upon it: surely the people is grass. The grass withereth, the flower fadeth: but the word of our God shall stand for ever.
>
> (Isaiah 40:6–8)

JOHN GIBSON

Further Reading

W Barclay, *The New Testament* (reissued, London, 1988). The translation first appeared in 1968–9.

J Barr, *The Bible in the Modern World* (London, 1973). The Croall Lectures given in New College, Edinburgh, in November 1970.

D Daiches, *God and the Poets* (Oxford, 1984). Gifford Lectures 1983.

Billy Kay, *Scots the Mither Tongue* (Edinburgh, 1986; London, 1988).

A E Lewis (ed), *The Motherhood of God* (Edinburgh, 1984). A Report by a Study Group appointed by the Woman's Guild and the Panel on Doctrine on the invitation of the General Assembly of the Church of Scotland.

J Moffatt, *The Moffatt Translation of the Bible* (revised edition, London, 1935). The New Testament first appeared in 1913, the Old Testament in 1924.

A C Partridge, *English Biblical Translation* (London, 1973).

G A Smith, *The Historical Geography of the Holy Land* (25th edition, reprinted, London, 1966).

P Hately Waddell, *The Psalms Frae Hebrew Intil Scottis* (reissued with an introduction by Graham Tulloch, Aberdeen, 1987). The translation first appeared in 1871.

BIBLICAL INDEX

(References to biblical individuals, events and themes will be found in the General Index)

GENERAL INDEX